Essays in Seminary Education

Essays in Seminary Education

John Tracy Ellis

Professor of Church History
in the
University of San Francisco

Fides Publishers, Inc.
NOTRE DAME, INDIANA

Nihil Obstat: Louis J. Putz, C.S.C.
University of Notre Dame

Imprimatur: Leo A. Pursley, D.D.
Bishop of Fort Wayne-South Bend

Library of Congress Catalog Card Number: 67-24811

In loving memory of

Anthony Viéban, S.S. (1872-1944)

who for forty-six years served the
seminarians and clergy of his
adopted country as an exemplary
priest, a wise counselor, and a dedicated and self-sacrificing friend.

Acknowledgement

The essays in this volume have first appeared in other forms, for which acknowledgement is made: THE APOSTOLIC AGE TO TRENT, and FROM TRENT TO THE 1960's, in *Seminary Education in a Time of Change*, Fides, 1965; DIOCESAN THEOLOGICAL SEMINARIES IN THE MIDDLE WEST, 1811-1889, in its original form was read as a paper at the meeting of the American Society of Church History held at Concordia Seminary, Saint Louis, on April 24, 1965; THE SEMINARY IN THE SHADOW OF VATICAN II, Part I, is from the text of a sermon delivered at the diamond jubilee Mass of the seminary of Mount Angel Abbey, Saint Benedict, Oregon, on May 12, 1964, and published in the *American Benedictine Review*, XV (September, 1964), 303-315, and Part II is from an address delivered at the diamond jubilee dinner of Saint Paul's College, Washington, D.C., January 25, 1965, and published in *Chicago Studies*, IV (Summer, 1965), 115-135; and THE SEMINARY TODAY appeared in *The Voice of Saint Mary's Seminary* XLIV (Winter, 1966), 7-11; 89-94. THE PRIEST AS INTELLECTUAL will appear as a chapter in *The Secular Priest in the New Church*, Herder and Herder, edited by Gerard S. Sloyan of Temple University.

Preface

To state that the seminaries have taken a position high on the list of the institutions of the Catholic Church feeling the effects of the *aggiornamento* inaugurated by Pope John XXIII, Vatican Council II, and the general unrest that has characterized the people of God within the present decade, is to state a truism. In fact, it is doubtful if at any period since they were prescribed by the Council of Trent in 1563 the seminaries have been the object of closer scrutiny and the subject of more books and articles than they have during the 1960's. It might seem open to question, therefore, to bring together a collection of essays most of which had previously appeared in print. The suggestion that this be done arose with the publisher, not the author, and it is hoped that this volume may prove of sufficient assistance to those involved and interested in seminary education to warrant the publisher's judgment.

The same author writing at intervals on the same general theme will almost inevitably find himself turning back to certain source materials that he has used before, and the present volume is no exception. Yet rather than to delete these passages—which have usually been quotations from the sources—I have let them stand in the belief that they will not seriously detract from the reader's interest, since in one case only, namely, that of Austin Dowling's tribute to John B. Hogan, S.S., which is quoted in "Diocesan Theological Seminaries In The Middle West," "The Seminary

Today," and in "The Priest as Intellectual," was the passage more than a sentence or two in length.

While writing these essays I originally expressed my thanks in the footnotes to a number of people who had been kind and helpful in one way or another. I should like here to add my appreciation to three friends who were generous enough to read one or other of the essays and to give me the benefit of their criticism. For this service I am grateful to the Very Reverend Louis A. Arand, S.S., President of Divinity College of the Catholic University of America, to the Reverend Raymond G. Decker, Secretary of the Senate of Priests of the Archdiocese of San Francisco, and to the Right Reverend Mark J. Hurley, Vice Chancellor of the Archdiocese of San Francisco.

John Tracy Ellis

San Francisco
September 7, 1967

Contents

1.

The Apostolic Age to Trent

As he was walking by the sea of Galilee, he saw two brothers, Simon, who is called Peter, and his brother Andrew, casting a net into the sea (for they were fishermen). And he said to them, "Come, follow me, and I will make you fishers of men." And at once they left their nets, and followed him. And going farther on, he saw two other brothers, James the son of Zebedee, and his brother John, in a boat with Zebedee their father, mending their nets; and he called them. And immediately they left their nets and their father, and followed him.[1]

These words constitute a description of the founding of what may be called the Church's first seminary, for it was during the three years that followed this episode that the apostles received from the Lord their education for the priesthood that He conferred on them at the Last Supper. Nor is much else known about the nature of that education through and beyond the apostolic age, other than a few facts and inferences such as that noted by Newman to the effect that over and above the public assemblies of the faithful who were catechized by Saint John, the latter was recorded "to have had about him a number of students whom he familiarly instructed. . . ."[2] The *Acts of the Apostles* furnish the

---

[1] Matthew 4:18-22.
[2] John Henry Newman, "Universities and Seminaries L'Ecole des Hautes Etudes," *Historical Sketches* (London: Longmans, Green and Company, 1909), III, 241. This essay was one of a series written in 1854 for the *Catholic University Gazette* in Dublin.

1

names of certain other men who were attached to the apostolic band, the nature of whose work is seen, for example, in Saint Paul's selection of Saint Timothy whom the apostle "wished to go forth with him." The account then related, "as they passed through the cities, they delivered to the brethren for their observance the decisions arrived at by the apostles and presbyters in Jerusalem."[3] That care was exercised in selecting candidates for the ministry, is known from Paul's directive to Timothy that he should "not lay hands hastily upon anyone," and he then gave Timothy several other points to guide him in selecting these candidates when he said:

> Some men's sins are manifest even before investigation, other men's sins only afterwards. In like manner also the good works are manifest, and those that are otherwise cannot be hidden.[4]

But beyond these and few additional facts, lack of extant evidence does not permit one to speak in detail of the character and method of priestly education in the early Church.

At the outset it may be well to indicate the limitations of the present chapter and of the following one as well. Obviously, within the space allotted, an historian can hope to do no more than merely sketch in a broad fashion the development of clerical education during the Church's more than nineteen centuries. After a quick survey of the principal factors at work in the education of priests from the apostolic age to the Catholic Reformation of the late sixteenth century, the pioneer efforts of the chief architects of the modern seminary will be summarized. For the first half of the seventeenth century the emphasis will necessarily fall on France where a galaxy of zealous and able churchmen fixed seminary patterns so firmly—and, generally speaking, so satisfactorily in view of *their* times and of *their* milieu—that they have endured substantially unchanged to our own day.

---

[3] Acts of the Apostles 16:4.
[4] 1 Timothy 5:22, 24-25.

Once one passes the mid-seventeenth century, however, the note of originality and experimentation that marked the late 1550s and early 1660s disappears. It is generally agreed that the Church's loss of the intellectual classes was climaxed in the eighteenth century, and that she has since failed to regain them. For that sad fact the seminaries must bear a share of the blame for neglecting to bring their thinking abreast of contemporary developments, and for failing to equip priests for a really effective encounter with their own particular moment in time, so that each period of the modern age might find reasons to respect, if not to adhere, to the Catholic faith. In that connection the words of a prominent English priest written nearly three-quarters of a century ago are still pertinent:

> Laymen and men of the world will never be influenced for long by those who seem to them below their own level in acquirements and general culture. They will argue from things secular to things religious; and if they detect, at it appears to them, ignorance or narrow-mindedness in respect of matters outside the sanctuary, we may rest assured that they will turn a deaf ear to the preacher when he mounts the pulpit.[5]

Unfortunately, the seminaries failed to move with time, so that only the very recent past has witnessed really serious and responsible efforts to bring about an *aggiornamento* within the Church's schools of clerical education. To return to the contents of these two historical chapters, following some generalizations concerning the character and spirit of that training before and after Trent, a final section will be devoted to an outline of the main features of Catholic seminary history in the United States, with a few concluding observations about the present status of the seminaries of the American Church in the light of their history.

From Saint Augustine to the Early Middle Ages

Throughout antiquity and well into the Middle Ages var-

[5] William Barry, "Isaac Hecker," *Dublin Review* (Fourth Series), II (July, 1892), 84.

ious methods were employed to enlist those who were to exercise the ministry, such as the case of Saint Matthias who was elected by the drawing of lots just before Pentecost,[6] and the choice by popular acclaim, or *ex abrupto*, as one writer has termed it,[7] of Saint Ambrose as Bishop of Milan in 374 and of Saint Augustine for the priesthood in 391. Aside, however, from certain rather vague suggestions that there may have existed schools for prospective priests in the homes of some bishops in the East—for example, Meletius, Bishop of Antioch, with whom the future Saint John Chrysostom became associated about 367—it was generally true that before the time of Saint Augustine, "no trace can be found of any special institutions for the education of the clergy."[8]

About a half century before Augustine organized his clerical community in North Africa, according to Saint Ambrose, Saint Eusebius, who was Bishop of Vercelli from his election in 340 by the clergy and people of that city until his death in 371, became the first bishop in the West to combine monastic discipline with a common life for the parochial clergy with whom he lived personally. Saint Paulinus also established a similar system in Nola in 395

---

[6] Acts of the Apostles 1:15-26.

[7] This phrase was used by the late Benjamin F. Marcetteau, S.S., in an unpublished essay entitled, "Historical Sketch of Clerical Training and History of the Society of Saint Sulpice," p. 2. Father Marcetteau's work was thoughtfully suggested to the writer by the Reverend Lyman A. Fenn, S.S., of Saint Patrick's Seminary, Menlo Park, California, and he is grateful as well to the Reverend John F. Mattingly, S.S., of the same institution for loaning him a copy of this fifty-five page essay.

[8] Anthony Viéban, S.S., "Ecclesiastical Seminary," *Catholic Encyclopedia*, (New York: Universal Knowledge Foundation, Inc., 1912), XIII, 695. The evidence concerning schools for prospective priests in the homes of bishops of the early Church is nowhere very ample or precise. See, for example, Johannes Quasten, *Patrology* (Westminster, Md.: Newman, 1960), III, 424-425; Alexander Kerrigan, O.F.M., *St. Cyril of Alexandria. Interpreter of the Old Testament.* (Rome: Pontificio Istituto Biblico, 1952), pp. 7-11; Frederik van der Meer, *Augustine the Bishop*, translated by Brian Battershaw and G. R. Lamb. (London: Sheed and Ward, 1961), pp. 225-234.

and continued to follow it after his election to that See about 409. A community life for the clergy would not, therefore, have been altogether strange to Saint Augustine who returned to Africa in 388 from Italy and who has been said to have recognized,

> that he could render no greater service to the Church in his part of the world than by creating a new elite, educated under his supervision, in his own house and largely by his own efforts, for there was quite obviously a shortage of priests with adequate intellectual training.[9]

True, at first the men who were drawn to Augustine's little monastery with its adjacent garden at Tagaste, would seem to have been ordained priests, but that in no way detracted from the education they received—and that they needed. After he became bishop in 396, the success which Augustine enjoyed in maintaining the principle of a monastic life combined with parochial activity, was ultimately responsible for a widespread clerical reform in Africa. His episcopal residence at Hippo was the school for the superiors of a good many monastic houses as well as for a considerable number of diocesan bishops, and in this way his clerical community became a model for imitation elsewhere. The improvement was centered, it is true, almost entirely in the cities, with the country clergy remaining largely without benefit of the superior advantages of their urban brothers. Yet there was a notable heightening in the moral tone of African clerical life in general, even if occasionally disciplinary infractions were still encountered among some of Au-

---

[9] van der Meer, *op. cit.*, p. 200. Nearly 1500 years later an interesting experiment begun by Herbert Vaughan, Bishop of Salford, shortly after his consecration in October, 1872, was reminiscent of Augustine's system. Vaughan assembled the newly ordained priests of his diocese in his own house for a year's training under his personal supervision. For a description of this "pastoral seminary" as Vaughan called it, see J. G. Snead-Cox, *The Life of Cardinal Vaughan* (London: Herbert and Daniel, 1910), I, 252-259.

gustine's own household. Of the moral uplift that followed
the great bishop's carefully supervised education of the
clergy, then, there could be no doubt, and it was not an exaggeration for one of his recent biographers to conclude:

> The saint left behind him a seedbed of sanctity and what was
> really the first seminary for priests. It was an imperfect thing,
> but its essential features were to be repeated through the ages.
> Augustine could not know what Genseric and Huneric had in
> store for the African clergy, but though their churches were
> destroyed their spirit survived and has continued to be ef-
> fective to this day.[10]

During this destruction of Roman civilization begun in
Saint Augustine's declining years and which followed his
death, the clergy were about the only class within whose
ranks education, or a desire for such, remained alive. In
the roughly 1,000 years that stretched between the death of
Saint Benedict around 547 and the opening of the Roman
College of Saint Ignatius Loyola in 1551, clerical education
underwent a number of significant changes which can be
summarized under the following headings: (1) monastic
schools; (2) episcopal schools; (3) universities.

The story of Saint Benedict's establishment of "a school of
the Lord's service," as he called his foundation, first a
Subiaco and then at Monte Cassino, is too well know to
need retelling here. Suffice it to say, from the earliest years
it was customary for the Benedictines to receive boys in their
monasteries for the purpose of educating them to become
monks, and it was from this practice that there arose the
monastic schools that ultimately expanded over all the western world. Thus prompted by Benedict's warning that idle-
ness was the enemy of man's soul and, therefore, that the
monks should be occupied at stated times in manual labor,

---

[10] van der Meer, *op. cit.*, p. 234.

"and at other fixed hours in sacred reading,"[11] but far more by the impetus to learning given by Cassiodorus in his monastery at Vivarium to which he retired in 540, the monastic school gradually took shape. It was in such a school at Wearmouth and Jarrow in Northumberland, for instance, that Saint Bede was placed at the age of seven (c. 680), and the intellectual aspects of the monastic community were neatly summarized by Bede when he stated in 731 that

> spending all the days of my life, in the mansion of the same monastery, I applied all my study to the meditation of holy scripture: and observing withal the regular discipline, and keeping the daily singing of God's service in the church, the rest of my time, I was delighted always, to learn of others, to teach myself, or else to write.[12]

THE EARLY MIDDLE AGES

Here, then, was the institution wherein many priests of early medieval Europe received instruction in the *trivium* and the *quadrivium* which were adaptations from classical times and which served as an introduction to the study of philosophy and theology. Full development of the theological curriculum, however, came only later after scholasticism had secured its victory in the scheme and method of clerical studies. Meanwhile the network of monastic schools spread through most of Christendom, and in the case of some of these schools a celebrated reputation was acquired. For example, less than a decade after the death of Saint Bede

---

[11] *The Rule of St. Benedict* translated by Dom Justin McCann and edited with a commentary by Dom Paul Delatte. (New York: Benziger Brothers, 1921), p. 304. In another place Benedict stated that from Easter to the calends of October the monks should labor from the first to the fourth hour of the day "at whatever is necessary," to which he added, "From the fourth hour until close upon the sixth let them apply themselves to reading." (p. 311).

[12] *The Ecclesiastical History of the English People by the Venerable Bede,* translated by Thomas Stapleton and edited by Philip Hereford. (London: Burns, Oates and Washbourne, 1935), p. 334.

his fellow Englishman, Saint Boniface, brought about in March, 744, the foundation of a monastery at Fulda under Saint Sturminus which, in turn, gave birth to numerous daughter houses and schools. Toward the end of the same eighth century monastic education likewise received a boon from Emperor Charlemagne, inspired probably by his learned English friend, Alcuin, in a series of decrees that provided that all clerics, secular and regular, must show an ability to read and write, as well as sufficient knowledge to fulfill their professional duties, and this under pain for suspension and deprivation of office. Moreover, reading schools were to be erected for the priesthood, and bishops were commanded to examine the clergy periodically to determine their compliance with the law. True, Charlemagne's decrees were often honored more in the breach than in the observance, yet, they were helpful in that dark age when so little emphasis was otherwise given to the things of the mind. Of the monastic type of school it has been said: "All the enlightened ecclesiastics of the time were educated in monasteries and most of them were monks: it was from the monasteries that the episcopal schools derived their teachers."[13]

Allowing for the exaggeration here—Alcuin, for one, was a product of the cathedral school of York and was not directly connected with monastic education until a few years before he died—the monastic schools were generally in the front rank. But the activities and personnel of the monastic and episcopal or cathedral schools, as well as those of the

---

[13] Hastings Rashdall, *The Universities of Europe in the Middle Ages.* Edited by F. M. Powicke and A. B. Emden. (Oxford: Clarendon Press, 1936), I, 29. Another writer has said that, "Primarily and originally his [Charlemagne's] aim was purely ecclesiastical, to drag the clergy of his day out of their abysmal ignorance of the tenets of their own faith. But the movement spread beyond those narrow limits. Learning began to be appreciated somewhat for its own sake. . . . More, there appeared here and there schools for the instruction of a limited number of lay pupils in connection with the monasteries." Nathan Schachner, *The Medieval Universities.* (New York: Stokes, 1938), p. 9.

early universities, were closely intertwined, and at times it is not easy for the historian to keep the lines distinct. The point may be illustrated from the lives of prominent church-men who lived during the centuries between the priestly ordination of Saint Augustine (391) and that of Saint John Fisher (1491). Thus, for example, Augustine himself relates that he was a student of the schools of Tagaste and Madaura before he went on to study at Carthage and then crossed to Italy where he both studied and taught, and where eventual-ly the influence of Saint Ambrose, the prayers of his mother, Saint Monica, and his own meditation and study brought him in 386 to embrace the faith. Over three centuries later a famous teacher like Alcuin, as has been seen, received his education at York's cathedral school, which for fifteen years he also served as principal master before the fateful meeting with Charlemagne at Parma in March, 781, changed the course of his life. The famous Palace School that Alcuin established at Aachen under Charlemagne's aegis was ob-viously neither monastic nor episcopal, but late in life he had experience of the former when in 796 the emperor agreed to his request to retire and appointed him abbot of the Abbey of Saint Martin at Tours where for eight years before his death in May, 804, Alcuin's time was absorbed in laying the foundations of a model monastic school.

Numerous other examples come to mind, but it will suffice to mention three renowned teachers whose preparation for the priesthood in the period before the Council of Trent showed such varied patterns. Thus Lanfranc's schooling be-gan in his native Pavia with a centuries-old reputation as a center of learning that went back to Roman times. Lanfranc finished his elementary and legal training there before he crossed the Alps and came first to Avranches in Normandy where he studied and taught and then about 1042 to the newly established abbey of Bec where as founder and prin-cipal master of the monastic school he had even greater success. Students were drawn to Bec from afar, among whom was Lanfranc's most famous student, Anselm of Aosta. Indeed, Saint Anselm's intellectual formation was due more to Lanfranc than to any other man; ultimately Saint Anselm succeeded his professor both as Prior of Bec and as Archbishop of Canterbury. Saint Thomas Aquinas's earliest schooling was likewise in a monastic setting, his family having placed him at Monte Cassino c. 1230 when he was only about five years of age. There under Benedictine auspices the Angelic Doctor was prepared for the advanced studies that he later pursued at the Universities of Naples, Paris, and Cologne. Finally, Saint John Fisher, one of the most illustrious Englishmen of his day in intellectual circles, did not receive his first instruction from monks but from secular canons who conducted the school attached to the Collegiate Church of Saint John in his native Beverley. It was there that he got his preparation for Michaelhouse at Cambridge where he won degrees in grammar and the arts before his ordination as a priest in December, 1491.

The vast majority of priests who had the benefit of formal education during the early Middle Ages—for many were ordained after no more than a brief period of informal and practical instruction under the direction of a priest—received it, therefore, in one or other of the monastic, episcopal, or cathedral schools that flourished before the advent of the universities. A further word should be said about the monastic school's companion institution, the episcopal school, and its offspring, the cathedral school. The birth of the episcopal school occurred very early in the history of the Church when, as was seen in the case of Saint Augustine at Hippo, a school was started in the house of a bishop. It was —and it remained—an episcopal enterprise, for though successive popes issued repeated exhortations and commands to the bishops of their time about the need for exercising vigilance in admitting men to holy orders, there was relatively little papal legislation of a specific nature and of universal application on this subject. Consequently, the presence or the absence of an episcopal school, its strength or its weakness—and the same pertained *mutatis mutandis* to its daughter institution, the cathedral school attached to the principal church of a diocese—normally depended on the individual bishop.

Among the numerous episcopal and cathedral schools of the Middle Ages, some won an enduring place in the history of education, such as those attached to the cathedrals of Chartres and Paris. Another school that exercised a widespread influence on clerical education was that of Seville which owed its origin to Saint Leander, himself a Benedictine monk, who after he became Archbishop of Seville in 579 put his monastic learning and experience to profitable use in the school that he opened near his cathedral. Under Leander's brother and successor in the See of Seville, the immensely learned Saint Isidore, the cathedral school achieved even greater prestige. Isidore further strengthened clerical education beyond his see city when as presiding prelate at the Fourth Council of Toledo in 633 he supported a law which made it obligatory for young men who intended to study for the priesthood to dwell in a single building near the church (cathedral). The influence of Toledo's conciliar legislation is well known, and it was illustrated in this particular case when over a century later (c. 755) Saint Chrodegang, Bishop of Metz, wrote a work for his clergy entitled *Regula Canonicorum*, wherein he quoted verbatim the Toledo decree of 633 concerning the obligation of common residence for aspirants to the priesthood.

In none of the schools mentioned thus far, nor in their contemporary educational institutions conducted under ecclesiastical auspices, such as the collegiate, chantry, guild, and hospital schools, was there the degree of uniformity in curriculum and method, or in over-all supervision, that one associates with the Church's seminaries today. And this was as true on the more advanced level of philosophy and theology as it was in the liberal arts, although on both levels, needless to say, there was a general similarity from one country or region to another. To put the point in terms readily understandable to a twentieth-century Catholic, there was then nothing to approximate the central control and direction of clerical education exercised by the Holy See's Sacred Congregation of Seminaries and Universities. In fact, the earliest forerunner of that branch of the Roman Curia came into existence only in January, 1588, when Pope Sixtus V erected a congregation that dealt largely with studies in the University of Rome. Actually, it was less than a half century ago that the congregation that has jurisdiction over the seminaries and universities of the Catholic world received its present form by a *motu proprio* of Pope Benedict XV in November, 1915.

MEDIEVAL UNIVERSITIES AND CLERICAL EDUCATION

But to return to the changing patterns of clerical education in the twelfth century, the medieval universities took their rise from a great variety of circumstances which differed from place to place, the details of which need not detain the reader here. It is worth noting, however, that foundations of this kind usually had direct links with the schools which have already been discussed. For example, it was famous professors like Peter Abelard, Peter Lombard, John of Salisbury, and William of Champeaux who drew students to Paris in great numbers where they attended these men's lectures in the Cathedral School of Notre Dame, the School of Sainte Geneviéve, Champeaux's establishment at the Abbey of Saint Victor, and similar institutions. It was out of this concentration of professors and students that the University of Paris was born in the early years of the thirteenth century.

At Oxford, to name only one other instance, the eighth-century monastery of Saint Frideswide had gained for the town an early reputation as a center of learning, a reputation which it had managed to retain so that by the late twelfth century there were large numbers of students attending Oxford's schools. But it was the coming of the new mendicant orders like the Franciscans, Carmelites, Dominicans, and Augustinians—and the impetus to renewed intellectual fervor that these friars furnished to older monastic orders like the Benedictines and the Carthusians, with the subsequent establishment by both the old and the new orders of houses of study—that laid the foundation for the first of the famous colleges out of which the University of Oxford finally emerged. Moreover, one of the factors which determined whether a particular group of scholars might eventually give birth to a university was the permanence they enjoyed by virtue of the *licentia docendi,* a privilege which was granted by a clerical official known by various titles as magiscola, chancellor, or archdeacon. The significant point, it has been said, was that by the end of the twelfth century, "the ecclesiastical sanction behind the license to teach was undisputed."[14] Regardless of their origin, then, all the early universities had ecclesiastical connections, a fact which should be remembered, said an historian of the institutions, as "the first of the conditions which determined, at least in northern Europe, the form of the intellectual movement out of which the universities grew and the shape of the university-system itself.[15]

Yet it did not necessarily follow that the universities created an ideal atmosphere for the education of priests. Unquestionably, for those who pursued their philosophical and theological studies in the new universities, there was an intellectual gain. Generally speaking, students in the cathe-

---

[14] Rashdall, *op. cit.*, I, 21.
[15] *Ibid.*, I, 29-30.

dral and monastic schools had been limited to the rather narrow approach of their professors' commentaries on the principal textbook, Peter Lombard's *Book of Sentences,* written in the late 1140's. The flowering of scholasticism, the first signs of which were seen as early as Saint Anselm— his *Cur Deus Homo* was finished in 1098—came only with the rebirth of Aristotle, and may be said to have reached its apogee in the early 1250s at the University of Paris when both Saints Thomas Aquinas and Bonaventure were lecturing there. This proved indeed to be an advance, both in content and method, over anything yet seen in medieval philosophy and theology. What was equally true was the progress of canon law which gradually won its autonomy from theology, and which provided a vital part of the academic background for most of the leading churchmen of the period.[16]

At no time, however, was there more than a small minority of the entire clerical body then under instruction of one kind or another with the priesthood in mind, who attended the universities. And only a small proportion of the numerous priests in the environs of the cathedrals and principal churches, therefore, had taken a degree, while many of them had no university training at all. That was one of the reasons why during what one might call the youth of the mendicant orders, the latter swept all before them with their zeal, their eagerness for knowledge, and their systematic training for holy orders in the houses of study opened by their superiors in and around the universities. And for the masses the friars' appeal was also enhanced by their poverty and by a kind of mystique concerning their way of life which created a vogue in European parochial circles that lasted beyond the mid-

---

[16] In that connection Rashdall remarked, "The idea of making a man a bishop or an archdeacon on account of his zeal, his energy, and success in the humble round of parochial duty is one which would hardly have occurred to sensible men in medieval times." (III, 447).

fourteenth century when they, too, began to undergo a decline.

A further factor militating against the universities as training centers for priests was the length of time demanded to complete the theological course. Normally the arts faculty was, so to speak, the preparatory school for theology and the other higher faculties, and students were usually fourteen or fifteen years of age when they began the study of the arts. This would mean that at the University of Paris, where the doctorate in theology often took fifteen or sixteen years to complete,[17] a man would be in his thirties by the time he had finished his education. Obviously, few could afford either the time or the expense involved in a program of this kind. Actually, an arts degree was not an absolute essential for the higher faculties, nor was a doctor's degree necessary for a candidate for the priesthood, unless he wished to become a professor of theology. Academic requirements varied a great deal from university to university, and at times even within the same university; consequently students for the priesthood were found to terminate their university studies at different times according to their individual circumstances. Moreover, except for candidates for degrees in theology, a cleric pursuing university studies with the priesthood as his ultimate goal, might well have come up to ordination with relatively little knowledge of theology. Allowing for Rashdall's tendency to exaggerate, there was yet considerable truth when in speaking about the priestly candidate at the university, he said:

> Except in so far as it taught him to construe his breviary and qualified him to read a provincial constitution or an episcopal mandate in Latin, there was no relation between the studies of the artist and the work of the ecclesiastical order. That education might be a good—even an indispensable—foundation for the studies of the theologian; but in a large majority of cases

---

[17] *Ibid.*, I, 474.

that foundation must have remained with little or no super-structure. Even when college foundations had multiplied, but a small minority of the clergy could have obtained theological fellowships or bursaries within their walls. Outside the colleges, the wealthier and more ambitious students betook themselves to canon law rather than to theology; the poorer must have left the university with a degree in arts or with no degree at all, and consequently without even the rudiments of a theological education.[18]

In so far as the spiritual formation of candidates for the priesthood was concerned, the universities assumed no responsibility on that score. Members of religious orders residing in a house of study of their community in a university neighborhood, were normally well served in their spiritual life by the carefully supervised living of their rule. But such was not the case with candidates for the diocesan priesthood. The latter's piety might, or might not, be nourished at the university, depending on the circumstances in which they happened to find themselves and, of course, on their personal initiative and disposition. In some clerical residence halls and colleges a fairly regular and systematic order of spiritual exercises obtained. In others there was little of this, with the consequence that it was possible for a university candidate for the priesthood to gain intellectually while he was losing ground in the virtues necessary for the priestly ministry.

THE RENAISSANCE

That clerical life had become sadly lacking in the qualities which made for an edifying and fruitful apostolate was painfully evident as the Middle Ages drew to a close. A pervad-

---

[18] *Ibid.*, III, 449-450. Rashdall later added, "The whole medieval university system, even the college system in the developed form which it had attained by the end of the fifteenth century, was about as unlike the modern seminary as anything that can well be imagined." (III, 451).

ing laxity had overtaken the religious orders as well as the secular priests—with high prelates the worst offenders of all—and the result was a situation unparalleled for clerical scandal since the so-called dark ages. Once again, limitation of space forbids more than a summary of the conditions of the priesthood during the Renaissance and the first years of the sixteenth-century religious revolt. The causes for this miserable state of affairs were many and varied, but one of the principal reasons for the collapse of morals among the clergy was traceable to the absence of institutions of priestly formation where a high standard of conduct was maintained and where abuses were quickly detected and eliminated before irreparable harm had been inflicted on candidates for holy orders.

Needless to say, as in every period of history there were exceptions. Even in the darkest corners of the Church of the Renaissance one would come upon sterling churchmen distressed over the havoc being wrought among souls and intent upon even heroic efforts to inaugurate reform. Such a person was Francisco Ximénez de Cisneros, Franciscan confessor to Queen Isabella of Castile, and after 1495 Archbishop of Toledo and Cardinal Primate of Spain. Ximénez was keenly aware of the deplorable conditions obtaining among so many of the Spanish clergy, conditions that had given rise to grave disorders throughout the Church generally, and to such anomalies, for example, as Francesco Piccolomini being Archbishop of Siena for over forty years before his election to the papacy in October, 1503, as Pius III, without having even been ordained a priest. In cases of this kind the sacral duties of the nominal bishop were usually performed by an auxiliary bishop, while the former received the revenues from the benefice by virtue of the favor he enjoyed with higher authorities, as was true of Piccolomini who had been named to Siena by his uncle, Pope Pius II. Locally, the situation within the ranks of the Spanish clergy was reflected in a decree of the Council or Aranda in 1473 that forbade the ordination of a man who was "ignorant of the Latin language," and in the remark of Peter Martyr who had come to Spain in 1487 at the invitation of Queen Isabella, to the effect that a Spanish clergyman of noble birth who could preach "was more scarce than a white crow."[19]

As has been said, Cardinal Ximénez was no stranger to clerical abuses, for in his travels as provincial of his order for Castile in the early 1490s he had observed much, and one of the things which had impressed itself on him most strongly was the need for more systematic education for the clergy, and especially for the sons of poor families. With the power and prestige of the primacy behind him after 1495, he began to devise remedial measures, the chief of which gradually took shape in the University of Alcalá. Having overcome the opposition and indifference that are the natural accompaniment of most ambitious projects of this character—and Ximénez probably experienced the greatest hostility to his plans from the jealous University of Salamanca—he laid the cornerstone of the first unit of the new university, the College of San Ildefonso, in 1500. The institution was formally opened in 1508 with a faculty of forty-two professors of whom six were assigned to teach theology, six to lecture in canon law, and eight to teach philosophy. In due time other colleges followed in one of which Ximénez provided scholarships for twenty-four needy students of whom eighteen were in theology.

---

[19] Quoted by Karl von Hefele, *The Life of Cardinal Ximénez*, translated by John Canon D'Alton. (London: Catholic Publishing and Bookkeeping, 1860), p. 198. Irregularities in episcopal administration were often due to the secular authorities, as was the case with Juan de Zumárraga, O.F.M., who was nominated as the first bishop for Mexico by King Charles I of Spain and sent on his way to the new world in August, 1528, although it was not until April, 1533, after many vicissitudes, that he finally received episcopal consecration at Valladolid in Spain.

Thus did the Primate of Spain give a splendid example of enlightened zeal and leadership at a time when corruption in high places had frequently thrust the bastard sons of royal and noble fathers into Spanish episcopal sees, with a similar spirit having made deep inroads into the lives of the clergy on all levels. In fact, although Ximénez accomplished a great deal for the moral and intellectual improvement of the Spanish Church before he died in 1517, even the power and persuasion of the cardinal primate failed at times to move some of the clergy to reform their lives, and of no single group, perhaps, was this more conspicuously true than the canons of his own cathedral chapter at Toledo among whom he vainly attempted in 1497 to bring about an improved way of life.[20] Among many of the Spanish religious there was likewise evidence to suggest that they may have known their finest hour, and what the greatest living historian of the religious orders of this period has said about them in England, was equally true on the continent. By the late thirteenth century, Knowles has said, not only had the monks and canons regular begun to diminish in numbers and zeal, but the mendicant friars, too, had reached their peak around 1300. The religious motivation that had characterized so much of the lives of medieval men generally, had by the opening of the fifteenth century greatly weakened, and thereafter

> when that world faded and was succeeded by a world in which money and property meant everything, and in which deep intellectual or spiritual interests were wanting, a world which was shortly to be shaken by the impact of new doctrines and new ideals, the monasteries and religious orders in general receded more and more from the forefront of society.[21]

---

[20] Reginald R. Merton, *Cardinal Ximénez and the Making of Spain.* (London: George Routledge and Sons, 1934), pp. 71-73.
[21] David Knowles, *The Religious Orders in England* (Cambridge: The University Press, 1959), III, 458.

LAXITY OF THE CLERGY: EARLY SIXTEENTH CENTURY

Just a week before the death of Cardinal Ximénez there took place at Wittenberg the historic episode of Martin Luther's nailing his theses to the door of the castle church, an action which heralded the Protestant Revolt. Humanly speaking, it would be difficult to see how the Church could have escaped the catastrophe of disunion when one considers the extent and depth of the scandal given by the corrupt lives of the clergy. And when the Fifth Lateran Council, convoked in 1512 for the purpose of inaugurating a reform, held its final session on March 16, 1517, with having done no more than to scratch the surface of the problem, it should have occasioned no surprise that less than eight months later Luther raised the standard of rebellion, and that many who had the Church's true interests at heart, should have almost felt a temptation to despair. In the meantime as the revolt spread rapidly beyond the Alps large numbers of the clergy defected, while at Rome the Medici Pope Leo X pursued his leisurely course until carried off by death in December, 1521, at the age of forty-six. The election of the Dutch cardinal, Adrian Dedel, as Adrian VI on January 9, 1522, seemed to offer renewed hope for the cause of reform, a hope born in no small measure from Adrian's honest admission of the gravity of clerical abuses and his forthright determination to do something about them. The pope's disposition was clearly revealed in the instructions he issued in November, 1522, for Francesco Chierigati, Bishop of Teramo, the nuncio whom he dispatched to the Diet of Nuremberg. In this document he was at pains to state:

> You are . . . to say that we frankly acknowledge that God permits this persecution of His Church on account of the sins of men, and especially of prelates and clergy. . . . Holy Scripture declares aloud that the sins of the people are the outcome of the sins of the priesthood. . . . We know well that for many years things deserving of abhorrence have gathered round the

Holy See; sacred things have been misused, ordinances trans-
gressed, so that in everything there has been a change for the
worse. . . .
We all, prelates and clergy, have gone astray from the right
way, and for long there is none that has done good; no, not
one. To God, therefore, we must give all the glory and humble
ourselves before Him; each one of us must consider how he
has fallen and be more ready to judge himself than to be
judged by God in the day of His wrath.[22]

But the hope enkindled by Adrian VI was not to be realized. Some months before his election the peace of western
Europe was disrupted by the outbreak of war between
Emperor Charles V and King Francis I of France, which
proved a major distraction from the business of ecclesiastical
reform; secondly, the leading bishops of the German world
where the Lutheran revolt was centered, either through
timidity or selfishness, declined to support the pope's initiative,[23] and in September, 1523, Adrian himself succumbed
after a reign of less than two years. He was succeeded by
another Medici, Clement VII, who for the next eleven years
faltered and procrastinated until all chance of genuine
reform had been dissipated. With the election of Alessandro
Farnese in October, 1534, as Pope Paul III, however, prospects brightened again and this time effective action was set
in motion. It is not too much to say that the widespread
moral laxity of the clergy and the absence of ardent zeal
for the Church on the part of clerics and hierarchs were
partially caused by weak, inefficient, ineffective, and often
nonexistent clerical education. Consequently it is more than
possible that zealous Trent later acted in perhaps an over-

---

[22] Adrian VI to Chierigati, November, 1522, in Ludwig Pastor, *The History
of the Popes* (St. Louis: B. Herder Book Company, 1910), IX, 134-135.
[23] Pastor was severe on these German prelates whom he characterized as
"weak-spirited" and so "steeped in worldliness" that they were heedless
of the needs of their time. "They thought more of worldly enjoyments,"
he said, "the banquet and the dance, than of the deliberations of the
Diet." (*ibid.*, IX, 140-141).

compensatory fashion in the matter of clerical education.

Thinking of these sixteenth-century religious movements solely in terms of clerical education—or its absence—the next significant step was taken when Paul III finally appointed the long deferred commission of reform in July, 1536. The nine members of the commission—four cardinals (Giovanni Carafa, Gasparo Contarini, Reginald Pole, and Jacopo Sadoleto), three bishops, one abbot, and one friar, with Contarini as president—held sessions from the autumn of that year through the early weeks of 1537, and on March 9 they submitted their report to the pope. The *Consilium delectorum cardinalium et aliorum prelatorum de emendanda ecclesia . . .,* as it was called, declared at the outset that the root of all ecclesiastical abuses was the exaggeration of papal authority by unscrupulous canonists. Woes had multiplied, said the report, until the Church had been brought to the brink of ruin and her clergy had gained an evil reputation among those outside the fold. The many scandals and the decline of clerical standards were traced to the laxity in admitting men to holy orders, and for that reason the commission recommended that in Rome and in other dioceses three virtuous and learned prelates should be appointed to supervise ordinations so that no candidate could be ordained except by or with the permission of the bishop of the diocese. In this way it was hoped every priest ordained would be the responsibility of a particular bishop and thus a step would have been taken toward eliminating the *vagi* or wandering clergymen. Moreover, every bishop should engage a teacher by whom his minor clerics should be instructed in letters and morals, and a strong remonstrance was likewise made against the appointment of men to benefices without regard to their worthiness for the clerical state.[24]

---

[24] Joannes Dominicus Mansi, *Sacrorum Conciliorum Nova et Amplissima Collectio* (Paris and Leipzig: Welter, 1902), XXXV, 347-355, con-

THE FIRST FOUR YEARS OF TRENT

The report of 1537 was a realistic scrutiny into the principal abuses of the clerical order; yet as much as the commission's members emphasized the necessity for vigilance in admitting men to holy orders, it did not seem to occur to them to suggest the prior need of institutions which would be devoted expressly to the spiritual and intellectual formation of future priests and bishops. Meanwhile the efforts of Paul III and the reforming element of the Roman Curia to convoke an ecumenical council for implementing this program of reform on a universal scale, met with one delay and disappointment after another. It is too intricate a story to attempt here even as a summary. Suffice it to say, the struggle to bring about a council continued for a quarter of a century. Only in the early days of December, 1545, was the Council of Trent finally able to get underway with four cardinals, four archbishops, and twenty-one bishops in attendance, and what the Church suffered by this delay has been suggested by the council's historian when he said:

If the Council of Trent had met in 1525 instead of 1545 it would only have been faced with a heresy and a popular movement instigated by it. At the former date Lutheran churches were not yet organized, the princes and towns who had embraced the new faith did not as yet constitute a political power, the ways of the people were still moulded by Catholic teaching and piety. A conciliar condemnation of Luther's teaching would probably have been accepted by the great majority of the German people and a reform decreed

tains the text of the commission's report. The notorious character of the lives of most of the high prelates of the period is too well known to need elaboration. Many would have shared the view quoted of Bartholomew Fernandez, O.P., Archbishop of Braga, a leader of the reform movement, "It is my opinion that their illustrious Lordships are in sore need of illustrious reform." H. Daniel-Rops, *The Catholic Reformation*, translated by John Warrington. (London : J.M. Dent and Sons, 1962), p. 101.

by the Council might yet have prevailed over the Lutheran one.[25]

Alas, many of those in authority showed no such clarity and determination, and when certain churchmen who did possess these qualities tried to inaugurate a move they were frequently thwarted by their rivals and enemies. Once the conciliar sessions opened on December 13, however, the subject of clerical reform could not be avoided, as the legates reflected several months later when in summarizing developments for Pope Paul III they remarked, "As to the Roman court, two things scandalize the world and deprive it of authority: one is avarice, the other its pomp and luxury."[26] Yet those of a reforming mentality had to move cautiously lest in their zeal all should be lost. The anomalous situation was well illustrated by the fact that not until February, 1547, did a plenary session of the fathers at Trent hear it stated in a speech of the president, Antonio Cardinal del Monte, "The aim of our reforming activity is the revival of the pastoral ministry—the cure of souls," which prompted Trent's historian to comment, "This was the first time that this purpose was clearly stated in a plenary assembly of the Council."[27] With the council in session for a year and two months before this basic principle was so much as enunciated in a plenary session, one can begin to understand why really effective action on clerical education was so many times put off, and why it should have been less than five months before the close of the eighteen-year assembly before it became a reality.

---

[25] Hubert Jedin, A History of the Council of Trent (London: Thomas Nelson and Sons, 1957), I, 580.

[26] Giovanni del Monte, Marcello Cervini, and Reginald Pole to Paul III, Trent, March 7, 1546, in Richard M. Douglas, Jacopo Sadoleto, 1477-1547. Humanist and Reformer. (Cambridge: Harvard University Press, 1959), p. 205.

[27] Jedin, op. cit., II, 356.

Indirectly, it is true, the conciliar debates touched several times on the question, for example, in the spring of 1546 when the neglect of the Scriptures in teaching and preaching was under discussion. One of the leaders on this occasion was Father Claude Le Jay, S.J., representative of Otto Cardinal Truchsess von Waldburg, Bishop of Augsburg. Le Jay had only recently come from several years of travel and observation in the German world where the lack of both an educated clergy and of vocations to the priesthood had made a deep impression on him. Speaking on April 6, he urged the necessity of establishing colleges wherein young men could be received and fittingly educated for the ministry in areas that were devoid of priests. Some days later the wretched situation was highlighted by the warning of Pedro Cardinal Pacheco, Bishop of Jaén, that the council should not compel priests to preach while so many of them were too ignorant to do so. Discussion continued until June 17 when the council finally passed a decree on the obligation of teaching and preaching the Scriptures, and called for the establishment of lectureships in connection with the cathedrals and principal churches (collegiate) of the large cities. Fundamentally, the decree was nothing more than a repetition of one enacted 331 years before at the Fourth Lateran Council of November, 1215.

It must have been a sore disappointment to the true reformers to witness nothing more accomplished for the training of future priests at this time than that embodied in the decree of June, 1546. This decree has been characterized as the council's only successful attempt to combine ecclesiastical reform with the elements of a sound Christian humanism. There were numerous humanists among the delegates—Marcello Cervini and Reginald Pole were two of the cardinal presidents—and in the humanists' eagerness to raise the educational standards of the clergy, as well as to emphasize the biblical approach in the teaching of theology, there was a

reflection of Renaissance thinking, about which *per se* there
was nothing wrong, but it produced no more than a restoration of the theological prebends prescribed over three centuries before. Obviously, the council was not yet ready to
break with the past, but as Jedin had said in concluding
this point: "As time went on it was seen that this measure
was inadequate; hence its historical bearing was very limited
. . . it was likewise seen that something new, something more
thorough must be done for the theological training and
the professional formation of the future priests."[28]

One of the tragic aspects of this story, however, was the
length of time it took the conciliar fathers to become convinced of this necessity. Meantime the council's own future
was jeopardized by the mounting tension between Charles
V and Paul III. The trouble was due to a number of causes,
among which was the emperor's insistence on treating religious questions with the German rulers without reference
to the Holy See. A second factor that endangered the assembly was the War of the Schmalkaldic League between
Charles and the Protestant princes, a conflict which constituted in the minds of a number of delegates at Trent a
menace to their personal safety; and thirdly, a further burden of anxiety was added in the early spring of 1547 when
typhus broke out in the city. The result was that in March
the question of a transfer to Bologna was put to a vote with
two-thirds (thirty-nine) in favor and a minority (fourteen)
opposed with five split votes. The fathers now broke ranks
with the majority moving to Bologna and a minority remaining at Trent.

At Bologna it was August 12 before there was another

---

[28] *Ibid.*, 122-123. Another recent treatment of this episode is James A.
O'Donohoe, *Tridentine Seminary Legislation. Its Sources and Its Formation.* (Louvain: Publications Universitaires de Louvain, 1957), pp. 33-
49. For all that pertains to seminaries in relation to Trent, the present
chapter is indebted to Father O'Donohoe's monograph, a complimentary
copy of which he generously furnished to the present writer.

airing of clerical abuses, this time in connection with the administration of the sacraments. But the subject was in no way advanced by del Monte's appointment of a special ten-bishop committee to deal with the problem, for they merely reiterated the judgment of Paul III's reform commission of ten years before that the ills of the clergy were due to a lack of vigilance in admitting men to holy orders. Nor was there anything new in the same committee's recommendation that candidates be submitted to an examination before being ordained. In other words, the discussion of late November, 1547, had added nothing of significance. And whatever slight hope there may have been for the enactment of even mild measures such as those talked about at Bologna, was extinguished by the increasingly embittered quarrel of Charles V and Paul III. The emperor had gained a signal victory over the Protestants at the Battle of Mühlberg on April 24, but it did nothing to heal the breach between him and the pope. And when the latter met with a flat refusal to his demand that Charles see to it that the prelates at Trent should proceed to Bologna, fearful of a schism if he severed all connections with his imperial adversary, Paul III capitulated to the extent of proroguing the assembly on September 13, 1549. Not until May 1, 1551 was Trent to witness further conciliar activity.

Saint Ignatius and the Early Jesuits

While the wheels of the council thus ground to a stop, progress was being made in another quarter. Thirty years before the renewal of Trent's sessions, Saint Ignatius Loyola had undergone the personal reform that was to lead him after many trials to the University of Paris. There he met a number of like-minded young men who joined him in August, 1534, in vowing their lives to Christ, and who ulti-mately went on to ordination to the priesthood and to constitute the original band of the Society of Jesus which won papal approval in September, 1540. Few churchmen of that time were more conscious than Ignatius and his early companions of the tragedy that had befallen the Church as a consequence of a corrupt and ignorant clergy, nor was there then any group within the Church that was better suited and equipped to apply a practical remedy than these university-trained priests of a new religious order. Their experience in conducting institutions fo the education of young men began early with the opening of a classical college at Messina in Sicily in April, 1548.

As is well known, from the outset the Jesuits attracted attention—favorable or otherwise—from everyone in ecclesiastical circles. It was no surpise, therefore, that a reforming prelate like Giovanni Cardinal Morone, who enjoyed high favor during the pontificates of Paul III and Julius III (1534-1555) should have conceived the idea of opening in Rome a college for educating candidates for the priesthood for the German lands with the Jesuits in charge. Morone knew at first hand the losses that had been suffered by the Church in the German-speaking world, having served at intervals through almost six years as nuncio to the court of Ferdinand, King of the Romans and brother of Charles V. His approach to Loyola won an immediate assent, and when the matter was referred to Pope Julius III he gave it his joyful approval. Saint Ignatius had been kept in close touch with German developments by several of his men who had been assigned to the German states, among them Peter Faber, Nicholas Bobadilla, and Claude Le Jay. During Le Jay's stay of over two years in Germany he became convinced that, much as he would rejoice at a restoration of the study of theology in the universities, it was futile to strive for it at that time. The extreme scarcity of clerical vocations there could only be remedied, he felt, by the individual bishops establishing colleges where they would gather the sons of the poor to study theology in preparation for the priesthood. Such was the substance of a letter which he wrote to his confrére, Alfonso Salmeron, S.J., in January, 1545, and such was the plan, as we have seen, that he continued to urge when he arrived at Trent the following year.

Long before Cardinal Morone made his proposal to Saint Ignatius, the latter had given sustained thought to the problems of ecclesiastical education, especially as they pertained to the members of his Society. In fact, as early as around 1543 he had begun to write his famous *Constitutiones,* a work which was substantially completed by 1551, although he continued to retouch it until the time of his death. In the *Constitutiones,* which were intended for the general government of the Society, Loyola worked out an elaborate program of studies, along with much detail on pedagogical methods and practical matters involving both teachers and students. The sound sense and balance that characterized his thought were present here, and we find him, for example, directing the rectors of the Society's colleges to weigh carefully all the factors that had to do with the students' promotion, such as age, differences in ability, and so forth. And that he was not afraid to encourage young men to strive for excellence was plain when he said: ". . . if some are old enough and have the ability, it is better that they should be advanced and distinguish themselves in all for the glory of God our Lord."[29] In like manner Loyola remarked that just as caution must be used lest zeal for learning should lead students to neglect their spiritual life, so also ". . . during the years of study too much place must not be given to mortification, prayers, and long meditations. For during this time of study, the pursuit of letters, undertaken with a pure intention of serving God, and demanding,

---

[29] *Constitutiones* of Saint Ignatius Loyola in a translation from the Spanish in an appendix to George E. Ganss, S.J., *Saint Ignatius' Idea of a Jesuit University.* (Milwaukee: Marquette University Press, 1954), p. 325.

so to speak, the whole man, will not be less pleasing to God
our Lord, but rather more so."[30]

Not only had Saint Ignatius thought in an original and
constructive way about the problems of clerical education;
he also acted on them in a practical manner. Intent that the
men who were to staff the Society's colleges should have as
good a training as possible, plans were set on foot by Loyola
and his associates to open a college in Rome. Such, in brief,
was the purpose of the Roman College which opened in
February, 1551, with an original faculty of fourteen Jesuits
whose instruction was at first confined to the liberal arts.
The institution was an immediate success, and this encour-
aging circumstance led in October, 1533, to the inauguration
of lectures in philosophy and theology, with twenty students
enrolled in the latter of whom some were young Jesuits
while others, as one historian has said, "were residents of the
German College which Ignatius had inaugurated the preceding year."[31] The ultimate success of the Roman college
was never seriously in doubt, and by 1565 nearly 1,000 students were in attendance at its courses.

Simultaneously plans were moving forward for the German College, the location of which had not been dictated
solely by the disturbed state of the German Church, but as
well by the fact that the Roman College was at hand where
the students could attend classes. For a summary of the aims
and spirit which brought the German College into existence,
it would be difficult to improve on Loyola's description
written to Le Jay less than three months before the opening
of the institution. Its purpose, he said, was to

> undertake the education and moral training of selected young
> men of good character who give promise of fruits of Christian
> piety and virtue . . . Measures will be taken to see that they

[30] *Ibid.*, p. 293.
[31] *Ibid.*, p. 158.

lack nothing in the way of necessities as to their dwelling, board, clothing, books and furnishings—in a word, anything that makes for student comfort. When they have made creditable progress in learning and virtue, they will be sent back to Germany and given ecclesiastical benefices. . . . Those who are intensely interested in the saving of Germany see in this college the surest and almost only means to support the tottering and—alas that we should have to say so, of many places at least—the collapsed Church in Germany.[32]

For this reason Saint Ignatius asked Le Jay to be on the alert for promising German youths who might be sent to Rome as students.

Formal sanction for the German College came in late August, 1552, in a bull issued by Pope Julius III, and it was opened in November. The student body gradually increased from the twenty-four who were in residence a month after the opening to sixty by 1554, and in March, 1555, Ignatius stated that there were then between seventy and eighty German students at the college with around fifty from other nations.[33] In the initial stages, the Jesuit founder experienced some uneasiness over finances, but when Father Jerome Nadal, S.J., reported that Ferdinand, King of the Romans, had agreed to pay all the expenses of forty-eight students for the academic year opening in the autumn of 1555, Loyola breathed more comfortably. It is also worthy of note that Saint Ignatius wrote out a set of regulations for the college which became something of a model for a number of later seminaries, especially those in Rome.[34]

---

[32] Loyola to Le Jay, Rome, July 30, 1552, in William J. Young (Trans. and Ed.), *Letters of St. Ignatius of Loyola*. (Chicago: Loyola University Press, 1959), pp. 259-260.

[33] Loyola to Gerard Hammontanus, Rome, March 22, 1555, *ibid.*, p. 378.

[34] The text of these regulations is contained in Frederico Schroeder, S.J., *Monumenta quae spectant Primordia Collegii Germanici et Hungarici collecta et illustrata*. (Roma: Cuggiani, 1896), pp. 60-74.

The Situation in England

By the time that the German College opened at Rome nearly twenty years had passed since England had been severed from complete papal union by the Act of Supremacy of 1534. Such a radical departure from the nation's religious past had not, of course, been accomplished without preparation of some kind. The age of the Tudors was more than a time of sharp religious change; profound economic changes were likewise at work which were not unrelated to the hardening attitude toward and falling away from the Church. What David Knowles has said of the national sentiment toward the religious orders, that "there was a new feeling of resentment abroad,"[35] could, *mutatis mutandis*, also be said of the English laity's temper toward the secular clergy. Clerical abuse and corruption, such as were prevalent on the continent, plus the keenness of the lay nobility and rising middle class for wealth and economic aggrandizement, served to fix an unfriendly gaze on the clergy generally. It was such a combination that accounted in part for the very mild opposition which Henry VIII encountered in his action against the Holy See. As is well known, of all the English hierarchy only John Fisher, Bishop of Rochester, withstood the royal will. And when a delegation of bishops visited him in the Bell Tower in the hope of persuading him to give way, the holy prelate deplored the loss of so many English Catholics to the faith, and then in direct reference to the hierarchy's defection he asked his visitors: "And seeing that judgment is begone at the home of God, what hope is there left, if we fall, that the rest shall stand? The fort is betrayed even by them that should have defended it."[36] No one realized the depth of that betrayal better than Saint John

---

[35] Knowles, *op. cit.*, p. 458.
[36] Quoted from Fisher's first (anonymous) biographer by Ernest E. Reynolds, *Saint John Fisher*. (New York: P. J. Kenedy and Sons, 1955), pp. 241-242.

Fisher's fellow prisoner in the Bell Tower, Saint Thomas More. With equal perception the fallen chancellor put his finger on one of the keys to the tragedy when he told Margaret Roper:

> And surely, daughter, it is greate pitye that any Christian prince should by a flexible Councell ready to followe his affections, and by a weake Cleargie lackinge grace constantly to stand to their learninge, with Flatterye be so shamefully abused.[37]

The comments of the two great martyrs sounded once again the Church's crying need in England as elsewhere for a properly trained and instructed clergy.

After Saints John Fisher and Thomas More, few English Catholics of that generation have left a more attractive memory than Reginald Pole. He was a second cousin to Henry VIII and his early years were wreathed in the favor of the crown. Following his elementary schooling under the Carthusians at Sheen, about 1512 Pole was sent to Magdalen College, Oxford, where fifteen years before the future Cardinal Wolsey had been elected a fellow before his ordination as a priest in March, 1498. In 1521 Pole proceeded to Padua where there began his long and affectionate relationship with Italy. His return home in 1527 brought him to England just as knowledge of the King's desire for Anne Boleyn had begun to cast a long shadow over the Church, and in the course of the divorce proceedings that followed, Pole, finding himself unable in conscience to accept his royal cousin's claim as supreme head of the Church, set out a second time for Padua in 1532. Here he became absorbed in the humanistic studies that he so much loved until 1536 when Paul III summoned him to Rome and in the consistory of December 22 of that year made him a cardinal.

---

[37] Elsie Vaughan Hitchcock (Ed.), *The Life of Sir Thomas More, Knights written by William Roper, Esquire* [Early English Text Society]. (London: Oxford University Press, 1935), p. 78.

As has been previously seen, in the following year Cardinal Pole was appointed a member of the papal reform commission, and when at last the ecumenical council assembled at Trent the Cardinal of England was one of the three legates of Paul III. On the death of that pontiff in November, 1549, Pole came within three votes of the necessary two-thirds majority of the forty-one cardinals voting, before the arrival of the French cardinals turned the tide in favor of Giomarria del Monte who was elected and took the name of Julius III. It was the death four years later of Edward VI of England, however, that gave a truly decisive turning to Pole's life, for almost immediately the pope named his legate to England, and after sitting out a long interval during which imperial politics prevented his crossing the channel, Emperor Charles V finally relented and he landed at Dover in November, 1554.

It had been twenty-two years since Cardinal Pole had seen his native land, and he was now anxious to use his legatine powers not only to restore the country to the obedience of Rome but, too, to help the Church regain its status in Catholic Christendom and to restore the clergy to the reputation they once enjoyed for respectable morals and sound discipline. With this in mind he summoned a national council which held its first session on November 4, 1555, and continued to meet until February 10, 1556. The ecclesiastical oddities of the age were exemplified in Pole's own life. In spite of the numerous clerical offices and assignments with which he had been associated during the previous thirty years, he had not as yet been ordained a priest. Only when the deprivation and burning of Thomas Cranmer, Archbishop of Canterbury, for heresy in March, 1556, created a vacancy in the primatial see to which Pope Paul IV named Pole, was his ordination to the priesthood brought about on March 10, 1557, two days in advance of his consecration as a bishop and only a year and eight months before his death.

If Cardinal Pole's career has been dwelt on, it has been because of the paramount importance of his name in the history of the modern seminary. The cardinal's long residence in Italy had brought him an acquaintance with all the leading ecclesiastical personalities of the age. including Saint Ignatius with whom Pole was on friendly terms. Two months after the latter reached England, Loyola sent him a report on both the Roman and German Colleges, noting that at the latter there was an English student, while an Irishman was enrolled at the Roman College. He then said:

> If your Eminence thinks fit to send some youth of talent and well-fitted for training in letters to the one college or the other, we hope that in a short time we should be able to send them back to you with good profit in life and learning and well-grounded in our holy faith. . . .[38].

There could be no question about Pole's thinking it altogether fit to do so, but conditions being what they then were, where was he to find them? In fact, it was with the hope of supplying that precise need that the cardinal was at pains in the national council to sponsor in its eleventh decree a law whose title read "that in cathedrals there be educated a certain number of beginners, from which, as from a seed-

---

[38] Loyola to Pole, January 24, 1555, Joseph H. Crehan, S.J., Saint Ignatius and Cardinal Pole," *Archivum Historicum Societatis Jesu*, XXV (1956), 84. In an appendix Crehan published an undated (c. 1572) letter by an unnamed writer, described as "some Italian friend of Pole's" and thought possibly to have been Niccolò Ormaneto, later Bishop of Padua, an intimate friend who served the cardinal over a long period as secretary. It was addressed to Pope Gregory XIII who was told that Pole had entertained the idea of converting the English Hospice at Rome into a college such as that opened shortly before (1568) at Douai. Actually, the English College, Rome, had its beginnings in this same hospice in 1576. Incidentally, the statement frequently made (*Catholic Encyclopedia*, XIII, 695), that Pole's decree was the first time that the word '*seminarium*' (seedbed) had been used in relation to seminaries, is no longer held to be true.

bed, priests may be chosen who can worthily be placed in charge of the churches."[39]

At last a canonical assembly had enacted a practical and realistic measure which seemed to give promise of meeting the Church's needs. Although in the strict sense there was little that was original about the decree—a fact which Pole explicitly stated—the general directive for the establishment of an institution to educate candidates for the priesthood, combined with the accompanying details on students' entrance requirements (favoring the sons of the poor), a program of studies which made due allowance for students' differing ages and intellectual abilities, qualifications to be met by the professors, and the sources from which financial support might be drawn, constituted one of the most complete and feasible plans to date for the improvement of clerical life. In drawing up the decree Pole had leaned on the enactments of earlier councils, the experience of the English cathedral schools, and the section of the *Reformatio legum ecclesiasticarum* of 1553. This latter document, intended for Parliament's consideration, had dealt with ways of improving those schools and had owed most to Cranmer, Anglican Archbishop of Canterbury.[40]

THE SEMINARY LEGISLATION OF TRENT

As it turned out, the English conciliar decree's most important contribution was the influence which it exerted on the final action taken at Trent over seven years later. Not since the decree on lectureships in Scripture of June, 1546, had the ecumenical council done anything worthy of note on this subject. Moreover, nothing was accomplished during

---

[39] Francis Cardinal Bourne, *Ecclesiastical Education.* (New York: Benziger Brothers, 1926), p. 74. The full text of the decree is given here in an appendix (pp. 74-77).

[40] For a summary of Pole's decree and its significance, see O'Donohoe, *op. cit.*, pp. 89-120.

the council's second period from May, 1551, to April, 1552, whereupon for a number of reasons, including Pope Paul IV's disinclination to reassemble the council and the opposition of the secular powers regarding its location, there ensued an interval of nearly a decade. Only with the election on December 26, 1559, of Giovanni Cardinal Medici who took the name of Pius IV and who had the extraordinary good fortune to have as his Secretary of State his nephew, Saint Charles Borromeo, was hope of the council revived. After overcoming a great many obstacles the assembly opened for its third and final period in January, 1562. But over a year passed before the appointment in February, 1563, of a committee of ten bishops who gave the subject of clerical reform new life with their probing into abuses connected with the Sacrament of Holy Orders.

This committee now received various proposals to remedy the evils that beset the clergy. Among the more important of these proposals were those of Emperor Ferdinand I which showed signs of the influence of Claude Le Jay, S.J.; another set of suggestions came from Luigi Beccadelli, Bishop of Ragusa, and a third from Charles de Guise, Cardinal of Lorraine and Archbishop of Rheims. It is not necessary to analyze the different approaches employed in these proposals. Suffice it to say, along with a number of other plans, they formed the basis for both the private discussions of the spring of 1563 and, too, for the public debates which began on May 10 when Nicolas Psaume, Bishop of Verdun, brought the subject before the council. During the two months that followed the fathers debated clerical reform along with other matters, and finally on July 15 in the twenty-third session the decree on seminaries received the council's approval with only seven bishops having reservations of one kind or another.

Given the struggle that it had taken to bring about this instrument for remedying the long-standing abuses in clerical life, it is little wonder that Pius IV should have thought of the decree as having been divinely inspired and have expressed the wish to be the first to put it into execution.[41] One of the council's first historians remarked that many were of the mind that whatever other good remained undone, this alone recompensed for all the labors and the anxieties which the fathers had experienced.[42] Since most of the clerical education of the modern Church looks to Trent as to its source and inspiration, it will be well to review the decree in some detail.[43]

That the substance of Trent's legislation was owed to the decree of Cardinal Pole of seven years before, is evident. With only a few verbal differences the first draft introduced for consideration in May, 1563, was practically verbatim that of the English national council, so much so, that a recent historian has stated that its composer did not even take the pains "to adapt the terms of the decree of Pole to the ensemble of the other articles for reform presented elsewhere in the same draft."[44] True, as the debate proceeded changes were made and amended drafts introduced, but the law that emerged on July 15, 1563, was basically the one which had come from Pole's council in February, 1556. Its principal provisions may be summarized as follows. Every cathedral and metropolitan church was obliged to erect a special institution—or seminary—for the education of future priests, an obligation from which the smaller and poorer jurisdictions might be absolved by several dioceses joining together to found what has come to be called a provincial or interdiocesan seminary. While the law called for a seminary in each diocese, it is worth noting that it did

---

[41] Pallavicino Sforza, *Istoria del Concilio di Trento*. (Francescantonio Zaccaria, Ed.). (Mendrisio: Minerva Ticinese, 1836), X, 223.

[42] *Ibid.*, IX, p. 254.

[43] The decree may be found in Henry J. Schroeder, O.P. (Ed.), *Canons and Decrees of the Council of Trent*, Original Text with English Translation. (St. Louis: B. Herder Book Company, 1941), pp. 175-179.

[44] O'Donohoe, *op. cit.*, pp. 139-140.

not specify that every candidate whom a bishop ordained must be educated in a seminary.

In regard to the entrance requirements, candidates should be at least twelve years of age, have a certain competence in reading and writing, and possess the kind of character which would suggest a fit man for the ministry. Moreover, as we have seen in the case of the English decree, preference was to be given to the sons of the poor. On the matter of the intellectual requirements, the legislation was quite vague, nor was there any division suggested according to the individual student's age and abilities. Beyond the statement that they were to study letters, the humanities, chant, and the science of "ecclesiastical computation," students were also to be taught Scripture, dogmatic, moral, and pastoral theology, and the rubrics. Specifications regarding the student's spiritual formation included the wearing of the clerical garb, receiving tonsure on entrance, assisting at daily Mass, going to confession once a month, and to holy Communion according to the advice of his spiritual director.

Finally, as for the faculty and administration, one can get an idea of the tenor of the decree from what was said in regard to the former. It was stated that

> . . . those offices or dignities, which are called professorships, shall not be conferred except on doctors or masters or licentiates of sacred Scripture or canon law and on other competent persons who can personally discharge that office; any appointment made otherwise shall be null and void, all privileges and customs whatsoever, even though immemorial, notwithstanding.[45]

The importance assigned to administration may be gauged by the fact that of four printed pages occupied by the decree —except for an introductory half page and the regulations governing the students and faculty—the rest of the space was devoted to administration. There were rather minute direc-

---

[45] Schroeder, *op. cit.*, p. 178.

tions, for example, about how to raise revenue for the seminary's support, as well as details concerning the two committees—one for spiritual and disciplinary matters, the other for temporal concerns—that were to function under the bishop as supreme administrator of the institution.

With the advantage of those who view Trent's legislation through the perspective of four centuries, it is easy to agree with a contemporary historian who has characterized the decree on seminaries as, "the most original and probably the most important creation of the Council."[46] Allowing full recognition of the enactment of 1563 as a victory for Catholic reform, it should not be forgotten that it was very late in coming, and that from the viewpoint of the spiritual and intellectual training of candidates for holy orders, its contents were disappointing with emphasis so largely directed to details of administration. Given the notorious lives of so many churchmen for a century or more prior to Trent, and the woeful inadequacy of their preparation for the priesthood, one would have thought that Luther's break in 1517 would have at last bestirred those in authority to strike at the root of so much of the Church's grief in the corrupt lives of her clergy. But, as has been seen, such was not the case. In fact, when finally the Fathers at Trent got around to taking action less than five months before the close of an assembly that had been meeting at intervals for nearly eighteen years, they would seem to have been motivated for the most part by ideas on clerical reform that, as has been said, were "concerned principally with preventing the ordination of the unsuitable rather than providing suitable training."[47]

---

[46] Pierre Janelle, *The Catholic Reformation.* (Milwaukee: Bruce Publishing Company, 1949), p. 97. Daniel-Rops has also stated that Trent's legislation on seminaries "proved to be among the most fruitful of its undertakings," *op. cit.,* p. 101.

[47] H. Outram Evennett in "Short Notices," *English Historical Review,* LXXIII (April, 1958), 349.

2.

From Trent to the 1960's

Early Post-Tridentine Seminaries

If the virtual indispensability of seminaries has long since been accepted throughout the Catholic world, it was otherwise in 1563. Indeed, a great deal of time passed before the decree on seminaries, or any of the laws of Trent, became operative in some countries. The point may be best illustrated by several examples. In Portugal where the reform-minded Archbishop of Braga, Bartholomew Fernandez, O.P., gave the lead, not too long a time elapsed before King Sebastian I in October, 1564, informed the Holy See that the Tridentine laws would be promulgated in such a way "as to ensure their undisputed and inviolate integrity."[1] And as was seen in the first chapter, in the Papal States where the pontiff's word was supreme, the Roman and German Colleges had anticipated Trent by almost a decade. The first Tridentine seminary in Italy was begun by Marcantonio Cardinal Amulio, Bishop of Rieti, in 1564, to be followed a year later by Pope Pius IV's Roman Seminary. Successive pontiffs gave generous support to these and kindred institutions both in the Eternal City and elsewhere when permitted by local rulers to do so. In northern Italy the nephew of Pius IV, Saint Charles Borromeo, was prompt to implement

---

[1] Sebastian I to Pius IV, October 2, 1954, in Pierre Janelle, *The Catholic Reformation* (Milwaukee: Bruce Publishing Company, 1949), p. 108.

41

the decrees of Trent throughout the immense ecclesiastical
Province of Milan over which he presided as metropolitan.
Not long after he took command in the north he summoned
his fifteen suffragan bishops to a provincial council, for as
he wisely remarked to his uncle, Pius IV: "I have decided
to begin the reform prescribed by Trent with the prelates.
This seems to be the best means to obtain obedience in our
diocese. We must be the first to march; our subjects will
follow the more readily."[2]

Charles Borromeo was, indeed, the first to march insofar
as a major undertaking in behalf of priestly education in
northern Italy was concerned. In December, 1564, he opened in Milan the first of several seminaries with an initial
faculty of fourteen Jesuits and thirty-four students in residence, while about 100 more students came from outside
to attend the classes. After eight years this seminary grew
to a student body of 140, with around sixty students enrolled
in another seminary which Borromeo had begun for less
intellectually gifted candidates. The Cardinal Archbishop of
Milan also drew up in 1569 a set of regulations for his seminaries which, though it was not a finished document, proved
serviceable a half century later in offering guidance to seminary pioneers like Father Jean-Jacques Olier and Saint
Vincent de Paul who, it has been said, "were inspired by
the example of Saint Charles, and introduced into priestly
life those devotional practices which Saint Charles had first
used and adopted from the *Spiritual Exercises* of Saint
Ignatius."[3]

The first seminary in the German world after the close of
the Council of Trent was begun in 1564 at Eichstädt in
Bavaria. As for England, Ireland, and Scotland, by the end
of the conciliar sessions at Trent the Catholics of these

---

[2] Borromeo to Pius IV, October 18, 1565, in Cesare Orsenigo, *Life of St.
Charles Borromeo* (Saint Louis: B. Herder Book Company, 1943), p. 83.
[3] *Ibid.*, p. 82.

countries had fallen on such evil days that the governments
of Elizabeth I and of James VI of Scotland would not allow
so much as a Catholic grammar school, to say nothing of
seminaries. But official proscription did not render the
priesthood of the three countries extinct. On the contrary,
only five years after Trent there was established at Douai
in the Low Countries the seminary that came to be known
as Douai College.[4] This institution which opened in September, 1568, was destined to become a center of English
Catholic ecclesiastical and intellectual life on the continent
for over a century, and also to serve as a model for a number
of other continental schools for the education of English,

---

[4] The English, Irish, and Scottish Catholics use the term college for a
seminary; for example, Saint Patrick's College, Maynooth, which was
founded in 1795 with financial assistance from the British government in
order to keep the Irish clergy from being influenced by French ideas in
the continental seminaries. A recent scholarly history of one of these
seminaries is David Milburn, *A History of Ushaw College* (Durham:
Ushaw Bookshop, 1964). An older work that deals with one of the English seminaries is Thomas Hooley, *A Seminary in the Making. Being a
History of the Foundation and Early Years of St. John's Diocean Seminary, Wonersh, 1889 to 1903* (London: Longmans, Green and Company,
1927). Francis Bourne, the future cardinal, was the first rector of this
institution which began at Henfield on August 3, 1889, with three students. Bourne had been educated by the Sulpicians in Paris, and Hooley
stated that Saint John's "owed a great deal to the influence of St. Sulpice
. . ." (p. viii). Mention has already been made of the house seminary begun by Herbert Vaughan soon after his consecration as Bishop
of Salford in October, 1872. Vaughan's biographer, J. G. Snead-Cox,
has two chapters that are pertinent to the history of seminaries, viz.,
"Vice-President of St. Edmund's," (I, 59-103) and "The Education
of the Priest," (II, 34-69). Snead-Cox quoted Vaughan's diary in
regard to what the latter described as "the severe system of discipline"
employed at the German College in Rome and at Saint Sulpice which,
he thought, would not do for Englishmen since he said, "We are naturally free; we care for our freedom more than any other nation. We are
willing to do good work, but we must not be forced to do it. . . .
English students should be guided without their knowing that they are
guided." He concluded, therefore, "Let us transplant the Sulpician or
German plant to England with enough earth to keep it alive, but then
let it be planted in English soil and develop according to the genius
of the country. Such was Newman's work in bringing the Roman
Oratory to England." Snead-Cox, *op. cit.*, I, 60.

Irish, and Scottish candidates for the diocesan priesthood. Douai was largely the inspiration and accomplishment of one man, William Allen, the future cardinal, and from this college and its sister institutions there went forth to their respective homelands a steady stream of zealous missionary priests. Through the ministrations of these men, and those of the English-speaking members of the religious orders, the faith was kept alive through the penal age. With the advent of the French Revolution in 1789 most of the continental colleges were forced to close temporarily, and it was at this time that several of them found refuge in England where the perennial hatred of Catholicism was monentarily eclipsed by the overriding national purpose to defeat revolutionary France. Thus Douai was moved to the mother country where the professors and students divided to establish in November, 1793, Saint Edmund's College, Old Hall, Ware, and in October, 1794, Saint Cuthbert's College, Ushaw, near Durham in the north. Both of these institutions are still flourishing as combined major and minor seminaries.

Unlike Portugal and the Italian states, however, the introduction of Trent's legislation into other Catholic lands proved painfully slow despite the fact the governments might well have been expected to insure its speedy and effective execution. True, King Philip II of Spain had even preceded his neighbor in Lisbon by several months in publishing the Tridentine decrees on July 19, 1564. But he was at pains to make it clear that this was being done only with the proviso that this action was without prejudice to the rights he claimed for the crown over the Church. What Philip had in mind became apparent as there unfolded the long struggle which he waged against both Pius IV and Pius V for the maintenance of ecclesiastical powers correctly described as "scarcely inferior to those which Henry VIII of England had claimed a few decades before."[5]

---

[5] Janelle, *op. cit.*, p. 108.

French Seminaries from Trent to the Revolution

France likewise illustrated the difficulty. The previous essay discussed the activity of that ambiguous figure, the Cardinal of Lorraine, who in closing months at Trent, urged the correction of clerical abuses and other reform measures. After the close of the council he tried to have the decrees immediately published in France. However, he found himself thwarted by the queen mother, Catherine de' Medici, who during the thirty years that spanned the reigns of her three weak sons (1559-1589), was the most powerful figure at court. Catherine's vacillation in all that pertained to the Protestants dictated her caution in launching a true reform of the French Church, for in her reckoning Trent's vigorous condemnation of the Huguenots made the conciliar decrees dangerous from a political point of view. Thus though the next forty years witnessed repeated efforts on the part of the papal nuncios and others to win royal acceptance of the decrees, they were never officially promulgated. Finally, at the Assembly of the Clergy in 1615, the Bishop of Luçon, the future Cardinal Richelieu, made a memorable speech in behalf of their implementation which led to the clergy's issuing a solemn declaration in which they "received" the Tridentine laws and promised to comply with their provisions. While this constituted a step forward for the Catholic Reformation in France, the king's refusal to take official action prevented the reform movement from realizing its true potentialities, with the result that abuses such as those connected with benefices were perpetuated all through this century and on to the French Revolution.

The roles played in the Church-State questions of this period by the Cardinal of Lorraine and the later Cardinal Richelieu serve to demonstrate how tortuous was the path of French religious reform. Charles de Guise, named Archbishop of Rheims at the age of fourteen, became in 1547 the virtual founder of the University of Rheims. This university which was developed out of the Collège des Bons Enfants, soon expanded four faculties, including theology. Moreover, in 1572 the cardinal secured a bull from Pope Gregory XIII for the establishment of the University of Pont-à-Mousson in Lorraine, which was staffed by the Jesuits, and which has been described as an important center of Christian education, "especially in the training of future priests for France, and for Scotland too."[6] Deeply immersed as he was in politics, however, Cardinal de Guise's ambitions at times clashed with his reforming tendencies although there could be no gainsaying the fact that in 1562 he identified himself at Trent with the reforming elements. In so doing he was carrying out the throne's instructions in such matters as the support he gave to the reception of Holy Eucharist under both species and to the liturgy in the vernacular; but on a third point in the official program, a married clergy, he remained silent in his speech of January, 1563. The previous essay already mentioned the leading part that the cardinal took in the discussion on seminaries. Upon his return from the council he started a seminary in 1567 at Rheims. However, the fury and disruption caused by the religious wars that had begun seven years before, put an end to it as well as to most of his educational projects.

Thirty-four years after the death of the Cardinal of Lorraine the twenty-three year old Bishop of Luçon took pos-

---

[6] Martin P. Harney, S.J., *The Jesuits in History* (New York: America Press, 1941), p. 134. For a scholarly account of this churchman's activities at Trent, see H. Outram Evennett, *The Cardinal of Lorraine and the Council of Trent.* (Cambridge: The University Press, 1940). One of the less attractive sides of the cardinal's ecclesiastical policies was his reaction to the Saint Bartholomew's Day Massacre of August, 1572, when he enthusiastically initiated a celebration of the event at the Church of Saint Louis in Rome, wrote a letter of congratulation to King Charles IX, and later at a session of the Assembly of the Clergy with the king in attendance, heaped praise on Charles for his action. See Henry Dwight Sedgwick, *The House of Guise* (Indianapolis: Bobbs-Merrill Company, 1938), pp. 237-238.

session of his diocese. Richelieu had originally been intended for a military career. However, when his older brother decided to enter the Grand Chartreuse—thus forfeiting their mother's hope that he would carry out the contract agreed upon with his granduncle, Jacques du Plessis, to succeed him at Luçon and keep the income of some 18,000 *livres* in the family—the younger brother was induced to change the plan for his own future. Up to 1605 Richelieu had had no ecclesiastical education, but being a man who never did things in half measures, he now retired to the country with Philippe de Cospéan, Bishop of Aire, a doctor in theology from Louvain, as his tutor. After almost three years he felt the essentials had been mastered, and he then proceeded to Rome in April, 1607, for the next steps, namely, ordination and consecration as a bishop. Returning to Paris in October he stood for the doctoral examination in theology and then remained on for a year, after which he proceeded south and entered his see city on December 21, 1608.

Luçon was on of the poorest dioceses in France with around 100,000 souls and 428 priests among whom clerical abuses had become a commonplace. Quickly resolving in June, 1609, a long-standing dispute between the diocese and the canons of the cathedral chapter, the young bishop launched an energetic program of reform. With a view to tightening clerical standards he called several diocesan synods. That Richelieu's activities did not constitute supererogation may be implied from a regulation issued in 1606 by the Archbishop of Bordeaux, the metropolitan of the province, to the effect that before a priest could be admitted to the status of a *curé* he must satisfy the diocesan authorities that he possessed a copy of the Bible, the lives of the saints, Mailhard's *Guide des Curés*, the catechism of Trent, and copies of the conciliar legislation of the province. As one of the historians of Richelieu's early years remarked, it was clear from this requirement that a priest was expected to have "only the knowledge necessary for the administration of the sacraments."[7]

In the synods of 1609 and 1610 Richelieu sought to implement the reform by such measures as demanding that the priests assemble one day a week for instructions in what concerned the administration of the sacraments, and later to submit to an examination in these matters.[8] The young bishop went a step further, and in 1611 began plans for a seminary. For many reasons it was a formidable undertaking at that time, entailing as it did the necessity of securing letters patent from the king and a decree from the local *parlement,* and of fulfilling, as has been said, "twenty other formalities capable of discouraging the most ardent zeal and the most energetic will."[9] But Richelieu lacked nothing by way of a determined will, so he pushed ahead in spite of all obstacles. On March 12, 1612, with his own money he purchased a house near the cathedral and installed there the first students with a superior and professor. The seminary of Luçon did not prosper under the secular priests, however, and Richelieu therefore invited the Oratorians to take charge which they did early in 1617.

Had the Bishop of Luçon remained in his diocese he might well have succeeded in establishing a lasting work in this seminary. But by the year of the Oratorians' advent to Luçon he was already engaged in making his political fortune in Paris and he saw little or nothing of Luçon thereafter. In a short time a quarrel arose between the Oratorians and the canons of the cathedral. The canons did not want to support the seminary; the Oratorians, in turn, felt aggrieved at being expected to labor without compensation. They gradually withdrew, until by 1625 only one priest was

---

[7] L. Lacroix, *Richelieu a Luçon. Sa Jeunesse—Son Épiscopat* (Paris: Letouzey et Ané, 1890), p. 75.

[8] *Ibid.,* p. 80.

[9] *Ibid.,* p. 83.

left, and this in spite of a personal visit to Luçon on the part of Pierre de Bérulle, the founder and superior general of the congregation. The strong hand of Richelieu was missing and as a consequence the seminary collapsed. As the historian of his Luçon years remarked, "The intrigues of the court, political anxieties, and his personal ambition caused him to forget a work that at the outset had been so near to his heart and for which he had expended so much zeal and energy."[10]

Fortunately for France—and for the Universal Church—Richelieu's generation produced a group of priests whose exclusive commitment to their sacred calling enabled them to combine deep piety, a remarkable zeal for souls, and an extraordinary talent for organization in the reform of clerical morals and the establishment of a systematic program of preparation for the priesthood. Consequently these men served not only their own age and country but which have continued to produce good results in many lands down to the present day. It is not necessary to do more here than mention the names of the principal pioneers of France's seventeenth-century seminary movement, and to speak briefly of the work of several of their number. In the front rank of these men were Adrien Bourdoise, Pierre de Bérulle, Vincent de Paul, Jean-Jacques Olier, and Jean-Marie Eudes.

That over a half century after the close of the Council of Trent there should still be grave need for drastic action to uproot the evils in clerical life, was all too evident. The situation described to Vincent de Paul in 1642 by a respected

---

[10] *Ibid.*, p. 89. Another reform measure that Richelieu introduced into the Diocese of Luçon was that of bringing in the Capuchin friars who established several houses. He never entirely lost his interest in clerical reform and in 1642 he told Father François Bourgoing, third Superior General of the Oratorians, that he would give the sum of 3,000 *écus* to finance conferences for the clergy in the Oratorian houses. However the cardinal's death in December of that year, before he had had time to assign the money, rendered the project abortive. *Ibid.*, p. 89, n.l.

canon of a cathedral church was not uncommon:

> In this diocese the clergy is without discipline, the people
> without fear, and the priests without devotion and without
> charity; the pulpits without preachers, learning without honor,
> vice without chastisement; virtue is persecuted and the author-
> ity of the Church hated and despised; self-interest is the ord-
> inary scale by which things are weighed in the sanctuary, the
> most scandalous are the most powerful, and flesh and blood
> have thus supplanted the gospel and spirit of Jesus Christ.[11]

One bishop confessed his horror at the thought that almost
7,000 priests of his diocese ascended the altar every day
regardless of their sins of intemperance and sexual impurity;
another prelate stated that except for the canon theologian
of his cathedral, he was unable to find a priest among his
clergy who was capable of acquitting an ecclesiastical obligation.[12] With numerous reports of this kind reaching Saint
Vincent, it was little wonder that he should have declared
the Church in many places in a state of collapse by reason of
the evil lives of her priests. "It is they who are ruining and
destroying her," he said, "and the depravity of the ecclesiastical state is the chief cause of the ruin of God's Church."[13]

Yet the ultimate remedy for these conditions was not
found in the French seminaries of that date, opened as they
had been, according to the mind of Trent, to boys of twelve.
Rather amelioration was to come through later houses of
formation for more mature youths. The latter evolved only
very slowly with two influential priests, Pierre de Bérulle
(the future cardinal) and Adrien Bourdoise leading the way.
In November, 1611, de Bérulle founded the French Oratory
with several companions. The principal aim of the Oratory

---

[11] An unnamed canon quoted by Louis Abelly, *La Vie du Vénérable Ser-
viteur de Dieu Vincent de Paul* (Paris: Lambert, 1664), Sect. I, 213.
[12] *Ibid.*, Sect. I, 214.
[13] Quoted by Abelly, *op. cit.*, Sect. I, 213.

was the perfection of the priestly state. And since de Bérulle's main objection looked to a restoration of the pristine purity and beauty of the priesthood, it was natural that the Oratorians should have established early seminaries in Paris (1612) and in Langres (1616), and that de Bérulle, as has been seen, should have sent his men to take charge of Richelieu's seminary at Luçon in 1617.

Meanwhile de Bérulle's contemporary, Bourdoise, had opened a house with twelve other aspirants at Saint Nicolas de Chardonnet in 1612, the year before his own ordination to the priesthood. Here they sought to instruct themselves in the practical aspects of the ministry. Ordained the following year, Bourdoise began in 1618 to receive young men for more extended instruction, and two years thereafter his little company secured a permanent house in Paris. Both de Bérulle and Bourdoise exercised a deep influence in clerical circles, and it was from them that famous seminary founders like Vincent de Paul and Olier derived early inspiration and enlightenment for their own endeavors. Indeed, Vincent went as far as to state in August, 1659, that before Bourdoise men scarcely knew what a seminary meant.[14]

All the while conscientious churchmen were casting about for the best means to lift the moral tone of the clergy, and to test the fitness of those who presented themselves for ordination, since the norm of canonical adoption of a candidate by a particular bishop was still far from universally observed. As a consequence of a meeting between Vincent de Paul and Augustin Potier, Bishop of Beauvais, in July, 1628,

---

[14] Pierre Coste, C.M., (Ed.), *Saint Vincent de Paul: Correspondence, Entretiens, Documents* (Paris: Librairie Lecoffre. J. Gabalda, 1924), XII, 289. Vincent was in error in stating that Bourdoise was the first man to open a seminary, because Saints Ignatius Loyola and Charles Borromeo, as well as Cardinal de Guise at Rheims, to name only three, had preceded him. Hereafter this work will be referred to as: Coste, *Saint Vincent de Paul.*

there was inaugurated the system of ten-day retreats for ordinands. To be sure, relatively little could be done in so short a time to equip men adequately for their life work; yet these pre-ordination retreats were a step in the right direction. They afforded an opportunity for a briefing on both the spiritual and practical aspects of the ministry as, for example, the administration of the sacraments and the rubrics governing liturgical services. Moreover, the good these retreats accomplished was extended beyond Beauvais when Bishop Potier's initiative was taken up in 1631 by Jean-François de Gondi, Archbishop of Paris, and by other ordinaries. In 1659 Pope Alexander VII officially sanctioned the retreats for all candidates for major orders. Some bishops stretched the length of these exercises from ten days to two or three months, and thus as one writer has said, "the first seminaries were being gradually and almost unconsciously established."[15]

Up to 1641 the retreats for ordinands continued to be the principal means of preparing men for holy orders in the French Church; yet their originator, Vincent de Paul, was not content to rest there. About 1636 his Congregation of the Mission opened the Collège des Bons-Enfants in Paris to youths who showed an inclination toward the priesthood. But after a few years Vincent candidly declared that he was dissatisfied with the results, for as he told Father Bernard Codoing, experience had demonstrated that it was unwise to expect boys so young to persevere. Paying his respects to Trent's seminary legislation as having been inspired by the Holy Spirit, Vincent maintained, nonetheless, that those institutions that had followed the conciliar rule of admitting boys at the age of twelve, such as the seminaries of Bordeaux, Rheims, and Rouen, as well as most of those in Italy outside Rome and Milan, had not flourished. "It is other-

---

15 Marcetteau, *op. cit.*, p. 20.

wise," he said, "when they [students] are taken from twenty to twenty-five or thirty years of age."[16]

It was one thing to recognize a defect, however, and quite another to apply an effective remedy. Well aware of Cardinal Richelieu's keen interest in all that pertained to clerical life, Vincent de Paul not infrequently consulted the powerful minister of King Louis XIII. In this instance Richelieu was quickly won to Vincent's plan and gave him 1,000 crowns which enabled the latter to introduce early in 1642 an administrative change at the Collège des Bons-Enfants. One division of the institution remained devoted to boys, while the other was turned over to the instruction of more mature youths who were boarded and lodged gratis for the two years required to complete the course. Still other older youths of the same age were admitted on payment of a pension and on their promise to remain for at least one year. The change brought gratifying results, and in 1645 all the older students were moved to another building. Indeed, according to Vincent's biographers, his major contribution to seminary education, was his recognition of the fact that seminaries should be opened to young men as well as boys of twelve as prescribed by Trent.[17]

The 1640's proved to be an especially fruitful decade for French seminary education. Not only did the Jesuits, Oratorians, and Vincentians continue to expand their work, but new groups came into existence whose principal objective was the education of the clergy. For example, the Congregation of Jesus and Mary, or Eudists, founded in 1643 by Saint Jean-Marie Eudes, was to figure prominently in sem-

---

[16] Vincent de Paul to Codoing, Paris, May 13, 1644, in Coste, *Saint Vincent de Paul*, II, 459.
[17] Pierre Coste, C.M., *The Life and Works of Saint Vincent de Paul*, translated by Joseph Leonard, C.M. (London: Burns, Oates & Washbourne, 1934), I, 261-262. See also the latest work on the subject, Maurice A. Roche, C.M., *Saint Vincent de Paul and the Formation of Clerics* (Fribourg: The University Press, 1964), pp. 135-136.

inary education during succeeding decades. More widely known, however, were the Sulpicians whose founder, Father Jean-Jacques Olier, had been intimately associated with Saints Vincent de Paul and Jean-Marie Eudes, as well as with the Oratorians, Pierre de Bérulle and the latter's successor, Charles de Condren. It was on December 29, 1641, that Olier took up residence with two companions at Vaugirard near Paris where in a brief time he and four associates had under their direction a group of eight men, composed of both ordained priests anxious for more adequate training and clerics who hoped to be ordained.

From the outset the relations of the little company at Vaugirard with the local parish were cordial. Olier always placed high value on this relationship since he felt it was important for candidates for the priesthood to be associated as closely as possible with parochial activities which would occupy so great a part of their later lives. This same idea helped to influence Olier's judgment when after a few months at Vaugirard he was offered the pastorate of the large and important Church of Saint Sulpice in Paris. Upon his aceptance and subsequent taking of possession—in company with his priests associates and fourteen students in August, 1642—the famous Seminary of Saint Sulpice was born. The students attended classes at the Sorbonne while living at Saint Sulpice where for the ensuing fifteen years they profited from the spiritual direction of Olier until the founder's death in April, 1657, at the age of forty-eight. While Olier had been linked with Vincent de Paul as one who had made the retreat for ordinands and also—as co-author of the retreat discourses, his seminary was not so much an outgrowth of the retreats as it was a new institution.

All things considered, students at the Sulpician mother seminary were probably afforded at this time a superior intellectual training to that of most candidates for the

French diocesan clergy. This was true by reason of their enrollment in the University of Paris, although in sending them there Olier had also been motivated by the hope that their presence would be a source of edification and sanctification to the Sorbonne professors. In spite of the brilliant achievements of many Frenchmen of this age in literature and the arts, the emphasis in ecclesiastical educational circles, unfortunately, was often anti-intellectual. Vincent de Paul's latest historian has frankly admitted that the saint showed this tendency, and Vincent's mind was pretty well summed up on the matter in his remark that for a priest, "a general knowledge suffices, and everything that a man desires beyond that is to be feared rather than desired by the workers of the Gospel. . . ."[18] That this put a dangerous premium on intellectual mediocrity among the clergy, if not on outright ignorance, would seem to be obvious. In fact, less than a generation after Vincent's death this kind of thinking was carried to extremes by the fiery abbot of La Trappe, Jean-Armand de Rancé. In 1683 de Rancé published his *La Sainteté et les Devoirs de la Vie Monastique*, a work that evoked, after considerable hesitation and reluctance, the notable defense of the intellectual virtues from Jean Mabillon, O.S.B., the famous Maurist, in his *Traité des Etudes Monastiques* of 1693.[19]

If seminary education was a long time in striking roots in France, by the same token it is doubtful that any other country was ultimately to show a more widespread and lasting success in this regard. There were, of course, failures,

---

18 Vincent de Paul to Gaspard Stelle, Paris, July 18, 1659, Coste, *Saint Vincent de Paul*, VIII, 33.

19 For a summary of the de Rancé-Mabillon controversy, see the introduction to the English translation of Mabillon's *Traité des Etudes Monastiques* by Alcuin Siebenand, O.S.B., Isidore Botz, O.S.B., and Maurice Weber, O.S.B., which was carried in successive issues of *Scriptorium*, XVII (January, 1958), ff. [*Scriptorium* is a privately circulated journal of the clerics of Saint John's Abbey, Collegeville, Minnesota.]

i.e. institutions that lasted for only a brief span of years and then disappeared forever, such as happened in Luçon to the seminary that was first in charge of the diocesan clergy and then of the Oratorians. There were also temporary failures like the Sulpicians experienced in Nantes until a fresh start in 1728 put the institution there on a firm and enduring foundation. But the over-all achievement of both the French secular and regular clergy engaged in this work was truly extraordinary. Thus, for example, the Eudists opened a seminary in Coutances in 1650 and one at Lisieux three years later; the Sulpicians, who by Olier's death in 1657 had founded four seminaries besides the original one in Paris, on the eve of the Revolution 130 years later were staffing fourteen seminaries in various parts of France.

But the movement that had produced such excellent re-sults in the second half of the seventeenth and the early years of the eighteenth century, did not escape the general decline that beset Catholicism with the dawn of the age of the *philosophes*. It has rightly been said that from about 1715, the year that Louis XIV died, Catholic thought was no longer fashionable. Discussion of the great religious and social problems that had for so long taken place in a Christian context gave way to a day when, as a recent historian has remarked, "Voltaire and Rousseau . . . assumed the mantles of Bossuet and Pascal."[20] With Louis XV's banishment of the Society of Jesus from France and from its colonies in 1763 the new tendencies won a signal triumph, for with the Jesuits' removal the French Church lost the most effective champions of her interests against the Jansenists, Gallicians, and rationalists. The defeat was rendered universal ten years later when pressure on Pope Clement XIV from the Bourbon sovereigns succeeded in having the Society suppressed throughout the world. With the forces of

---

[20] Adrien Dansette, *Religious History of Modern France*, translated by John Dingle (New York: Herder and Herder, 1961), I, 5.

scepticism and of state absolutism thus riding high over both Church and State, it was not altogether a literary license when an ecclesiastical historian described authority in both realms at this time as having "bobbed around like corks as they were carried by the currents of the times towards the revolutionary maelstrom."[21]

As for the seminaries' fate in this changing pattern of events, the general havoc and disruption that were to befall them with the Revolution had a foreshadowing in the lands subject to the Emperor Joseph II who launched his ecclesiastical "reforms" soon after he ascended the throne of the Holy Roman Empire in 1780. During the next ten years one category after another of religious institutions was swept away by the emperor's determination to reduce the Church to a department of government which, in turn, led to a multiplication of restrictive measures such as forbidding seminarians to go to Rome to study. Needless to say, these policies aroused opposition. When a decree of October, 1786, suppressed the episcopal seminaries in the Low Countries and replaced them by two state seminaries at Louvain and Luxemburg—a system also put into effect in Vienna, Budapest, Pavia, Freiburg, and other cities—it set off student riots at Louvain that ended by most of the seminarians returning to their dioceses rather than to accept the government's terms.[22]

The widespread opposition to these measures throughout the imperial dominions, plus the difficulties encountered in financing the state seminaries, led Joseph II's brother and successor, Emperor Leopold II, to close these institutions in May, 1790. But the late emperor's ecclesiastical policies were substantially retained, with the result that interference

---

[21] *Ibid.*, I, 37.
[22] For Joseph II and the Church and what came to be called after him Josephism, see Ludwig von Pastor, *The History of the Popes* translated by E. F. Peeler (Saint Louis: B. Herder Book Company, 1952-1953), XXXIX, 421-481; XL, 1-86.

from the State continued to be a real factor in the German world as, for example, in Bavaria where the bishops' right to operate seminaries was not recognized until the concordat of 1817. Bismarck's *Kulturkampf* brought a renewed tightening of the State's control after 1873, a movement that was illustrated by the requirement that candidates for the priesthood spend three years at a state university and that they submit to an examination before a state inspector for an ecclesiastical appointment. The State's action should not, however, be interpreted as yielding only negative results, for there was support among some Catholics for the Catholic faculties of theology at the state universities in preference to the episcopal seminaries, because of the higher intellectual standard demanded at the universities. In the end, in spite of the State's interference and pressure, the episcopal seminaries managed to survive in places like Eichstadt, Fulda, and Mainz, with the result that the dual system of seminary education so familiar in the twentieth century became a permanent feature of German Catholic life.

ENGLISH AND IRISH SEMINARIES

It would be enlightening to trace the evolution of seminary education elsewhere in Europe, but limitation of space will allow for no more than mention of several broad lines of development before attention is turned to the American scene. Throughout most of the nineteenth century two opposing schools of thought on clerical education were discernible in England. One group felt that the Church's best interests were served by mixed student bodies of both seminarians and lay students, as was the situation at Saint Edmund's College, Ware, and at Saint Cuthbert's College near Durham. Another group were strongly opposed to having candidates for the priesthood in school with lay students, a position that was epitomized in 1869 by the action of

Henry Edward Manning, Archbishop of Westminster, when he removed his theology students from Saint Edmund's and found a strictly Tridentine seminary at Hammersmith, an institution which, however, enjoyed little lasting success and which was closed in 1892. In Ireland, on the other hand, it was mainly differences of opinion over government support for seminaries that divided churchmen in the last decade of the eighteenth century, when for the first time in over two centuries the opportunity presented itself to educate Irish candidates for the priesthood at home. A beginning on an independent basis was made at Carlow in 1793, but it was overshadowed two years later when a subsidy from the British government made possible the opening of what became Ireland's national seminary, Saint Patrick's College at Maynooth. And one should not speak of Irish seminary education without mentioning the extraordinary service rendered by the graduates of the missionary seminaries. A notable example of these institutions is All Hallows College in Dublin which since its founding in 1842 has supplied a total of approximately 3,200 priests to the English-speaking world, including fourteen bishops and nearly 1,200 priests who have served in the United States.

SEMINARY EDUCATION IN THE UNITED STATES

Background

It was not from England or Ireland that the original impetus arose for the inauguration of seminary education in the new Republic across the Atlantic, but rather from France. The external manifestation of power and prosperity which the Church of France displayed at the eighteenth century drew toward a close, was in reality only a facade that concealed numerous and grave weaknesses of long standing. Again, the story cannot be told in any detail in the limited

space available here. Suffice it to say, the convening of the
Estates General early in May, 1789, provided the occasion
for the gradual laying bare of the French Church's weaknesses, with the deep cleavage between the upper and lower
clergy one of the first aspects to manifest itself in the Estates
General. The intent of the Church's enemies was likewise
gradually unfolded as the Declaration of the Rights of Man
and the Citizen which was adopted in late August abolished
all clerical privileges. Events moved on swiftly to the secularization of ecclesiastical property, the suppression of the
religious orders, and ultimately to the passage on July 12,
1790, of the Civil Constitution of the Clergy. With this measure the French Church was to all practical purposes severed
from the See of Rome. A period of agonizing doubt and
indecision ensued for Pope Pius VI concerning what policy
to adopt, but finally in March, 1791, he issued a detailed
condemnation of the Civil Constitution of the Clergy. The
issue was now clearly drawn for the French clergy who
were faced with the dread alternative of taking the oath to
support the Constitution and thereby putting themselves in
schism, or of going into exile. Only a decade later was the
relentless warfare between the ecclesiastical and civil orders
brought to an end by the shrewd move of Napoleon Bonaparte in negotiating the concordat signed in July, 1801,
which ushered in a new chapter of Church-State relations
between Paris and Rome.[23]

---

[23] One of the latest scholarly accounts of the Church in this period is Jean
Lefon, *La Crise Révolutionnaire, 1789-1846* (Paris: Bloud & Gay, 1949).
The damage done to religion by Josephism and the French Revolution
was well illustrated in the case of the Benedictines, who at the beginning
of the fourteenth century were estimated to have had the enormous
number of around 37,000 monasteries—reduced by the Protestant Revolt
and religious wars of the sixteenth century to about 5,000—whereas by
the early part of the nineteenth century there were scarcely more than
fifty monasteries in the entire order. With the end of the close association
of Church and State that had obtained in France for centuries prior to
the Revolution of 1789, religious education in general was placed at a

Once the oath to support the Civil Constitution of the Clergy began to be enforced, the stream of clerical exiles leaving France swelled in all directions. By 1797 there were thirty French bishops and around 5,500 priests living in England alone, to say nothing of those who had found a haven in other countries. In the midst of the revolutionary turmoil the seminaries were closed, and Saint Sulpice in Paris temporarily escaped only through the astuteness of the Sulpician superior general, Father Jacques-André Emery, who managed by his clever tactics to appease the troops and members of the revolutionary clubs who occupied most of the building. But this was hardly the atmosphere in which to conduct a seminary, even if the professors and

---

distinct disadvantage. In fact, long before 1789, the ground was being prepared. As one writer has said, "The result of this was that religious education lost its place of primacy in the school, that it was separated from other education, that moral education was claimed as a function of the State, that Church control or supervision of general education was terminated, and that religious education, which had been formerly looked upon by both State and Church as a matter of grave importance and as a process which reached freely into every phase of life—social, intellectual, and political as well as religious—was now completely or largely ignored by the State and regarded as a matter of private concern, to be decided by the individual or the family and by the Church." Clarence E. Elwell, *The Influence of the Enlightenment on the Catholic Theory of Religious Education in France, 1750-1850* (Cambridge: Harvard University Press, 1944), p. 301. For an overview of the Church's struggle against the rising tide of infidelity between the Peace of Westphalia (1648) and the Revolution, see E. Preclin and E. Jarry, *Les luttes politiques at doctrinales aux XVIIᵉ et XVIIIᵉ siècles* (Paris: Bloud & Gay, 1956), pp. 703-802. Speaking of the disruption of the Church's educational system by the Revolution and Napoleon Bonaparte, Edward E. Y. Hales emphasized the great need for a restoration of the religious orders, and especially the Society of Jesus, and he then said, "An equally essential need was to make provision for seminaries for the training of priests. The widespread closure of the seminaries, the hostility displayed by many of the revolutionary governments towards the pursuit of vocations, and the involvement of most of the young manhood of Europe in war had created by the year 1815 a general shortage of priests, especially acute in France, and had also had a most deleterious effect upon the quality of theological study." *The Catholic Church in the Western World* (Garden City Hanover House, 1958), p. 74.

students were permitted to remain. Moreover, if for a time the perils from the civil and military authorities were circumvented, there was an added element of uneasiness from a schismatic Archbishop of Paris who was installed in March, 1791, as well as from a schismatic pastor appointed by him to take charge of the Church of Saint Sulpice. Under these circumstances it was understandable that Emery should have sought a refuge for his men where they would be able to pursue their apostolate of educating candidates for the priesthood free from the handicaps that had crippled their work in France.

Actually, far worse was in store for the clergy who remained in France. But Emery did not wait to act until the clerical ranks were further decimated by the arrests and massacres of September, 1792. Fortunately, an opportunity was found in the summer of 1790 when he turned for counsel to Archbishop Antonio Dugnani, Apostolic Nuncio to France. Dugnani suggested the United States as a desirable location for a seminary, and he added that John Carroll, who had been elected to the new See of Baltimore the previous November, was then in England for his consecration. Emery eagerly responded to the nuncio's suggestion and both men promptly wrote Carroll, the former stating, "The first condition of their [Sulpicians] crossing would be that it would cost neither you nor the residents of the United States anything; they themselves will find the means from their own resources to defray the expense of the undertaking."[24] Grateful as he was for the offer, Carroll at first hesitated because of the utter absence in his diocese of building, endowment, or students. But after Emery had sent Father François Nagot to London to explain in detail what the Sulpicians had in mind his misgivings were put to rest.

[24] Dugnani to Carroll, Paris, August 24, 1790, in Joseph W. Ruane, *The Beginnings of the Society of St. Sulpice in the United States, 1791-1829* (Washington: Catholic University of America Press, 1935), p. 22.

Just before he sailed for home the bishop informed his friend, Lord Arundell of Wardour, of his good fortune, remarking, "While I cannot but thank divine Providence for opening on us such a prospect, I feel great sorrow in the reflection, that we owe such a benefit to the distressed state of religion in France."[25]

Agreement having been reached between Bishop Carroll and the Society of Saint Sulpice, the latter's plans and preparations gradually matured and by early April, 1791, four priests, with Father Nagot as superior, were ready to sail with five seminarians who numbered two Englishmen, a Canadian, a recently converted American, and a Frenchman. After a tedious voyage of three months they landed at Baltimore on July 10, and after a few days spent in a temporary dwelling, Nagot rented a house known as the "One Mile Tavern" where on July 20 the first Mass was celebrated. In September the house and four adjoining acres of ground were purchased and here Saint Mary's Seminary, the mother seminary of the United States, had its humble beginnings.[26]

---

25 Carroll to Arundell, n.p., c. October 1, 1790, in *ibid.*, p. 32. That Emery was a truly remarkable man has been attested by all historians of the period both secular and ecclesiastical. A recent biographer of Napoleon mentioned the impasse created between Pius VII and the emperor over the investiture of the bishops nominated by the latter, and the need it entailed for a modification of the concordat of 1801. He then stated, "Emery, the leading spirit in this direction, had the courage to argue the matter with the Emperor for two hours in the presence of the ministers, State Council, cardinals and bishops." J. M. Thompson, *Napoleon Bonaparte* (New York: Oxford University Press, 1952), pp. 296-297. The most recent scholarly work on the Sulpician superior general is Jean Leflon, *Monsieur Emery* (Paris: Bonne Presse, 1945).

26 There had been no seminary in what became the United States previous to Saint Mary's in Baltimore. The closest approximation was the Franciscan novitiate at Saint Augustine in Florida which in 1607 had seven novices of whom two were diocesan priests. But soon thereafter it was closed and the novices were moved to Cuba. Juan de la Cabezas de Altamirano, O.P., Bishop of Santiago de Cuba, visited Florida in 1606 and in his report to the crown he mentioned a school at Saint Augustine which, says the historian of the Franciscans' Florida missions, "probably was a combination of school and seminary." Maynard Geiger, O.F.M.,

Bishop Carroll's originally favorable impression of the newcomers grew as time went on. After they had been nearly two years in Baltimore he described their work for Leonardo Cardinal Antonelli, Prefect of the Congregatio de Propaganda Fide: "The establishment of a seminary is certainly a new and extraordinary spectacle for the people of this country. . . ." By this time the Sulpicians had come to mean more to the diocese than just seminary professors, for he added, "All our hopes are founded on the Seminary of Baltimore. Since the arrival of the priests of Saint Sulpice, the celebration of the offices of the Church and the dignity of divine worship have made a great impression, so that, though the church of Baltimore is hardly worthy of the name of cathedral, if we consider its style and its size, it may be looked upon as an episcopal church in view of the number of its clergy."[27]

The fury of the revolutionary assaults against the Church increased during 1792, and that year six more Sulpicians set out for the new world, including three future bishops of the American Church. Several more seminarians also came in 1792 of whom one deacon, Stephen T. Badin, was to become on May 25, 1793, the first priest ordained in the United States in a ceremony performed by Bishop Carroll. Two years later the second priestly ordination in this country was for Demetrius Gallitzin, the Russian convert prince, and on March 29, 1800, Saint Mary's first native born American to

---

The Franciscan Conquest of Florida, 1573-1618 (Washington: Catholic University of America Press, 1937), p. 201; see also pp. 219, 235-238. Fifty-seven years after Cabezas de Altamirano's visit, François de Montmorency de Laval, first Bishop of Quebec, began a seminary which has been in existence for over three centuries, and in 1668 he supplemented this institution by a minor seminary. The Quebec seminaries educated a good number of priests who served in the Great Lakes region, the Mississippi Valley, and Louisiana during the eighteenth century. However, neither the French nor the Spaniards, both of whom had many missions in parts of what became the United States, had anything approaching a real seminary.

[27] Carroll to Antonelli, Baltimore, April 23, 1792, in Ruane, *op. cit.*, p. 36.

reach the priesthood, William Matthews, was ordained. Actually, for almost two decades after its opening the seminary's fate hung in the balance for lack of clerical vocations, there being at no time during the academic years 1799-1802 more than two students. One can easily understand, therefore, why the Sulpicians had practically decided by 1803 to close the institution and to return to France, a decision with which Father Emery, their superior general, was inclined to agree. But just as they were about to act Pope Pius VII arrived in Paris in the closing days of November, 1804, for the coronation of Emperor Napoleon. Emery sought and was accorded a lengthy audience during which he discussed a number of pressing problems with the pontiff, among which was the difficulty with the American seminary and the intention to close it. Pius VII was quoted as having replied, "My son, let it remain; yes, let that seminary exist; for it will bear its fruit in time. In recalling the directors to employ them in France at other houses would be to rob Peter to pay Paul."[28] Saint Mary's was thus saved, and in less than a decade the pope's judgment was vindicated, for beginning with the six students of 1803 the number rose steadily until in 1810 there were twenty-four, and of the forty-six who entered the seminary between 1800 and 1810 twenty-three were ultimately ordained priests.

Types of Pre-Civil War Seminaries

For many years Saint Mary's of Baltimore remained the principal center for the education of candidates for the

---

[28] Jean-Edme-August Gosselin, *Vie de M. Emery* (Paris: Joubay (1962), II, 148. Details of the Sulpician superior's lengthy audience of Pius VII were furnished by Emery himself to Clausel de Coussergues who covered the pope's sojourn in Paris for the *Gazette de France*. The journalist identified his source in a letter of March 20, 1843, to Etienne Michel Faillon, S.S., the church historian who, incidentally, came to the United States twice in the 1840's and 1850's as official visitor to the Sulpicians.

diocesan priesthood in the country, and even today it retains
something of a national character with a student body of
400 representing fifty-four dioceses. Yet it was not alone in
the field for very long and, in fact, of the forty-three dioceses
erected in the United States between the establishment of
the hierarchy in 1789 and the Second Plenary Council of
Baltimore in 1866, more than half undertook a seminary at
one time or another with the widest variety of results.
Among the different types of institutions begun between
1789 and 1866—apart from major as distinct from minor
seminaries—a number of broad categories emerged. For
example, there was the institution begun primarily to satisfy
the needs of a particular diocese such as the Philosophical
and Classical Seminary of Charleston opened in January,
1822, by John England, first Bishop of Charleston, which
passed through many trials, yet by 1833 had produced
twenty priests. In the early years little distinction was made
between major and minor divisions in American seminaries,
although ultimately most of those that lasted divided the
students in the classics and liberal arts (minor) from those
studying philosophy and theology (major). Thus with the
opening of Saint Mary's College at Baltimore in 1799 which
received lay students as well as those whom it was hoped
would go on to the seminary, the Sulpicians distinguished
between the two types of clerical candidates, a distinction
which was even more sharply drawn in 1848 when they
established Saint Charles College at Ellicott City, Maryland,
as solely a minor seminary.

A second category of American seminary—with again no
distinct division at first between major and minor seminarians—was that conducted by secular clergy, often assisted
by a few lay masters. This type of seminary was intended
to educate students for the diocesan priesthood; however it
was not the foundation of any particular diocese. The earliest and best example of this type was the institution that

made its appearance in 1808 near the tiny village of Emmitsburg in western Maryland under the auspices of the Sulpician Fathers and was called Mount Saint Mary's College.
What was originally intended as a minor seminary gradually
evolved into a school for boys in which several young laymen
who were engaged to teach in time expressed a desire to
be priests. In order to retain their services as teachers, and
at the same time enable them to make progress toward the
priesthood, the administrators sought and secured permission in 1820 from Ambrose Maréchal, S.S., Archbishop of
Baltimore, to introduce classes in theology. Two years thereafter the Emmitsburg institution was separated from the
Society of Saint Sulpice, and thenceforth pursued its independent course as both a college for lay boys and minor
seminarians, and also as a major seminary. That there should
have been relatively little intellectual emphasis in these
early seminaries was understandable if not altogether commendable. The point was well illustrated by Archbishop
Maréchal in counseling a young American-born convert
priest who was in Paris to make his Sulpician solitude (novitiate). The archbishop advised him that his principal object should be that of penetrating himself with the spirit of
Saint Sulpice, to which he added, "and be well persuaded,
my dear friend, that if you come here having imbibed all
of that, this immense advantage will be for you and for the
Church in the United States, infinitely preferable to all the
knowledge that you can acquire during your sojourn in
Europe. . . . [29]

---

[29] Maréchal to Samuel Eccleston, Baltimore, February 12, 1826, in Columba E. Halsey, O.S.B., "The Life of Samuel Eccleston, S.S. Fifth
Archbishop of Baltimore, 1801-1851," unpublished master's thesis, The
Catholic University of America, 1963, pp. 19-20. The only extensive account of Mount Saint Mary's College and Seminary is the outdated and
poorly organized work of Mary M. Meline and Edward F.X. McSweeny,
The Story of the Mountain, 2 vols. (Emmitsburg: Weekly Chronicle,
1911).

A third category of seminary not infrequently found in this country before the Civil War was much like that of the household of Saint Augustine, namely, a house or domestic seminary where a group of clerics assembled in the home of a bishop and were personally instructed either solely by the bishop or by the bishop assisted by one or two of his priests. Clerical education in the Diocese of Boston began that way, a circumstance brought about by the War of 1812 which put Baltimore in the war zone and made Boston parents uneasy about having their sons at Saint Mary's. It was Father François Matignon, the most famous priest of early Boston Catholicism, who suggested to the parents of two youths who had been in Baltimore that they be permitted to continue their education in the home of Boston's first bishop, Jean Cheverus. With this the domestic seminary was born, and it continued on through most of the administration of Cheverus' successor, Benedict J. Fenwick. In describing his seminary for the Jesuit superior, Francis Dzierozinski, in 1826, Fenwick said, "I have two young men 21 and 22 years old [James Fitton and William Wiley] who are very promising, to whom I give lessons twice a day. They are the foundation of my Seminary. I would send them to your college [Georgetown] and pay for their education, if I were not afraid that you would persuade them to be Jesuits. . . ."[30]

The same type of institution was the forerunner of Saint Charles Borromeo Seminary in Philadelphia. In this instance a gift of $4,803 to the diocese in October, 1831, from the Leopoldinen Association of Vienna, a Catholic immigrant aid society, enabled the bishop, Francis Patrick Kenrick, in the following June to receive Patrick Bradley into his house on South Fifth Street. That September the bishop told Carlo Cardinal Pedicini, Prefect of Propaganda, that while he had

---

[30] Fenwick to Dzierozinski, n.p., April 11, 1826, in John E. Sexton and Arthur J. Riley, *History of Saint John's Seminary, Brighton* (Boston: Roman Catholic Archbishop of Boston, 1945), p. 25.

not as yet been able to erect a seminary, he had received three young men into his house, "to make sacred studies," as he expressed it, after they had been trained in philosophy by an excellent teacher, Father Francis Guth, who was in charge of the German congregation at Holy Trinity Church.[31] And in appealing for funds for the seminary in a pastoral letter of January, 1834, the bishop informed his people that he had received six students into his house of whom four were then engaged "in the study of divinity" under himself and several of his priests.

In proceeding in this manner Bishop Kenrick went contrary to the advice of a majority of his clergy and many of the laity who favored a seminary combined with a college for lay students such as had developed at Emmitsburg. One of his biographers maintains that in holding for a purely clerical student body, Kenrick was probably less influenced by what were regarded as the directives of Trent than he was by observation of what had happened at Saint Joseph's College in Bardstown, Kentucky, where he had taught after he first arrived in the United States in 1821. Martin J. Spalding, later Bishop of Louisville, had been both professor and president of Saint Joseph's in the 1830's and he later stated, "Experience, however, showed that many of the seminarians had their vocations shaken by being thrown so much in contact with youth of the world; while scarcely a candidate for the ministry was obtained among those who received their education in the college."[32] In any case, the house

---

31 Kenrick to Pedicini, Philadelphia, September 7, 1832, in Hugh J. Nolan, *The Most Reverend Francis Patrick Kenrick, Third Bishop of Philadelphia, 1830-1851* (Washington: Catholic University of America Press, 1948), p. 153. For Guth, see George E. O'Donnell, "Rev. Francis X. Guth and the Founding of St. Charles Seminary, Philadelphia," *Records of the Amreican Catholic Historical Society of Philadelphia,* LXXIV (December, 1963), 227-232.

32 Martin J. Spalding, *Sketches of the Life, Times and Character of the Rt. Rev. Benedict Joseph Flaget, First Bishop of Louisville* (Louisville: Webb & Levering, 1852), p. 300. For seminary developments in the

seminary served Philadelphia until the diocese was financial-
ly able to support Saint Charles Borromeo Seminary which
was occupied in January, 1839, by ten students under the
direction of Michael O'Connor, the future first Bishop of
Pittsburgh.

One more seminary of the early nineteenth century is
worthy of mention because of the unusual circumstances
surrounding its origin. In April, 1808, Rome created an
ecclesiastical province in the United States, raising Baltimore to metropolitan rank and erecting four new dioceses
as suffragan sees, among which was Bardstown in Kentucky.
Due to the Napoleonic wars and to other causes, long delays
ensued before its first bishop, the French-born Sulpician,
Benedict Flaget, was ready in May, 1811, to start for his
western see with a little party consisting of his fellow Sulpician, Father John B. David, and three seminarians—all of
European birth—Guy Chabrat, Jacques Derigaud, and Pierre
Schaefer. Of these three, Chabrat was already a sub-deacon.

The travelers proceeded by stagecoach to Pittsburgh
where on May 22 they started down the Ohio River, thus
lending substance to the remark of the historian of the first
seminary west of the Alleghenies to the effect that the institution had been born "on a flatboat at the Pittsburgh
docks."[33] David was made head of the seminary, and later

---

early Diocese of New York, see Thomas F. O'Connor, "Pioneer Catholic
Seminaries in New York," *New York History*, XXIV (April, 1943),
211-219. The earliest attempts to establish seminaries at Nyack and
Lafargeville, New York, in 1834 and 1838 respectively were both failures
and only with the opening of Saint Joseph's Seminary at Fordham in
1840 was a permanent foundation made.

[33] William J. Howlett, *Historical Tribute to St. Thomas' Seminary at Poplar
Neck near Bardstown, Kentucky* (Saint Louis: B. Herder Book Company, 1906), p. 26. Flaget himself stated, "The boat, on which we
descended the Ohio, became the cradle of the seminary and of the
Church of Kentucky. Our cabin was, at the same time, chapel, dormitory,
study-room and refectory," (*ibid.*, p. 28). It was in the little seminary
chapel on the Howard farm on December 12, 1812, that the two first
members of the Sisters of Charity of Nazareth made their vows and

in describing its early days for the Sulpician superior general he embodied an account of the rough frontier conditions that the Church then faced in the West. Speaking of how Flaget from the outset had been determined to establish a seminary, David then continued,

This is, in fact what Bishop Flaget has done. It is the only way he has to get missionaries for his diocese, which is almost entirely lacking in them. We left Baltimore, May 13, 1811, taking with us the elements of a Seminary, i.e., Chabrat and Derigaud, whom Bishop Flaget brought from France, and a young Frenchman of Philadelphia [Schaeffer] who had long desired to have some priest test his vocation to the priesthood. We arrived June 4 at Louisville, on the Ohio, 38 miles from Bardstown, whither we went the following Saturday. From Bardstown we went to take lodgings with Badin [Father Stephen T. Badin], who had built a log house of one room for the Bishop. This was called, without irony, the 'Bishop's Palace.' The seminarians lodged in another log cabin, and I in a small closet. Chabrat, then a sub-deacon, taught the other seminarians till he was ordained to the priesthood. Meanwhile, I took charge of three or four congregations which were in need of a priest. I prepared them for Chabrat, who was destined to take them over as soon as he should be ordained. A pious layman, Thomas Howard, has left by will a fine plantation to the Bishop of Bardstown for a Seminary. But the Church could get actual possession of only the half of it, because the widow had been given a life tenure of the other half. This good woman, eager to see the wishes of her husband realized without delay, urged the Bishop to accept the whole estate, or to establish a Seminary in the house she lived in. Her offer was accepted, and our seminarians, then five in number, moved there December 5. I went there the same day

---

were joined in a few weeks by Catherine Spalding who became the first superior. The initial work of these women was the making and repairing of the clothes for the bishop, priests, and seminarians. For a brief treatment of their first superior, see David Spalding, C.F.X., "The Character of Mother Catherine Spalding," *Records of the American Catholic Historical Society of Philadelphia*, LXXIII (December, 1962), 67-76.

from my post on the missions and took charge of the nascent Seminary.[34]

A fourth category of seminary which arose in the United States was the national seminary. At the time that Saint Thomas Seminary had its beginnings the Catholic minority in this country was still largely composed of the descendants of the colonial families of Maryland and Pennsylvania, with a considerable number of French who were refugees from the political disturbances in their homeland. But long before the Kentucky seminary closed its useful service in October, 1869, the American Catholic community had undergone a profound change in personnel. Once immigration from Europe had begun in earnest, the native Catholic population, numbering in 1820 around 195,000, was quickly submerged. In the half century between 1820 and 1870 an estimated total of 1,683,791 Irish Catholics reached these shores along with 606,791 German Catholics, to speak only of the two predominant immigrant groups. Here, then, was the principal fact with which the Church of the United States had to cope throughout the remainder of the century. It was little wonder, therefore, that this difficulty should have been reflected in clerical education and have given rise to a new type of institution, namely, the seminary intended for educating youths of a particular nationality.

For obvious reasons Irish youths found no linguistic problem when they sought to test their vocation in one of the existing seminaries. But it was otherwise with their German counterparts. In 1741 two German Jesuits in colonial Pennsylvania were brought to America at the instance of the German Catholic settlers in Philadelphia and in the rural areas to the west. In 1787 their fellow countrymen's initi-

---

[34] David to Antoine Duclaux, n.p., September 14, 1814, in Lloyd P. McDonald, S.S., *The Seminary Movement in the United States: Projects, Foundations and Early Development, 1784-1833* (Washington: Catholic University of America Press, 1927), pp. 39-40.

ative ended in the establishment of the first national congregation of the American Catholics at Holy Trinity Church
in Philadelphia. For these and other German Catholics in
the new world, the German tradition of an intimate association of their religious faith with their mother tongue had
been a prime reality in their lives. And nowhere did this
become more evident in the nineteenth century than in
Wisconsin where the Germans settled in such large numbers.
The first Bishop of Milwaukee, the Swiss-born John Martin
Henni, was conscious of this fact, and less than three weeks
after his arrival in his see city, in a letter to the Abbey of
Einsiedln in his native Switzerland he asked,

> When and how shall I satisfy all the needs, yea, even the most
> urgent? To mention one case, where will I get a sufficient
> number of priests, who will be obliged to speak both English
> and German, and in some cases, also French, for the ever
> increasing number of immigrants? . . . without a well-organ-
> ized German seminary the dioceses of the Northwestern part
> of the United States are only half taken care of. In this sem-
> inary chiefly only young men of German extraction could be
> made familiar with the English language and trained for the
> priesthood. This conviction I have entertained for a long
> time—indeed as time goes on the more convinced I am that
> such an institution is really wanted. How is it to be accom-
> plished?[35]

If the monks of Einsiedln did not have the answers to
Bishop Henni's questions, it was not long before his own
zeal and ingenuity provided an answer. Beginning in a very
modest fashion in 1845 with several young men brought
into his own home where he, Father Michael Heiss, and
Father William Quinn were the professors, the seeds of the
future Saint Francis Seminary were sown. These seeds
slowly developed in a number of different locations and

---

[35] Henni to the Monks of Einsiedln, Milwaukee, [May 22, 1844], Peter Leo
Johnson, *Halcyon Days. Story of St. Francis Seminary, Milwaukee, 1856-
1956* (Milwaukee: Bruce Publishing Company, 1956), p. 22.

circumstances over the next decade until the cornerstone of a separate and permanent building was laid in July, 1855. By this time twenty-eight priests had been ordained, and in the year that the Civil War ended there was a student body of 102. From the beginning, as the historian of Saint Francis Seminary makes clear, there was a strong Jesuit influence in the curriculum and in the textbooks used, and once the theological faculty of the University of Innsbruck, Austria, was reopened in 1858 under Jesuit auspices the influence was, perhaps, even more marked. The first rector, Michael Heiss, had been a student in the 1830's at the Gregorianum, the seminary attached to the University of Munich, where the stimulating ideas of Johann Adam Möhler had aroused a renewed interest in scholasticism. Heiss brought this spirit with him to Milwaukee, so that when Pope Leo VIII issued his encyclical *Aeterni Patris* in August, 1879, calling for a revival of scholasticism, it found one of the readiest American echoes at Saint Francis.

Nor was the Milwaukee seminary the only American institution of predominantly German character. In 1875 a school for German youths who wished to become priests was opened. This institution ultimately found a permanent home near Columbus, Ohio, and in 1892 was placed directly under the Holy See with the name Pontifical College Josephinum. Later in the century as other national groups within the American Catholic community acquired numbers and strength they, too, founded ecclesiastical institutions for their own people. Thus, for example, the Poles opened Saints Cyril and Methodius Seminary in 1886, first at Detroit and then in 1909 moved to its present location in Orchard Lake, Michigan, where in 1927 a combined college and minor seminary was added and called Saint Mary's College. Both institutions have produced a large number of priests of Polish birth or descent who have served the Church in this country.

THE CONCEPT OF A NATIONAL CENTRAL SEMINARY: PRE-CIVIL WAR

Of the remaining seminaries supported by the American Catholics, something should be said about three types: (1) the national or provincial seminary; (2) institutions outside the United States; (3) houses of study of the religious orders and congregations. As to the first, at an early date the suggestion was made that the apostolate would be greatly furthered by a central or national seminary. It was Bishop Fenwick of Boston who raised the question in September, 1828, with James Whitfield, Archbishop of Baltimore, more than a year in advance of the hierarchy's first council. Fenwick conceived the projected council as a proper medium for promoting what he had in mind. Among the Church's needs he saw the supply of more priests as one of the most pressing, a need which would be served, he said, "by the establishment of a central college or seminary to be under the worthy gentlemen of St. Sulpice in which the education shall be purely ecclesiastical, and to whose support, as it would be for the benefit of all, every diocese shall contribute in proportion to the number of students each shall send to it."[36] John England, Bishop of Charleston, expressed himself similarly to Archbishop Whitfield in suggesting "the propriety and practicability of having a common College, besides our Diocesan Seminaries."[37]

But once the First Provincial Council of Baltimore got underway on October 3, 1829, opposition to the idea arose among the eight bishops in attendance. Flaget considered it too costly an undertaking to patronize at his great distance from Baltimore. Joseph Rosati, C.M., Bishop of Saint Louis,

[36] Fenwick to Whitfield, n.p., September 10, 1828, in Sexton-Riley, *op. cit.*, p. 28.

[37] England to Whitfield, n.p., December 26, 1828, in Peter Guilday, *The Life and Times of John England, First Bishop of Charleston, 1786-1842,* (New York: America Press, 1927), II, 117.

was not sympathetic. In the end England withdrew his support. The subject came up again in the Second Provincial Council of October, 1833—this time with England's strong backing—but once more the central or national seminary failed to materialize. It was not that the more advanced churchmen did not give the matter of clerical education serious thought, for as early as 1851, nearly forty years before such became a reality, Archbishop John B. Purcell of Cincinnati raised the question of a Catholic university at a time when plans were being made for the hierarchy's first plenary council. He asked Archbishop Kenrick of Baltimore, "Is it expedient and practicable to found a Catholic University? And if not, how shall we otherwise provide for the education of such a clergy as the peculiar circumstances of this country require?"[38] Actually it was only in 1884 when a wealthy young laywoman pledged $300,000 to the bishops that the latter showed a will to have a university. As a consequence of her benefaction there opened in November, 1889, The Catholic University of America which was at first exclusively a school of theology, although on a graduate level.[39]

The American hierarchy were not without precedents for a central or national seminary, for in 1795, to mention one example with which most of the bishops were familiar, Saint

---

[38] Archives of the Archdiocese of Baltimore, 31-B-4, Purcell to Kenrick, Cincinnati, November 20, 1851, in John P. Marschall, C.S.V., "Francis Patrick Kenrick. The Baltimore Years," unpublished doctoral dissertation, The Catholic University of America, 1965, p. 12.

[39] For the University's theological school, see John Tracy Ellis, *The Formative Years of the Catholic University of America* (Washington: American Catholic Historical Association, 1946); Patrick H. Ahern, *The Catholic University of America, 1887-1896: The Rectorship of John J. Keane* (Washington: Catholic University of America, 1948); Peter E. Hogan, S.S.J., *The Catholic University of America, 1896-1903: The Rectorship of Thomas J. Conaty* (Washington: Catholic University of America Press, 1949); and Colman J. Barry, O.S.B., *The Catholic University of America, 1903-1909: The Rectorship of Denis J. O'Connell* (Washington: Catholic University of America Press, 1950).

Patrick's College had been established at Maynooth, Ireland for the entire Irish Church. It was an institution that was to exert a widespread influence in the English-speaking world by reason of its numerous alumni scattered through various countries.[40] Had a central seminary for the United States been founded any time prior to 1846, it would have been at the same time provincial in scope, since until that year the country had but the one ecclesiastical Province of Baltimore. By 1853, however, there were seven provinces, and in none of them was there more persistent and successful effort for a seminary supported by both the metropolitan see and its suffragan dioceses than in the Province of Cincinnati. Seminary education had been inaugurated in Cincinnati as early as 1829, but not until October, 1852, did Archbishop Purcell witness the full realization of his dreams in the opening of Mount Saint Mary's Seminary of the West. Four years later Purcell offered the institution to the suffragans of his province, and with their acceptance a board of bishops was appointed to administer it.

That the Province of Cincinnati made more rapid progress in Catholic education at all levels than most of its sister provinces, there was little doubt,[41] a fact that would be difficult to account for apart from its forward-looking metropolitan. Purcell was not discouraged by the failure of the First Plenary Council to take any action in regard to a university; in fact, it was probably in part the reason why he petitioned the Holy See for permission to grant theological

---

[40] For a charge that Gallican influences were present in Maynooth, see Henry F. Neville, "Theology, Past and Present, at Maynooth," *Dublin Review* 3rd Series, XXXIII (October, 1879), 449-464; which drew a spirited defense of the college from its vice rector, William J. Walsh, The "Alleged Gallicanism of Maynooth and of the Irish Clergy," *ibid.*, 3rd Series, XXXIV (April, 1880), 210-253. Neville was Rector of the Catholic University of Ireland from 1879 to 1883.

[41] See Edward A. Connaughton, *A History of Educational Legislation and Administration in the Archdiocese of Cincinnati* (Washington: Catholic University of America Press, 1946).

degrees in his own seminary. The request was refused, however, in June, 1858, on the ground that the American College, then being planned for Rome, would afford students the opportunity to acquire degrees.[42] In any case, in time Cincinnati's provincial seminary found imitators as, for example, Saint Joseph's Seminary at Troy, New York, which opened in October, 1864, for the Province of New York. Saint Paul Seminary established in 1894 by Archbishop John Ireland answered a like need for that vast province. And in the present generation Saint John's Seminary at Plymouth, Michigan, has served the Province of Detroit since 1949, as does Mount Saint Bernard Seminary, founded in 1951, that of the Province of Dubuque.

AMERICAN CLERICAL EDUCATION IN FOREIGN INSTITUTIONS: PRE-CIVIL WAR

Throughout the colonial period and up to 1791 the several hundred priests who exercised their ministry within the present boundaries of the United States were all products of foreign seminaries, as were most of the new republic's early bishops, including the founder of the hierarchy, the native-born John Carroll, who made his priestly studies at the Jesuit scholasticate in Liége. And this remained true of large numbers of priests well after the establishment of seminaries in this country, men who were already ordained when they arrived to care for the spiritual needs of the swelling ranks of immigrant Catholics who were coming from many lands. A case in point is that of the French-speaking immigrants. In the half century between 1820 and 1870 there was an estimated net Catholic immigration from France of 137,417 with 9,668 Belgians, most of whom like-

---

[42] Pius IX to Purcell, Rome, June 14, 1858, in John H. Lamott, *History of the Archdiocese of Cincinnati, 1821-1921* (New York: Frederick Pustet Company, Inc.. 1921), p. 292. Lamott discussed the Cincinnati seminaries in general, *ibid.*, pp. 287-295.

wise spoke French. Together they constituted a body of the faithful for whom, perhaps, a higher proportionate number of priests came to the United States than was true of other language groups.

Before the Civil War many of these French and Belgian priests settled among their fellow countrymen in the Middle West as, for example, in the Belgian colonies of the Diocese of Detroit where the apostolic administrator of the see, Bishop Peter Paul Lefevere, had himself been born in Belgium. Among Lefevere's Belgian priests was Father Peter Kindekens whom he had ordained in 1842, a man with a strong missionary spirit which he used to good advantage in promoting the Church's interests in the Diocese of Detroit. The Bishop of Louisville at the time was Martin Spalding who had been deeply influenced while still a boy by a Belgian priest, Father Charles Nerinckx, one of Kentucky's pioneer missionaries. It was from Nerinckx that Spalding derived a lasting admiration for the Belgians. The story of the origins of the American College at Louvain is too complicated to retell here. Suffice it to say, it grew out of a combination of events, including a visit to Belgium by Spalding in 1853 in search of teachers, and Kindeken's trip to Rome three years later as the agent of Francis Patrick Kenrick, Archbishop of Baltimore, in behalf of an American seminary in the Eternal City.

Having failed in his mission to Rome, Father Kindekens went on to Belgium where he found the bishops favorably disposed toward the establishment of a seminary at Louvain for the missions of the United States. The idea won the hearty and practical support of Bishops Spalding and Lefevere who became its chief sponsors, with the consequence that in March, 1857, the American College opened at Louvain with Kindekens as its first rector. At first the students were recruited mainly among Europeans who wished to do missionary work in this country, although almost from

the outset certain American seminarians were sent to study
there. Among the first of these was the future Bishop of
Peoria, John Lancaster Spalding, who arrived in October,
1859, and who was joined two years later by Patrick W.
Riordan, future Archbishop of San Francisco. Like all enterprises of this kind the institution met with opposition, not
the least of which was the indifference, or hostility, of some
bishops who did not believe in an American seminary on
foreign soil. But the obstacles having been gradually surmounted, the American Church has ever since profited
from the ministry of numerous priests educated at a seminary with the immediate environs of what was then, and
perhaps still remains, the greatest Catholic university center
in the world.[43]

Although, as previously mentioned, Father Kindekens was
unable in 1856 to win support at Rome for an American
seminary in the Eternal City, his failure was due to external
circumstances and in no way to papal disapproval of the
idea. On the contrary, the original suggestion for such an
institution had come two years before from a member of the
papal diplomatic corps. In June, 1853, Gaetano Bedini,
Archbishop of Thebes and Apostolic Nuncio to Brazil, arrived in New York as the representative of Pope Pius IX
for what proved to be an exciting and turbulent eight-
months visit. It is not of interest here to recount the un-
pleasantness experienced by the nuncio at the hands of the
Know-Nothings, but only to examine the recommendations
that Bedini was prepared to make to the Holy See upon his
departure in February, 1854. These were summarized for
John Hughes, Archbishop of New York, by the nuncio's

---

[43] On the Louvain seminary there is J. Van der Heyden, *The Louvain
American College, 1857-1907* (Louvain: Ceuterick, 1909), which has for
the most part been superseded by the scholarly volume of John D. Sauter,
The American College of Louvain, 1857-1898 (Louvain: Publications
Universitaires de Louvain, 1959).

English secretary, Father John Virtue, after the latter had reached London. He said, "He [the nuncio] looks mainly to two [effects of his trip] and with earnestness and confidence. . . . They are, the establishment of a nuncio or other Representative of the Holy See at Washington and the foundation of an American College in Rome. If these can be obtained, the Mission will not certainly have been in vain."[44]

In the lengthy report which Archbishop Bedini submitted to Filippo Cardinal Fransoni, Prefect of Propaganda, he went into detail concerning the need for the college he was proposing at Rome, and gave as one of the principal reasons the improvement of the seminary education he had observed in the United States.

> It would offer a wider, more complete and more solid education to the American Clergy than they now get, he said. I was present at some examinations and scholastic exercises, or concursus, and I was not at all satisfied with the results. I have already noted . . . that the young priest, once ordained, has no time to continue his studies because he is distracted by so many other matters of his ministry. The occasions and encouragements are lacking for one to further his studies. The most outstanding priest is the one that has built the most churches and begun the most institutions.[45]

While Bedini's last point will occasion little surprise even today, it did not follow that the transfer of American students to Rome in the 1850's would necessarily assure them an education greatly superior to that they might receive at home. Less than eight years before, John Henry Newman, then a student at the Urban College of Propaganda, re-

44 Virtue to Hughes, London, May 24, 1854, in Robert F. McNamara, *The American College in Rome, 1855-1951* (Rochester: Christopher Press, 1956), p. 6.
45 Bedini to Fransoni, Rome, July 12, 1854, James F. Connelly, *The Visit of Archbishop Gaetano Bedini to the United States of America, June, 1853-February, 1854* (Roma: Libreria Editrice dell'Università Gregoriana, 1960), p. 244. The full text of the report is given here, pp. 193-287.

marked that James Robert Hope had told him that "we should find very little theology here, and a talk we had yesterday with one of the Jesuit fathers here shows we shall find little philosophy."[46] Moreover, Newman's opinion did not improve with time, for some months later he confided to Richard Stanton,

> Again (let me say it to *yourself*, for I don't like to say it aloud) you will not, cannot, get education here—not simply from the many objects there are to take you off your studies, but because you are not a boy. The lecturers are men quite up with their subject, but the course takes *four* years—if you don't stay that time, you only go through a part of it—and any how you go, lecture after lecture, to drawl through a few tedious pages. All this is quite necessary for boys, not for grown men. I should think (still in confidence) you will do as much sitting at home at Maryvale.[47]

Needless to say, Newman was not insensitive to the unique intellectual and cultural opportunities that Rome afforded, quite apart from the ecclesiastical schools. Like his fellow Englishman, Wilfrid Ward, who studied briefly at the same Urban College thirty years after Newman, and who held a similarly low view of clerical education in the Eternal City, he fully recognized Rome's riches for one who, as Ward said, wished to study antiquity, the history of the Church, and the lives of the saints.[48] Nor were there then lacking in

---

[46] Newman to John D. Dalgairns, Rome, November 22, 1846, Charles Stephen Dessain, (Ed.), *The Letters and Diaries of John Henry Newman* (London: Thomas Nelson and Sons Ltd., 1961), XI, 279.

[47] Newman to Stanton, Rome, February 21, 1847, *ibid.*, XII, 48.

[48] From a memoir of Ward's for the years 1877-1882 reprinted by his daughter in Maisie Ward, *The Wilfrid Wards and the Transition* (New York: Sheed & Ward, 1934), p. 62; the full text is found on pp. 54-86. Speaking of the sceptic's disparagement of human reason, Ward remarked concerning the teaching he had observed during his eight-month stay at the Urban College (October, 1877-May, 1878): "But philosophy was taught to us in Rome in a way which seemed to me equally a *reductio ad absurdum* of the human reason. In the one case reason is pressed to a point which discredits itself, in the other authority held the

the Church of the United States those who appreciated Rome's special advantages, even if philosophical and theological instruction there left much to be desired by way of originality of thought, critical approach, and the other pedagogical methods that stimulate young minds.[49] In January, 1855, Pope Pius IX addressed a letter to Archbishop Hughes in which the pontiff expressed the desire that there should be an American seminary in Rome. As in the case of Louvain several years before, there was at first, to use the phrase of the historian of the college, a quite "uncertain response."[50] But again like Louvain, the Roman project found several enthusiastic supporters in the hierarchy, in this instance principally two alumni of the Urban College, Bishop O'Connor of Pittsburgh and Archbishop Kenrick of Baltimore. To be sure, many obstacles had to be overcome before the inauguration of the American College on December 8, 1859. And though the institution drew only twelve students at its

---

field so exclusively that it was evoked to prove the reasons alleged for its validity—an equal disparagement of the functions and powers of reason. We were taught the various philosophical positions as the 'right view' and if any of us did not find those positions convincing we were accounted heterodox. Thus philosophy which professed to prove the rational duty of accepting Theism and revelation was not really enforced by reason but by authority. It was really learnt by rote and by sheer memory. Those students were best thought of who learnt best by heart. Genuine philosophic thought annoyed our Professors. The man with whom I had the opportunity of arguing at close quarters was Don Corti, our clever little *Ripetitore*, and I was equally impressed by his readiness in replying and by his failure ever really to understand or even to consider one's objections." (p. 66). For a quite complimentary judgment on Roman education by an English seminarian of the years 1868-1873, see William Barry, "Roman Memories of 1870," *Dublin Review*, CLXVII (October, 1920), 232-248, an article which Barry later enlarged and included in his volume, *Memories and Opinions* (New York: Putnam, 1926), pp. 64 ff. He had been especially impressed by the two Italian moralists, Antonio Ballerini, S.J., and Domenico Palmieri, S.J.

[49] The best recent scholarly treatment of Roman clerical education during this period is Roger Aubert, *Le pontificat de Pie IX, 1846-1878* (Paris: Bloud & Gay, 1952), pp. 184-223.

[50] McNamara, *op. cit.*, p. 19.

birth, its opening marked a victory for the sponsors. The
heavy trails that still lay ahead were ultimately surmounted
and the college has in the last 105 years contributed approximately 2,000 priests to the Church of the United States, and
has long since come to have an accepted place in American
Catholic life.

Mention has already been made of Innsbruck, Austria, to
which some American bishops assigned students after the
theological faculty there was reestablished in 1858. Still
other youths were educated by the Sulpicians in Montreal,
or attended one or the other of the German, Italian, Spanish,
or French seminaries as, for example, two two future bishops, John Ireland and Thomas O'Gorman, whose superior,
Thomas L. Grace, Bishop of Saint Paul, enrolled them in
1853 at the seminary of Mexmieux in France. By reason of
the heavy German immigration, however, more thought was
probably given at this time to securing priests familiar with
that language than with other continental tongues. And that
it was a subject of concern on both sides of the Atlantic we
know from a letter of Purcell of Cincinnati to John Hughes
in which he said,

> Another capital point of consideration is the constant desire
> of the Coadj. (Rass) [Andreas Räss] of Strasburgh [*sic*], to
> establish a German Seminary, in his own, or one of the adjoin-
> ing dioceses, for the education of American Missionaries. Such
> is his zeal that he is willing, nay anxious, to live in the Semin-
> ary, even as a Professor, to promote its success. He suggests
> that two priests might be found in the U. States, who would
> be willing and capable to teach in the Seminary and give
> seminarians accurate views of men and things here. Were I
> selected for such a purpose, I would consent so to serve all
> my days. Let this last be (entrenous). I feel, however, that
> priests could be found who would at the same time be more
> competent. If two, or three American Prelates would unite in
> writing to him, the means wd. soon be forthcoming—and if
> such a good work is not done, what shall become of our in-

creasing German population? I would want ten more German priests just now.[51]

By the time the American College had opened at Rome the deepening crisis over slavery had cast a long shadow over the homeland. In the years that followed the firing on Fort Sumter the seminary movement made little or no progress. But as one historian of education has said, not even the secular college found "the answers to the questions raised by the rising tide of democracy until after the Civil War. Nor did it, until then, begin effectively to grapple with the question of quality, of standards, of excellence."[52] If such was true in secular circles, how much more likely was the static curriculum and the seminary's strong hold of tradition to induce a similar situation in ecclesiastical education. For the immediate post-war years detailed statistics are not available; however the *Catholic Directory* for 1868 counted fifty institutions for the education of both the diocesan and regular clergy with a combined student enrollment of 913.[53] This surely was a very small total, for a Church whose adherents had passed 4,500,000 by 1870, and who was being so rapidly augmented by immigration from abroad. Like all institutions, the seminaries of the period had their defects, one of which was the proliferation of small and feeble foundations which drained off much of the Church's limited personnel and financial resources. It was a weakness that had not gone undetected, for as early as the summer of 1834 John Hughes, the future archbishop, in writing to his former professor, Simon Bruté, Bishop-elect of Vincennes, remarked,

---

51 Archives of the Archdiocese of New York, A-12, Purcell to Hughes, Cincinnati, January 24, 1842, microfilm copy, Manuscript Collections, The Catholic University of America.

52 Frederick Rudoph, *The American College and University. A History* (New York: Alfred A. Knopf, 1962), p. 221.

53 *Sadlier's Catholic Directory, Almanac, and Ordo. . . .* (New York: Sadlier and Company, 1868), p. 426.

With regard to any thing's being done for the education of
clergymen, I despair of it until the bishops and colleges, or
college, shall understand each other and themselves better.
It is a subject on which there is too great a variety of opinion,
and on which each superior looks only to the boundaries of
his own jurisdiction.[54]

Religious Houses of Study

Obviously, the expanding Church of the United States
needed additional seminaries, with the Catholic population
by the end of the century having passed the 12,000,000
mark; however it was doubtful if the best interests of ecclesiastical education were served in having the fifty seminaries
of 1868 more than double to 109 by 1900. Of these 109,
thirty were for the secular priesthood with a total of 2,630
students, while the seventy-nine scholasticates and houses
of study for the regular clergy enrolled 1,998 students.[55]
Seminaries for the religious congregations and orders had
long been a familiar part of the American Catholic scene.
Among the first were the Vincentians who were induced to
come to this country by Bishop Louis William Dubourg.
They arrived at Perryville, or the Barrens at it was called, a
small settlement about eighty miles south of Saint Louis, in
September, 1818. By the following March there were ten
students being taught mainly by Father Rosati, the future
bishop. In the Vincentians' seminary, which served both
their own candidates as well as Dubourg's few diocesan
students, the costs were found to be so high and the income
so meager that with reluctance Rosati introduced in November, 1822, the plan already adopted elsewhere of com-

---

[54] Hughes to Bruté, n.p., June 10, 1834, in John R. G. Hassard, *Life of the
Most Reverend John Hughes, First Archbishop of New York* (New York:
D. Appleton and Company, 1866), p. 149.

[55] *The Catholic Directory, Almanac and Clergy List — Quarterly for the
Year of Our Lord 1900* (Milwaukee: M. H. Wiltzius & Company, 1900),
insert opposite p. 820.

bining a school for lay students with the seminary, so that the students of the latter might be used for teaching in the former.[56]

One of the reasons for the increase of religious communities was the pressing need of missionaries for various national immigrant groups, for example, the Germans for whom a pioneer band of six Redemptorists reached New York in June, 1832. When that congregation's first American seminary was established at Cumberland, Maryland, in 1851 it reflected this German emphasis, as was likewise true at the institution's other locations in Annapolis and in Ilchester, Maryland, where a new building was occupied in September, 1868.[57] Much the same background lay behind the coming of the Benedictines, led by a group of eighteen who were invested with the habit in October, 1846, by Boniface Wimmer, O.S.B., the man who had been the soul of the enterprise. The setting for the ceremony was the little Saint Vincent Priory, a rural foundation about forty miles east of Pittsburgh, where within two years the monks had a seminary and a school for boys. The other pioneer Benedictine communities have much the same story, such as Saint Meinrad's in southern Indiana which from its beginning in July, 1854, had a seminary as its principal objective; Saint John's in Minnesota, which was established two years later; and Saint Benedict's in Kansas which was founded in 1857.[58]

[56] Frederick J. Easterly, C.M., *The Life of Rt. Rev. Joseph Rosati, C.M., First Bishop of St. Louis, 1789-1843* (Washington: Catholic University of America, 1942), pp. 45-63.

[57] John F. Byrne, C.Ss.R., *The Redemptorist Centenaries* (Philadelphia: Dolphin Press, 1932), pp. 419-433.

[58] For these monastic communities, see Albert Kleber, O.S.B., *History of St. Meinrad Archabbey, 1854-1954* (St. Meinrad: Grail Publication, 1954); Colman J. Barry, O.S.B., *Worship and Work* (Collegeville: Saint John's Abbey, 1956); and Peter Beckman, O.S.B., *Kansas Monks. A History of St. Benedict's Abbey* (Atchison: Abbey Student Press, 1957). In contrast to the black monks, the two first permanent foundations of male contemplatives, Gethsemani in Kentucky (1848) and New Melleray near Dubuque (1849)—both of which in time had seminaries

Before leaving the seminaries for the religious, something should be said about clerical education among the largest of the teaching communities in the American Church, the Jesuits. Once the ex-Jesuits in this country had gained permission to affiliate with the Russian province in 1805, their progress was rapid. Though externally flourishing, within there was a good deal of stress and strain brought on by the Society having become overcommitted to conducting colleges and schools, as well as by the tendency of some superiors to ignore the rules governing the intellectual formation of the members. One Jesuit writer has characterized the situation as constituting "internal confusion and disarray," and as he explained it,

> In order to suit practical needs of the moment, the long, systematic training program for her members was stretched out and deformed beyond reason. Except for those sent to the European continent to pursue their studies, the normal young Jesuit's personal education had to contend for time with simultaneous teaching and prefecting duties.[59]

It is not possible here to describe the several educational improvisations in the Jesuits' seminary program up to 1860. Suffice it to say, in July of that year the scholastics were sent to Boston where, it was hoped, a solution to the difficulties might be found in a central seminary. But the Boston experiment did not work, and only with the purchase of a

---

for their own men—had come to the new world not only because of the promise it offered for their apostolate, but primarily because of the dim prospects of a politically disturbed France and a famine-ridden Ireland. These reasons, more than the intention of filling the spiritual needs of the immigrants, accounted for the new American houses of the Cistercians. On the Kentucky Trappists, see Thomas Merton, *The Waters of Siloe* (New York: Harcourt, Brace and Company, 1949) and M. Raymond [Flanagan], O.S.C.O., *Burnt Out Incense* (New York: P. J. Kenedy and Sons, 1949); and for the Dubuque abbey, Matthias M. Hoffman, *Arms and the Monk! The Trappist Saga in Mid-America* (Dubuque: William C. Brown Company, 1952).

[59] F. Gerard Drummond, S.J., "The Origins of Woodstock College, 1859-1869," *The Philosopher* [Publication of the students of Fordham University College of Philosophy and Letters] XI (May, 1964), 101.

farm near Woodstock, Maryland, in January, 1866, was ecclesiastical education for the Society in the United States
put on the road to a permanent and satisfactory solution.
There in September, 1869, Woodstock College was opened
as a central seminary for the Jesuits' American members with
seventeen students in theology and thirty in philosophy. The
faculty was composed principally of exiled Italian Jesuits
from the Turin Province, the most noted of whom was the
first prefect of studies and professor of dogmatic theology,
Camillo Mazzella, the future cardinal in Curia.[60]

THE PROBLEM OF SEMINARY PROLIFERATION

The sheer multiplication of houses of priestly formation
in the United States in the present century has been aston-
ishing. By January, 1964, the grand total of seminaries of
all kinds had reached 571, of which 112 enrolling 17,061
students were exclusively diocesan in character, with an
additional 9,640 candidates for the diocesan priesthood
under instrution in other seminaries, making a total of
26,701. At the same time there were 459 scholasticates and
houses of study of the religious orders and congregations
with 22,049 students, which added to the diocesan candidates, meant that in January, 1964, there were 48,750 students engaged in studies for the priesthood in this country.[61]
These are, indeed, impressive figures; however when it is
recalled that an investigation made in 1959 revealed that
over forty percent of the seminaries in the United States
had less than fifty students, questions may be legitimately
be raised as to the quality of instruction, educational facilities, and equipment of institutions of this size, and as to
whether the general cause of clerical education would not

---

60 See Patrick J. Dooley, S.J., *Woodstock and Its Makers* (Woodstock:
   College Press, 1927). A centennial history of the college is at present in
   progress by Francis G. McManamin, S.J., of Loyola College, Baltimore.
61 *The Official Catholic Directory, Anno Domini 1964* (New York: P. J.
   Kenedy and Sons, 1964), General summary, p. 1.

be better served by fewer seminaries with more highly
trained personnel and endowment.[62]

---

[62] "Statistical Report on Catholic Seminaries in the United States," Seminary Departments, National Catholic Educational Association (August, 1959), p. 3. This report accompanied the departments' *Seminary Newsletter*, I (October, 1959). One of the most recent writers to treat this weakness was Joseph O'Donoghue, "A Greater Role for Laymen? Reforming the Seminaries," *The Commonweal*, LXXXI (November 6, 1964), 194-196. The problems associated with small and isolated seminaries have a long history in practically all American churches. For example, in the early 1880's the scarcity of able Protestant ministers prompted Charles W. Eliot, President of Harvard, to support a revitalizing movement within the Divinity School with the two-fold object of making the bachelor of divinity degree inaccessible to all except students who had been thoroughly prepared, and to exclude entirely those who were unable to meet the new academic standards. Eliot felt the Divinity School required special protection since, as he put it, "it is liable to be seriously discredited by the crude public performances of incompetent young preachers . . ." He was hopeful, therefore, that the decline of Protestant denominationalism would permit students of Harvard's Divinity School to study theology "without having committed themselves in advance to any theory, creed, or set of opinions on controverted points." Until that came about, he saw little prospect of the clerical profession recovering its lost prestige, and the dearth of able ministers, acknowledged by practically all Protestant churches, would continue, he said, "so long as young men of independent spirit and mental virility are repelled from the profession at the very threshold, as they now are." Eliot expressed his solution in this way, "A partial remedy for this evil is likely to be found in the conduct of theological education at universities, or other centres of diversified intellectual activity, instead of in isolated denominational seminaries, and with the same academic freedom for teacher and pupil which is allowed in other great departments of study." [*Annual Reports of the President and Treasurer of Harvard College, 1881-82* (Cambridge: University Press: John Wilson and Son, 1882), pp. 27, 29-30]. A generation later the Secretary of Yale University, Anson Phelps Stokes, pleading for an end to the proliferation of small and inadequate Protestant seminaries, voiced the same idea. Remarking the disadvantages of the majority of seminaries being located at a distance from any college or university, he said, "It follows that relatively few of our students of theology have during their days of preparation the quickening influences which come from living in an atmosphere freighted with the spirit of learning and of a broad outlook on life." ["University Schools of Religion," *Religious Education*, IX (August, 1914), 325.] In discussing the relationship of professional schools to the university, Abraham Flexner dismissed the seminaries with a phrase when he said, "Of the professional faculties, a clear case can, I think, be made out for law and medicine, not for denominational religion, which involves a bias. . . ." [*Universities, American English, German* (New York: Oxford University Press, 1930), p. 29].

In any case, it is a simple matter to reckon the number of seminaries and their student populations; it is quite another thing to present a balanced and objective analysis of their quality as centers of spiritual formation and as educational institutions where young men's intellectual capacities meet the cultivation and challenge that they merit. Criticism of one kind or another about seminaries has been a fairly constant theme from the earliest days of the organized American Church. For example, John Carroll, the first bishop, sincerely welcomed the Sulpicians in 1791, even if the formative period of Saint Mary's Seminary left some doubts in his mind about their methods of instruction. He remarked to his old friend, Father Charles Plowden, in December, 1804, that the seminary then had twelve students, and if they continued at that rate they would be able to supply all the congregations with priests. He then added,

> But whether the Sulpicians and their mode of studies are calculated to produce eminent scholars, is a doubt with me. In the meantime, if they form virtuous priests with divinity enough to perform the functions of the ministry and guide the souls committed to their care, we must be satisfied, till time and opportunity give the means of introducing a more solid and comprehensive system of education.[63]

Close observation over the next few years by the critical eye of this ex-Jesuit professor, as well as more practical experience of what was called for in the Church at the time, caused him to place another emphasis on the Sulpicians' services. In January, 1812, he told the same English friend, "Too much praise cannot be given by me to the priests of Saint Sulpice here for their zeal and sacrifices to the public cause. They now maintain and educate at their own expense twenty-two Seminarians for the ministry."[64]

---

[63] Carroll to Plowden, n.p., December 7, 1804, in Peter Guilday, *The Life and Times of John Carroll, Archbishop of Baltimore, 1735-1815*, (New York: Encyclopedia Press, 1922), II, 754.

[64] Same to same, n.p., January 27, 1812, *ibid.*, II, 755. At this time Carroll

CRITICISM OF SEMINARY EDUCATION: NINETEENTH CENTURY

The present writer has already noted opinions about seminaries among some of Carroll's successors, such as Bishops Benedict Fenwick, John Purcell, and John Hughes; the number could easily be increased.[65] If certain bishops and lesser churchmen have manifested a perpetual anxiety on this score, it has been in part due to a realization from the American Church's earliest days of the validity of an idea beautifully expressed by Saint Pius X. In his first encyclical, *E supremi apostolatus*, of October 4, 1903, he urged the bishops of the world, "Let your first care be to form Christ in those who are destined by the duty of their vocation to form Him in others." Exhorting the world's hierarchies to exercise vigilance over their seminaries, the pontiff then added,

> All other tasks must yield to this one. Your greatest diligence, therefore, will be directed towards the right government and ordering of your seminaries, so that they may flourish both in sound doctrine and upright morals. Look upon your seminary as the delight of your heart. . . . Bear carefully in mind that as a general rule the faithful will be such as are those whom you call to the priesthood.[66]

Needless to say, comment on the seminaries has not always been judicious and constructive. A case in point was

---

was still in an unhappy mood over the way things were going at Georgetown College, and he followed his praise of Saint Mary's by saying, "I wish as favorable an account could be given of the College of Geo.-Town, which has sunk to the lowest degree of discredit."

[65] For example, see Bishop England's strictures on the Sulpicians' American seminaries in the chapter, "The Diocesan Seminary of Charleston, 1822-1832," *passim,* in Guilday, *John England,* I, 474-516.

[66] Vincent A. Yzermans, (Ed.), *All Things in Christ: Encyclicals and Selected Documents of Saint Pius X* (Westminster, Md.: Newman Press, 1954), p. 9 The pope added, "Furthermore be most solicitous for young priests who have just left the seminary. From the bottom of Our heart We urge you to draw them often close to you, in order to enkindle them and inspire them so that they may aspire only after God and the salvation of souls." (*ibid.*).

Jeremiah W. Cummings, founder and first pastor of Saint Stephen's Parish in New York, a priest of whom it was said that, "by an amusing cynicism of speech and a contrariness of views he became the critic of clerical life, saying the things and doing the things which irritate and flout popular opinion." This same Cummins, "a man of independent spirit and of imperious temper,"[67] published an article in October, 1860, that was highly critical of the failure of the American Church to produce more native vocations, as well as of the fitness to serve in the United States of many priests educated in European seminaries. Granted that it was, indeed, preferable to have native-born priests, it was scarcely helpful to state, as Cummings did, "There are dwelling-places of seculars and regulars on the European continent, which allow themselves to be turned into cheap priest factories on the principle that John or Thomas is not fit to be ordained if he is to stay at home; but he will make a good enough priest for America."[68] This kind of comment not only gave offense, but it proved harmful to the cause which it was intended to improve.

The remarks of Doctor Cummings, however, should not be thought typical either of his time, or any other period in the life of the Church of the United States. Insofar as the American clergy's concept of a seminary was known, it was more closely attuned to the idea expressed by Newman in a sermon preached at the dedication of Saint Bernard's Seminary in Birmingham in October, 1873. With his almost unerring gift for discerning the course of the future, he warned of a major evil coming upon the Church which he described as "that plague of infidelity," and which, he said, for the first time in its history would confront Christianity

---

[67] John Talbot Smith, *The Catholic Church in New York* (New York: Hall & Locke 1905), I, 170-171; II, 393.

[68] J.W.C. [Jeremiah W. Cummings], "Our Future Clergy: An Inquiry into Vocations to the Priesthood in the United States," *Brownson's Quarterly Review* [Third New York Series] I (October, 1860), 507.

with a world "simply irreligious." To combat this peril Newman would have the clergy cultivate an ecclesiastical spirit
of which the practice of the presence of God and an elevation of mind were essential ingredients. It was in this connection he stated, "A seminary is the only true guarantee
for the creation of the ecclesiastical spirit."[69]

SEMINARIES AND THE THIRD PLENARY COUNCIL

That Newman's concept expressed the mind of most
American Catholic leaders was evident a decade later in
connection with the Third Plenary Council. Both the metro-
politans' preliminary discussions at Rome in the autumn of
1883, and the exchange of opinions that took place during
the ensuing year, revealed the bishops and their theological
advisers as keenly aware of the role that the seminary should
play in the creation of a proper ecclesiastical spirit. In the
council itself, which was in session from November 6 to
December 7, 1884, considerable time and attention were
devoted to the education of the clergy. In the end forty-six
decrees pertaining to minor and major seminaries were
enacted, as well as additional decrees which adumbrated a
seminarium principale of university.[70]

---

[69] "The Infidelity of the Future," *Faith and Prejudice and Other Unpublished Sermons of Cardinal Newman* edited by the Birmingham Oratory
(New York: Sheed and Ward, 1956), pp. 124-125; 127.
[70] *Acta et Decreta Concilii Plenarii Baltimorensis Tertii* (Baltimore: John
Murphy Company, 1886), pp. 69-94. The two preceding plenary councils
had little of an original character to say about seminaries. In 1852 one
decree was passed that merely counseled those bishops who could not
support a seminary of their own to join with others in the same province
so that there would be at least one seminary in every province. *Concilium
plenarium totius Americae septentrionalis Foederatae Baltimori habitum
anno 1852* (Baltimore: John Murphy Company, 1853), pp. 45-47. The
council of 1866 had a chapter on seminaries, although. much of what
was said was a repetition either of Trent's legislation or of previous
American enactments. See *Concilii Plenarii Baltimorensis II. . . . Acta et
Decreta* (Baltimore: John Murphy Company, 1868), pp. 105-110. On
this occasion the bishops also had special praise for the American Col-

There is space here for only a brief account of the debates and the contents of the conciliar decrees. In regard to the minor seminary, most of the discussion related to the course of studies which was not to be less than six years in length. The traditional subjects of a minor seminary curriculum were mentioned with general agreement on the need for thorough education in English, in enough Greek to enable students to read the New Testament in that language, and in instruction in at least one modern foreign language. There was also, of course, agreement on the need for Latin, although a difference developed over the amount of emphasis it should receive. Bishops John Lancaster Spalding and Bernard J. McQuaid contended that the schema gave too much stress to Latin, but in the end they were overruled and the final wording remained substantially as it had appeared in the original draft.

The debates on the major seminary were on the whole along conventional lines, except that the majority of bishops made it clear that they were not disposed to introduce here the European practice of summer villas for seminarians. The bishops believed that seminarians would profit from contact with the world during their summer holidays. The council declared that seminary professorships were not to be entrusted to those who had only a temporary interest in the work, but rather to men who were eager to teach and who were ready to sacrifice themselves to that end. In delineating how the various courses were to be conducted, the legislation was quite conservative and revealed more of an apologetic than a critical or scientific tone and approach. Thus the professor of Scripture was counseled to begin his instruction by vindicating the authenticity and canonical authority of each of the books of the Bible, and then proceed to an-

lege both in Rome and Louvain, as well as for All Hallows College in Dublin, and they likewise mentioned the advantages for clerical education to be derived from a university when the opportune time would come (pp. 227-228).

alyze their contents in such a way as to both nourish the students' piety and provide them with the biblical weaponry with which to defend religion. In the same vein the professor of Church history was directed to aim at establishing the truths of history against the false views that had hitherto been accepted as truth, and at showing how much good had been derived from ecclesiastical institutions in past ages.[71]

THE NATIONAL SEMINARY: POST-THIRD COUNCIL

Of the fifty conciliar decrees of 1884 which were devoted to clerical education, only the last four dealing with the *seminarium principale* represented any real advance. In the recent past the perennial talk about improving education for priests had begun to center more around the idea of a graduate school of theology or a university. And in the years after the plenary council it was this aspect of the problem that gave substance to the continuing dialogue, since the education of the laity entered hardly at all into the discussion.[72] The widest variety of opinion was expressed, running all the way from the complacent views of James F. Loughlin, former professor in Saint Charles Seminary, Philadelphia, who stated in 1890 that he saw "no reason why we should not pronounce that the Catholic clergy of the United States are a highly intellectual, well-educated body of men,"[73] to Bishop McQuaid's declaration seven years later that he felt Catholics efforts in seminary work were "still elementary in

---

[71] For the council's treatment of seminaries, see Francis P. Cassidy, "Catholic Education in the Third Plenary Council of Baltimore," *Catholic Historical Review*, XXXIV (October, 1948), 275-290.

[72] For a summary of opinion on a Catholic university at this time, see the present writer's chapter, "The Growth of an Idea," in *The Formative Years of the Catholic University of America*, pp. 15-86.

[73] James F. Loughlin, "The Higher and Lower Education of The American Priesthood," *American Catholic Quarterly Review*, XV (January, 1890), 106.

more ways than one."[74] To Loughlin's mind the best prospect for improving the seminaries lay in giving effect "as speedily as practicable to the admirable injunctions and provisions of the Third Plenary Council."[75] McQuaid, on the other hand, while respectful of the council, would in some respects make a clear break with the past because, as he said, "There is no justifiable reason why Church authorities in America should be hampered by the customs and usages of older countries, where innovations are looked on in the light of sacrileges."[76]

Thus the subject continued to be aired in the Catholic press, in clerical journals, and in the private correspondence of churchmen, especially that of the bishops who were chiefly responsible for what was done, or was not done, in the way of seminary education. For example, in the spring of 1891, Patrick W. Riordan, Archbishop of San Francisco, told John J. Keane, Rector of The Catholic University of America, that in his judgment seminary faculties should aim to be as good as that of the University's school of theology. Showing an uncommon awareness of the disservice done to superior students by the seminary's failure to offer them an intellectual challenge worthy of their talents, Riordan declared, "A good student loses his time and weakens his mental health in being obliged to pass three years in pursuing so called preliminary studies, which are as a rule of the most elementary character, [and] which consist in giving them a number of facts, instead of giving them the great principles underlying facts."[77]

---

[74] Bernard J. McQuaid, "Our American Seminaries," *American Ecclesiastical Review*, XVI (May, 1897), 463.

[75] Loughlin, *op. cit.*, p. 111.

[76] McQuaid, *op. cit.*, pp. 464-465.

[77] Archives of the Catholic University of America, Keane Papers, Riordan to Keane, San Francisco, April 2, 1891. The present writer owes this reference to the kindness of the Reverend James P. Gaffey, Superintendent of Schools of the Diocese of Santa Rosa, who has written the life of Archbishop Riordan. At the time of the latter's silver episcopal jubilee in

All things considered, the two most widely known and influential Catholic prelates of the late century were Cardinal Gibbons and Archbishop Ireland, both of whom held pronouncedly friendly attitudes toward the American civil order, as well as sharing a general openmindedness that deplored unnecessary ecclesiastical condemnations and censures. This attitude was reflected in the address given by the cardinal on October 28, 1891, at the centennial of Saint Mary's Seminary. He first paid an extraordinary tribute to the Sulpicians who were mostly Frenchborn, as well as to all the apostolic priests who had come to the United States from abroad. But painfully aware as he was of the nationalist dissension then rife within the Church of the United States, he availed himself of the occasion to emphasize the values of a native priesthood. "If the Church is to take deep roots in the country and to flourish," he said, "it must be sustained by men racy of the soil, educated at home, breathing the spirit of the country, growing with its growth, and in harmony with its civil and political institutions."[78] The cardinal would be the first to discount his own ability as an educational theorist; yet five years thereafter his book, *The Ambassador of Christ*, revealed a mind that had given much thought to the factors involved in spiritual and intellectual preparation for the priesthood. In fact, twelve chapters, or nearly half of the nearly 400 pages, were devoted to the intellectual standards a priest should maintain in the various aspects of his ministry.[79]

October, 1908, he remarked that he hoped the ceremony in Saint Mary's Cathedral would be especially impressed on the minds of the seminarians who were present. "If I have done nothing more," he said, "I feel proud that I have accomplished the great work of establishing St. Patrick's Seminary at Menlo Park, where young men reared in this State can become servants." *The Great Archbishop* (San Francisco: Nash, 1935), p. 10; this is a reprint from *The Monitor* of October 17, 1908.

[78] Quoted in Allen Sinclair Will, *Life of Cardinal Gibbons, Archbishop of Baltimore*, (New York: Dutton, 1922) I, 530.

[79] *The Ambassador of Christ* (Baltimore: John Murphy Company, 1886), pp. 164-348.

In all of this, of course, the Archbishop of Saint Paul heartily agreed. If one were to wonder what kind of a spirit lay behind the launching of the Saint Paul Seminary in September, 1894, a partial answer was at hand in the sermon that John Ireland delivered at Gibbons' silver episcopal jubilee a year before. On this occasion Ireland was at pains to emphasize the need for an open and broad approach on the part of churchmen to the world in which they lived. Acknowledging the grave damage done to religion by the French Revolution and its aftermath, which had understandably prompted many clergymen to turn their backs on the world, the archbishop yet felt that this policy had been seriously detrimental to the Church's obligations and to her best interests. Of these men he said.

> The age passed beyond them. There were a few Lacordaires, who recognized and proclaimed the duties of the hour: but timid companions abandoned them; reactionaries accused them of dangerous liberalism, of semi-heresy; and they were forced to be silent. . . . The age, abandoned to itself and to false and mischievous guides, irritated by the isolation and unfriendliness of the Church, became hardened in its secularism, and taught itself to despise and hate religion.[80]

Ireland's words were a happy augury for the seminary he was to open the following September. If this type of thinking had prevailed in Catholic seminaries generally, some of the unfortunate consequences which their isolation and aloofness induced might have been avoided.

That Ireland's breath of view obtained among a number of seminary administrators and professors, as well as among certain priests not directly engaged in seminary work, was true. Two notable examples near the end of the century were John Talbot Smith, a priest of the Archdiocese of New

---

[80] Ireland called the sermon preached on October 18, 1893, "The Church and the Age," *The Church and Modern Society*, (Saint Paul: Pioneer Press, 1905), I, 110-111.

York, who did a great deal of writing, and John B. Hogan,
S.S., Rector of Saint John's Seminary in Boston. In 1896 the
former published a volume which he called *Our Seminaries.
An Essay on Clerical Training* wherein the following six-fold
division told something of the author's method and approach:
'The Standard'; 'Health, Strength and Manners'; 'Certain
Arts of Expression'; 'The Spiritual Life'; and 'The Missionary
Spirit.' The final division of eight chapters took up nearly
one fourth of the volume and was called 'The Intellectual
Life.'[81] Smith felt especially moved on this last aspect of the
problem, and that he did not hesitate to speak plainly, as
was evident when he lamented the priest's lack of articulate-
ness and remarked, "The habits of intellectual life in the
seminary have dwarfed him. The curriculum rarely recognizes anything but theology and philosophy, and these often
isolated from present conditions and without practical application."[82]

Father Hogan had begun his analysis in May, 1891, in a
series of articles in the *American Ecclesiastical Review*; they
were subsequently published in book form two years after
Smith's volume appeared.[83] Like Smith, he gave due emphasis to the spiritual and moral aspects of the candidate's
"training"; but he, too, made a strong plea for the seminary
to develop the student's intellectual capacities, as well as an
appeal to the young priest to continue to study after his

---

[81] The book was published in New York by William H. Young & Company;
it appeared in a second edition in 1908 with a new title, *The Training of
a Priest.*

[82] *Ibid.*, p. 251. For a gift copy of Smith's work, now long out of print, the
present writer is grateful to John R. Sullivan, S.S., of Saint Mary's
Seminary, Roland Park, Baltimore. Some notion of the relative scarcity
of significant writings on seminaries can be had from the general index
of the leading Catholic journal of the last quarter of the century, the
American Catholic Quarterly Review. The index covered the issues from
the *Review's* beginning in January, 1876, to October, 1900; the *Review*
ceased publication with the issue of April, 1924.

[83] The first of the series was called, "The Curriculum," *American Ecclesiastical Review*, IV (May, 1891), 342-349.

ordination. "In reality there is room, even in the busy existence of a priest," he maintained, "for much more serious study than is commonly thought." He believed that if priests would only try, they would soon discover how much more they could do than they had been doing. "Day after day they will feel their powers expand with the effort," he continued, "and the evergrowing, varied knowledge will become one of the happy necessities of their existence . . ."[84]

In the course of his articles Hogan treated each subject in the seminary curriculum in detail, revealing throughout an expanse of mind and critical attitude which were exceptional in ecclesiastical circles at that time. What he had to say about the history of the Church will serve to illustrate the tone and spirit of his contribution. He quoted with approval Cicero's remark that ignorance of history kept a man "in the condition of perpetual boyhood," and he then went on to stress the emancipating effect that history can have on the human mind in freeing it from narrowness and insular confinement. Hogan further made his own the statement of the English Church historian, William Stubbs, to the effect that not the least of history's lessons was to learn,

> that there are many points on which no decision as to right or wrong, good or evil, acquittal or condemnation, is to be looked for, and on which we may say that, as often the height of courage is to say I dare not, and the height of love is to say I will not, so the height of wisdom is to have learned to say, I do not know.[85]

---

[84] John B. Hogan, S.S., *Clerical Studies* (Boston: Marlier, Callanan & Company, 1898), pp. v-vi. The present writer wishes to express his thanks to the Reverend William G. Woods, former librarian of Saint Patrick's Seminary, Menlo Park, California, for a gift copy of this work which has long been out of print.

[85] *Ibid.*, pp. 371-372. The quotation from Stubbs was taken from the latter's lecture, "Methods of Historical Study," delivered on May 18, 1877, and contained in his *Seventeen Lectures on the Study of Medieval and Modern History* (Oxford: At the Clarendon Press, 1886), p. 95. In contrast to Hogan's attitude toward church history, was the emphasis on its apologetic value in the paper of Daniel J. Kennedy, O.P., of the Dominican

Mention has already been made of the views of James Loughlin who early in 1890 expressed general satisfaction with the present state of clerical education. He felt, however, that the seminaries would be strengthened if their faculties could be rescued from what he termed their "unorganized isolation" and formed into a confederation.[86] Seven years passed before that hope was realized through the initiative of the Rector of The Catholic University of America, Thomas J. Conaty. Conaty had two principal objectives in mind: (a) to affiliate the seminaries of the country to the new University in Washington; (b) to find a remedy for the deficiencies of students who came to the University after a seminary education that left them unfit to meet the requirements for the S.T.B. degree without loss of time in making up prerequisities.

In October, 1897, Monsignor Conaty took a step forward when he asked permission of the Board of Trustees to approach the seminary authorities for the purpose of organizing them and thus drawing them closer to the University. Permission was granted. As a consequence of Conaty's invitation ten rectors met at Saint Joseph's Seminary, Dun-

House of Studies, Washington, called "The Importance of History in the Study of Dogma," read at the third annual meeting of the National Catholic Educational Association in Cleveland on July 12, 1906. Kennedy quoted the constitution *Dei Filius* of Vatican Council I as indicating what he termed "the apologetic value of history. . . .," and he later stated, "History must be the weapon of defense, which, at all times, useful, is especially necessary in our times, when the enemies of the Church are arming themselves with all instruments of attack that can be found as fabricated by those who devote themselves to historical research." *Catholic Educational Association. Report of the Proceedings and Addresses of the Third Annual Meeting, Cleveland, Ohio, July 9, 10, 11 and 13, 1906* (Columbus, Ohio: Published by the Association. Secretary's Office, 1906), pp. 251-252. Two days before, however, the same meeting heard Patrick R. Heffron, Rector of Saint Paul Seminary, speak in a much more mature and helpful manner about church history when he said it "must be studied in the light of contemporary sources. All the acumen of a well-trained mind must be brought to bear on the application of the canons of historical criticism." (*ibid.*, p. 217).

[86] Loughlin, *op. cit.*, pp. 111-112.

woodie, New York, on May 25, 1898, while the heads of five other seminaries sent word of their approval of the idea. In addressing the assembled rectors, Conaty said,

> Our young cleric must be prepared to meet the issues of the hour—issues no longer between the true Church of Christ and the sects, but between revealed religion and all forms of agnosticism and false individualism . . . He must also be prepared to enter into the field of social and economic reform . . . The battle of the future is to be a philosophical battle, as well as scientific and historical. It will be a defense of the very foundations of belief . . .[87]

Before departing from New York, the seminary administrators voted to set up a permanent organization to which they gave the name Educational Conference of Seminary Faculties. That autumn Conaty's actions received emphatic endorsement from the Rector of Saint John's Seminary, Brighton, in an article in the *American Ecclesiastical Review*. In fact, Hogan went beyond the original idea and outlined a method by which he believed academically superior students might be singled out and afforded advanced instruction along the lines of the German seminar. Showing that he understood and sympathized with the plight of able young minds caught in the system's rule that all seminarians follow exactly the same academic program, he said,

> It is easy to see how, by following such a method bright students would be lifted up from the depression into which the ordinary routine of work casts them when unrelieved, and rid from the temptation of seeking relief in indiscriminate reading and other distractions; how they would soon develop a taste for deeper knowledge and reveal their aptitudes for special lines of study, which are the natural signs of a vocation to the University. At the same time this special discipline,

---

[87] "Educational Conference of Seminary Presidents," *Catholic University Bulletin*, IV (July, 1898), 401.

carried on during the whole course of theology, would be the best possible preparation for University work.[88]

The Hogan article should have furnished a constructive program of action for the seminaries. Yet such was not to be, for after a second meeting at Saint Charles Seminary in Philadelphia on September 1, 1899, the Educational Conference of Seminary Faculties lapsed into a state of quiescence for the next five years. Only in July, 1904, was it revived in response to a call from Conaty's successor at the University, Monsignor Denis J. O'Connell. To the meeting held in Saint Louis, there had been invited not only the seminary rectors, but also representatives of the elementary schools and delegates of the Association of Catholic Colleges. On this occasion the seminary organization's perpetuity was assisted, if not absolutely assured, when it joined with the people from the elementary schools and the colleges to form the Catholic Educational Association which thereafter held regular annual meetings of which the seminaries were an integral part.[89]

QUALITY OF SEMINARY EDUCATION IN THE TWENTIETH CENTURY

One of the accepted norms for determining the quality and value of a system of education, or of an educational institution, is the number of men of enduring reputation it has produced. Judged by this standard, the Catholic seminaries of the United States over the 174 years that have passed since the opening of Saint Mary's in Baltimore, have not

---

[88] John B. Hogan, S.S., "Seminary and University Studies," *American Ecclesiastical Review*, XIX (October, 1898), 368-369. Hogan had been vetoed by the faculty for the chair of apologetics at the University in 1894 and was still unacceptable to some. Ahern, *op. cit.*, p. 68, n. 17.

[89] The origins of the National Catholic Educational Association and the part played by the seminaries in its first years, are outlined in Hogan, *op. cit.*, pp. 65-80; and Barry, *op. cit.*, pp. 215-235.

had a distinguished record. [90] To be sure, the American Church has had in her midst able theologians, exegists, philosophers, and Church historians. To mention only a few conspicuous names in the first category by way of illustration, there have been theologians like Francis Patrick Kenrick, James A. Corcoran, Aloysius Sabetti, S.J., Camillo Mazzella, S.J., Herman J. Heuser, and Adolph A. Tanquerey, S.S. But with the single exception of Corcoran, these men were born abroad and received most or all of their education outside the United States, so the American seminaries cannot fully claim them as they might had they been educated in this country. Only within the last few decades has there come to be a sizeable corps of native American seminary professors whose superior graduate training and productive research have enhanced the ecclesiastical sciences. Especially has this been the case in the field of Scripture where of late Americans have more than held their own with their counterparts abroad in the scholarly *Catholic Biblical Quarterly* and in other learned journals.[91]

There are many explanations for the dearth of American-born Catholic scholars in the ecclesiastical sciences, as well as the severe shortage of priests who are both learned and articulate in theology and its allied sciences. It is much too complicated a question, however, to attempt anything more

---

[90] See Gustave Weigel, S.J., "American Catholic Intellectualism—A Theologian's Reflections," *Review of Politics*, XIX (July, 1957), pp. 275-307.

[91] For a listing and partial assessment of the work of American Catholics in Scripture, see Robert North, S.J., "The American Scripture Century," *American Ecclesiastical Review*, CL (May, 1964), 314-345. Two able summaries of theological trends since Leo XIII are Roger Aubert, Aspects Divers du NeoThomisme sous le Pontificat de Léon XIII," Giuseppe Rossini (Ed.), *Aspetti della Cultura Cattolica nell' Età de Leone XIII. Atti del Convegno tenuto a Bologna il 27-28-29 Dicembre 1960* (Roma: Edizioni Cinque Lune, 1961), pp. 133-337, and the same writer's "La Théologie Catholique au Milieu du XXe Siècle," *La Revue Nouvelle*, XVII (Juin 15, 1953), 561-576. Canon Aubert continued his survey in subsequent issues of *La Revue Nouvelle* to that of October 15, 1953, where he treated existentialism and ecumenism (pp. 272-292).

here than to suggest several of the principal causes. One explanation springs from the fact that the native-born Catholic seminarian, priest, and prelate have been, and are, as thoroughly American as their non-Catholic fellow citizens. They, too, have acquired their share of the inhibiting influences and the hampering characteristics of the national life that have militated so strongly throughout American history against creative intellectual work. In other words, Catholic clerics have in no way been immune from the spirit described less than three years ago by an authority in American intellectual history when he said, "Again and again, but particularly in recent years, it has been noticed that intellect in America is resented as a kind of excellence, as a claim to distinction, as a challenge to egalitarianism, as a quality which almost certainly deprives a man or woman of the common touch."[92]

And if the national ethos has been a contributing factor to the seminaries' failure to produce more priests with a deep respect for learning and a love for books—for as professional schools it is not their business to produce scholars—it has been due among other reasons to several debilitating attitudes prevalent in those circles that are responsible for and control the seminaries. Of these attitudes, two may be said to have been peculiarly American. The first of these is a failure to take education in general in a really serious way rather than to treat it as a *pro forma process* through which one is obliged to pass in order to acquire the appropriate label for the performance of a certain practical task. One wonders if this point has not been exemplified for many years in the consistently high percentage of priest graduate students at The Catholic University of America whose superiors have sent them there to study canon law, social work, and education. And a second factor closely related to the

---

[92] Richard Hofstadter, *Anti-Intellectualism in American Life* (New York: Alfred A. Knopf, 1963), p. 51.

first has been a lack of incentive from too many ecclesiastical superiors, that is, a failure on the part of the latter, whether diocesan or religious, to place a high premium on the outstanding intellectual achievement of their men in the seminary.

A third point has to do with a phenomenon that was not American in its origin. It pertains to the discouragement and even fright which has periodically overtaken intellectual endeavors in Catholic circles by reason of the presence—at times real and at times imagined—of what superiors have conceived as a danger to the religious faith of their subjects. The low state of ecclesiastical learning at Rome in the 1840's of which Newman spoke, was partly due to the siege mentality that had held so many of the Church's best minds captive since the French Revolution. But had Newman lived into the early years of the present century, he would have witnessed even a darker picture. No sincere and informed Catholic would attempt to deny that modernism was a real heresy, and that there was a moral obligation on the part of those in authority who understood its true character to take steps to rid the Church of the danger. But it was equally true that in the campaign to protect the Catholic world against the influence of this movement grave injury was done to innocent persons. Many scholars came to feel that it was better to cease all research and writing rather than to become the object of their superiors' anxiety or embarrassment, or the cause of scandal or suspicion to their colleagues and students.

Obviously, modernism took no significant hold upon the Catholic Church of the United States, any more than a few years before there had been any reality to the so-called heresy of Americanism that some European Catholics had fancied as a prelude to the modernist movement.[93] But it

---

[93] The modernist movement and its aftermath in relation to the American Catholics still awaits an historian. Thomas T. McAvoy, C.S.C., has treated

would be idle to deny that the Roman directives leading up
to and following Pius X's encyclical, *Pascendi dominici
gregis*, of September 8, 1907, did not produce a dampening
effect on the research, writing, and general intellectual efforts of many seminary professors in this country. How otherwise is one to account for such happenings as the sudden
death in the summer of 1908 of the *New York Review* edited
by professors of Saint Joseph's Seminary, Dunwoodie, a
journal that was the most learned periodical published to
date under American Catholic auspices? How likewise could
one explain the dismissal of the Dutch-born scholar, Henry
A. Poels, from his chair of Old Testament at The Catholic
University of America in April, 1910, and the question raised
the previous month—from Rome—concerning the orthodoxy
of Joseph Bruneau, S.S., of Saint Mary's Seminary in Baltimore?[94]

If episodes of this kind did not permanently kill Catholic
scholarly endeavor in Washington, Baltimore, and New York,
they served to induce an atmosphere that was threatening
and unsympathetic to creative thought and original research
in these institutions. Of the fear and anxiety that pervaded
the Catholic seminaries generally at this time, there can be
no doubt. Whatever prospective investigation that professors

Americanism thoroughly in his volume, *The Great Crisis in American
Catholic History, 1895-1900* (Chicago: Henry Regnery Company, 1957);
see also Robert D. Cross, *The Emergence of Liberal Catholicism in
America* (Cambridge: Harvard University Press, 1958).

[94] Some background for the *New York Review* is contained in the privately
printed letter of Edward R. Dyer, S.S., Vicar General of the Society of
Saint Sulpice for the United States, dated April 18, 1906, and addressed
to his own subjects in explanation of five Sulpician professors at Saint
Joseph's Seminary, Dunwoodie, leaving the Society. For the Poels and
Bruneau cases, see John Tracy Ellis, *The Life of James Cardinal Gibbons,
Archbishop of Baltimore, 1834-1921* (Milwaukee: Bruce Publishing
Company, 1952), II, 171-182; 475-476. The most recent treatment of
the modernist movement in the English-speaking world is Maisie Ward's
chapter, "The Modernist Crisis," *Unfinished Business* (New York: Sheed
and Ward, 1964), pp. 49-63.

may have been inclined to make the advance knowledge in their respective disciplines was blighted, and there came about here, as elsewhere throughout the Catholic world, the situation that was described so vividly, and so bravely, by Eudoxe-Irénée Mignot, Archbishop of Albi, in his memorable letter of October, 1914, to Domenico Cardinal Ferrata, Secretary of State to Pope Benedict XV. Picturing the disastrous effects that had followed from the spying and dishonorable reporting by certain agents of the former Secretary of State, Rafael Cardinal Merry del Val, Mignot said,

> The perpetuation of this state of things will mean an inferior clergy, more concerned with the externals of worship than with the spiritual realities of interior religion—a clergy which will understand nothing of the intellectual and moral difficulties of the time, or for the movement of ideas, and the Church will be the loser. Such a clergy will stand motionless amidst a world on the march, a world whose light they ought to be.[95]

Fortunately, the new pontiff shared Archbishop Mignot's anxiety, and in the first encyclical of his reign, *Ad beatissimi*, of November 1, 1914, Benedict XV warned against individual Catholics who attempted either to speak for the Church or to condemn the views of their coreligionists. On all questions where the Holy See had not pronounced judgment, and where free discussion was allowable, said the pope, "it is certainly lawful for everybody to say what he thinks and to uphold his opinion."[96] It was the herald of a happier time for the Church's thinkers and scholars, and thereafter the skies brightened perceptibly for them.

---

[95] Mignot to Ferrata, n.p., October, 1914, Nicolas Fontaine, *Saint Siège, Action française et Catholiques intégraux. Histoire critique avec Documents* (Paris: Librairie Universitaire. J. Gamber, 1928), p. 133. The entire text of the lengthy document is carried in an appendix (pp. 119-137). For this aspect of the early years of this pontificate, see Walter H. Peters' chapter, "Modernists and Integralists," *The Life of Benedict XV* (Milwaukee: Bruce, 1959), pp. 42-53.

[96] "First Encyclical of Benedict XV," *Catholic Mind*, XII (December 22, 1914), p. 746.

CONCLUSION*

During the half century since *Ad beatissimi,* American
seminaries have been gradually improving. They have
known moments of doubt and darkness when timid souls
have exaggerated the danger to the faith from free and open
exchange of ideas and expression of opinions. Yet progress in
clerical education has not been lacking, and he would be a
dull man, indeed, who would fail to have sensed the *aggior-*
namento currently at work within the seminary world.
Thoughtful men are agreed that the critical character of the
present time requires this up-dating if the Church is to have
relevance for the age, and a swelling chorus of her own sons
as well demands it.[97] In the period of change and adjustment that lies ahead for the seminaries, mistakes and errors
of judgment will almost inevitably occur, and that in spite
of the highest motives and intentions. But the wise administrator and the perceptive professor will not be disheartened
by that fact, because they will have beforehand accepted the
necessity for a certain amount of trial and error, for honest
experimentation, along avenues and paths as yet untrod.
These men who are destined to chart the future course of
the Catholic seminary world will have sensed the peculiar
pertinence for them in the striking call issued from the

---

[97] The literature on the subject of seminary reform has of late become so
extensive that it is impossible to do more here than to mention several
items which, in the judgment of the present writer, are especially helpful.
In the order of their appearance they are: Thomas Corbishley, S.J., "The
Intellectual Formation of the Religious," *Wiseman Review,* No. 493
(Autumn, 1962), 260-268, which, although directed to religious, is
equally applicable to those connected with the diocesan seminary; Denis
E. Hurley, "Pastoral Emphasis in Seminary Studies," *The Furrow,*
XIII (January, 1962), 16-30; John J. Wright, "Perseverance in the
Seminary: Problems and Remedies," *American Ecclesiastical Review,*
CXLVII (August, 1962), 73-87; Charles Davis, "Theology in Semi-
nary Confinement," *Downside Review,* LXXXI (October, 1963), 307-
316; Walter J. Burghardt, S.J., "The Intellectual Formation of the Future
Priest," *Bulletin of the National Catholic Educational Association,* LXI
(August, 1964), 58-68.

sacred precincts of Bethlehem in January, 1964, by Pope
Paul VI, a call in which their delicate task may be said to
have been reflected in the Holy Father's words when he
said,

> We are living at the historic hour when the Church of Christ
> must live its deep and visible unity. . . . We must give the life
> of the Church new attitudes of mind, new aims, new standards
> of behavior, make it rediscover a spiritual beauty in all its
> aspects: in the sphere of thought and word, in prayer and
> methods of education, in art and canon law. A unanimous
> effort is needed in which all groups must offer their co-oper-
> ation. May everyone hear the call which Christ is making to
> him through our voice.[98]

---

98 "Faith, Unity, and Peace. Pope Paul's Epiphany Message from Bethlehem," *The Tablet*, CCXVIII (January 11, 1964), 53.

* While writing the chapters on the history of the seminary,
the writer incurred a debt of gratitude to a number of persons,
several of whom have been mentioned in the footnotes. He wishes
to express special thanks, however, to his expert typist, Miss
Mary L. Randle, who performed her difficult task with complete
dedication and generosity, and to his former student and friend,
The Reverend John P. Marschall, C.S.V., who gave time and care
when he could ill afford to do so, to verifying references and
furnishing the writer with certain materials not immediately
available to him. For similar acts of kindness he would wish
likewise to mention Mr. John T. Appleby of the American Historical Association, and two former students and friends at
present working for their doctorates, the Reverends John Whit-
ney Evans at the University of Minnesota and Michael O'Neill
at Harvard University.

3.

Diocesan Theological Seminaries in the Middle West, 1811-1889

The boat on which we descended the Ohio became the cradle of the seminary, and of the church of Kentucky. Our cabin was, at the same time, chapel, dormitory, study room and refectory. An altar was erected on the boxes, and ornamented so far as circumstances would allow. The Bishop prescribed a regulation which fixed all the exercises, and in which each had a proper time. On Sundays, after prayers, every one went to confession; then the priests said Mass, and the others went to communion. After an agreeable navigation of thirteen days, we arrived at Louisville, next at Bardstown, and finally, at the residence of the Vicar General.[1]

Thus did John B. David, S.S., rector of the first Catholic theological school in the Middle West, Saint Thomas Seminary, located in its earliest years on a farm about three miles from Bardstown, Kentucky, describe its origin six years after the event. According to the historian of the seminary, it had been born on May 20, 1811, on a flatboat at the Pittsburgh docks when the new bishop, Benedict Joseph Flaget, his

---

[1] John B. David, S.S., to a friend in France, November 20, 1817, Martin J. Spalding, *Sketches of the Life, Times, and Character of the Rt. Rev. Benedict Joseph Flaget, First Bishop of Louisville* (Louisville: Webb & Levering. 1852), pp. 69-70. The writer wishes to thank his friend, the Reverend Columba E. Halsey, for checking the quotation from the Spalding book, a copy of which was not available at the time of writing.

fellow Sulpician and friend, David, and three seminarians came aboard for their voyage down the Ohio River.[2] It is easy enough, therefore, for the present day historian to date the beginnings of Catholic theological instruction in the Middle West when furnished with so clear a *terminus a quo*. As for the *terminus ad quem*, I have chosen 1889 which witnessed in November of that year the opening at Washington, D.C., of the Catholic University of America, an institution which at the beginning was exclusively a graduate school of theology for the clergy of the entire United States. A further link relating the University to the theme and geographical area to which the present discussions are confined, was the fact that its origins were owed to the progressive ideas and forceful initiative of churchmen of the Middle West, especially to the young, Kentucky-born prelate, John Lancaster Spalding, first Bishop of Peoria.[3]

So much, then, for the time and place of the chain of events that unfolded during the seventy-eight years between 1811 and 1889 in the Middle West, a region interpreted to mean, in the main, the double tier of states on opposite sides of the Mississippi River. By way of a further geographical refinement, one might say the territory running north to south from the Canadian frontier to the southern boundaries of Missouri, Illinois, and Kentucky, and east to west from the eastern limits of Michigan, Ohio, and Kentucky to the western boundaries of North Dakota, South Dakota, Nebraska, and Kansas, allowing a little leeway for

---

[2] William J. Howlett, *Historical Tribute to St. Thomas' Seminary at Poplar Neck near Bardstown, Kentucky* (Saint Louis: B. Herder Book Company. 1906), p. 26.
[3] For the state of Catholic theological education, and of Catholic higher education in general up to 1889, see the introductory chapter of John Tracy Ellis, *The Formative Years of the Catholic University of America* (Washington: American Catholic Historical Association. 1946), pp. 15-86.

brief excursions beyond these limits.[4] As for the third item in the familiar triology of time, place, and idea that the late professor of church history in the Catholic University of America, Peter Guilday, was fond of emphasizing, the idea might be delineated as follows. I have tried to survey the principal developments in the Catholic theological seminaries of this region for candidates for the diocesan priesthood, with a view to presenting a picture of their number and size, the peculiar circumstances that brought several of them into being, with as much said about certain other features of these institutions as the limited contemporary evidence will allow, for example, the type of education imparted, the textbooks used, the relation of these institutions to the Catholic colleges of the period, the kind of life experienced by the faculties and students, and the type of priests they produced for the Church of the Middle West up to the final decade of the last century. If the reader does not find here answers to certain questions that occur to him, it will be due in all likelihood to one of two causes: first, the present study is intended as a preliminary investigation and has been written largely from printed, not manuscript, sources; secondly, there are a number of points, I am convinced, whereon there simply is not sufficient evidence of any kind to warrant a judgment.

By way of another introductory idea or two, permit me to distinguish the kind of seminary with which we are here concerned, a distinction that can best be made, perhaps, by mentioning the types of Catholic seminaries that will not be treated. For example, little will be said about the houses

---

[4] In his volume, *The Holy See and the Nascent Church in the Middle Western United States, 1826-1850* (Rome: Gregorian University Press. 1962), Robert Trisco stated that he used the term 'Middle West,' "in the loose sense to mean the region stretching from the Alleghenies to the Rockies except the South." (p. 8). Reference will be made hereafter to the considerable amount of data in this work relating to mid-western seminaries.

of formation of the Church's numerous and varied religious orders and congregations, for in many particulars they were —and are—quite different from the seminaries engaged in training the diocesan or secular clergy. Secondly, I shall concentrate on what is termed in Catholic circles the 'major' seminary, that is, an institution that has normally comprised six years of instruction, two in philosophy and four in theology. Parenthetically, it might be mentioned that the current trend among American Catholics is strongly in the direction of what has come to be called the '4-4-4 plan,' that is, four years of high school, four years of college, and four years of theology, instruction in each of the three divisions to be received by the students in a separate institution. Our principal attention will be given, then, to the major seminaries established to train men for the diocesan priesthood in the Middle West between 1811 and 1889. There was a good deal of variety among them as to circumstances of origin, considerable variation as to location, size, and longevity, strong similarity as to programs for students' spiritual direction, and virtual unanimity in regard to curriculum and general pedagogical methods.

Students of ecclesiastical history do not need to be told that the system of seminary education of the Roman Catholic Church is of relatively recent origin in terms of her nearly 2,000 years of history. Only four years ago, in fact, there was celebrated the 400th anniversary of the formal sanction for the Church's seminaries as we know them, as it was embodied in the decrees passed at the twenty-third session of the Council of Trent in July, 1563. Moreover, at least a century passed before Trent's legislation could be said to have acquired anything like general application in the lands of Catholic Christendom. Thus the particular version of the seminary system from which the first institution of the kind in the United States, Saint Mary's Seminary of Baltimore, took its rise in July, 1791, had been inaugurated in France

only a century and a half before when Father Jean-Jacques
Olier and his little company who constituted the nucleus of
the Society of Saint Sulpice, took possession of the parish
church of that name in Paris in August, 1642.

In any case, the most significant of the reform decrees of
Trent pertaining to holy orders, was the one that called for
a seminary to be established in connection with every
cathedral church, each, as the decree stated

> according to its means and the extent of its diocese, to provide
> for, to educate in religion, and to train in ecclesiastical dis-
> cipline, a certain number of boys of their city and diocese, or,
> if they are not found there, of their province, in a college
> located near the said churches or in some other suitable place
> to be chosen by the bishop.[5]

But what was said of the time taken to implement this decree in Europe was *mutatis mutandis* true also of this country, for of the thirty-three dioceses established within the
years and the geographical area defined above, only eight
had major diocesan seminaries that lasted uninterruptedly
for a decade or more. That is not to say, however, that only
eight of the thirty-three dioceses attempted to found seminaries, or to make other provision for the education of candidates for the priesthood during the seventy-eight years
under review. On the contrary, if all the different schemes
set on foot for the theological education of the diocesan
clergy were included, probably twice that number could be
counted. The initiative that brought them into being came
at a time when throughout the Catholic world an extraordinary effort was being made to reorganize the training
centers for the priesthood. Referring to the restoration of
the religious orders that followed the French Revolution and

---

[5] H[enry] J. Schroeder, O.P. (Trans. and Ed.), *Canons and Decrees of
the Council of Trent* (Saint Louis: B. Herder Book Company. 1941),
p. 175.

the fall of Napoleon, a recent historian of the papacy has remarked:

> An equally essential need was to make provision for seminaries
> for the training of priests. The widespread closure of the
> seminaries, the hostility displayed by many of the revolution-
> ary governments towards the pursuit of vocations, and the in-
> volvement of most of the young manhood of Europe in war
> had created by the year 1815 a general shortage of priests,
> especially acute in France, and had also had a most deleterious
> effect upon the quality of theological study.[6]

And if the Middle West witnessed so few lasting Catholic
theological schools at this time, it was mainly due among
other reasons to the general poverty of the Catholic community and to the dearth of native vocations. These were
the prime factors that frequently dictated the simplest and
least expensive method of theological instruction, namely,
the so-called house seminary in which a number of frontier
bishops lived with small groups of generally foreign-born
seminarians whom they had recruited abroad. Basically that
was the type of the Catholics' first mid-western seminary
during the eight years that the theological students of the
Diocese of Bardstown continued to live on the Howard
Farm. It was only with their removal in the autumn of 1819
to Saint Joseph's Seminary in town that the diocese had a
separate theological school, the less advanced students hav-

---

[6] Edward E. Y. Hales, *The Catholic Church in the Modern World* (Garden City, New York: Hanover House. 1958), p. 74. The best recent treatment of the Catholic theological schools of this period is to be found
in Roger Aubert, *Le pontificat de Pie IX, 1846-1878* (Paris: Bloud &
Gay. 1952), pp. 184-223. Insofar as casulties among Catholic seminaries
was concerned, the phenomenon was not confined to the United States.
For example, of the seven diocesan seminaries established in England
between 1873 and 1891, only two survived viz., Saint John's, Wonersh,
in the Diocese of Southwark and Saint Joseph's, Upholland, in the
Diocese of Liverpool, two sees that were later raised to metropolitan
rank. David Milburn, *A History of Ushaw College* (Durham: Ushaw
Bookshop. 1964), pp. 263-264.

ing remained at Saint Thomas in the country. And even in Bardstown the seminarians occupied the same uncompleted building with Bishops Flaget and David and were employed as well in the boys' school that opened in the basement that same autumn. It was both lack of means and of vocations that likewise compelled Frederic Rese, first Bishop of Detroit, after taking possession of his see in January, 1834, to follow a similar arrangement for the few candidates whom he was able to gather about him, such as the Irish-born Thomas Cullen whom he had known in Cincinnati and who was ordained a priest in 1836.[7] Nor did the situation change much under Rese's successor, Bishop Peter Paul Lefevere, who, nonetheless, in 1846 gave the institution the name of Saint Thomas Seminary, a school that did not endure beyond 1854. The scarcity of native vocations was, in fact, so marked in the case of the Diocese of Detroit that it must have struck the third bishop, Caspar H. Borgess, when he entered upon his new duties in 1870 and found eighty-eight priests of whom only six were American-born.[8]

The same conditions obtained elsewhere in the Middle West. For example, poverty was a constant threat to the existence of the region's second Catholic seminary which opened in October, 1818, at the village of Perryville about eighty miles south of Saint Louis and which was called Saint Mary's of the Barrens. And in this instance further economies were effected by having the students for the diocesan priest-

---

[7] George Paré, *The Catholic Church in Detroit, 1701-1888* (Detroit: Gabriel Richard Press. 1951), p. 419.

[8] *Ibid.*, pp. 530, 652-654. One of the largest Catholic theological schools in the country had its origin in this fashion, Saint Charles Borromeo Seminary of the Archdiocese of Philadelphia. Under date of June 26, 1832, Bishop Kenrick entered in his diary, "I received into my own house Patrick Bradley, as a student of the Seminary. He had come here from the diocese of Derry in Ireland. . . ." [Francis E. Tourscher, O.S.A. (Trans. and Ed.)] *Diary and Visitation Record of the Rt. Rev. Francis Patrick Kenrick, Administrator and Bishop of Philadelphia, 1830-1851* (Philadelphia: The Editor 1916), p. 76.

hood live and take their classes with the candidates for the Congregation of the Mission [Vincentians or Lazarists] where both were in the charge of Italian Vincentians whose services Bishop Louis William Dubourg had enlisted during a trip to Europe. Yet the saving thus brought about was not sufficient to solve the problem, and after a four-year struggle the superior, Father Joseph Rosati, C.M., future first Bishop of Saint Louis, who was likewise professor of theology and of philosophy, finally abandoned hope of maintaining a seminary separate from all other activities. He felt compelled to resort to a device that had meant the difference between life and death to other institutions like Mount Saint Mary's in Emmitsburg, Maryland, namely, a school for lay boys taught by the seminarians. In announcing the innovation to his European superior Rosati said:

> Next Thursday we will commence classes for externs in a house near the Seminary, but in a manner that the externs will have no communication with the seminarians. . . . I would not have been able to obtain our principal objective, namely the education of the clergy, without these indispensable means.[9]

Obviously, this was anything but an ideal arrangement, but the fact that it had worked in other places probably encouraged Bishop Rosati to try it, and a measure of the success achieved in Missouri became known four and a half

---

[9] Rosati to Antonio Francesco Baccari, n.p., November 29, 1822, Frederick J. Easterly, C.M., *The Life of Rt. Rev. Joseph Rosati, C.M., First Bishop of St. Louis, 1789-1843* (Washington: The Catholic University of America Press. 1942), p. 61. At Emmitsburg the reverse order had been followed, i.e., the school for boys, Mount Saint Mary's College, had preceded the seminary, the former having begun in 1808 and the latter in 1820; but the same system obtained of having the theological students teach the lay boys. For the history of the Emmitsburg institutions, see Mary M. Meline and Edward F. X. McSweeny, *The Story of the Mountain, Mount Saint Mary's College and Seminary* 2 vols. (Emmitsburg: Weekly Chronicle. 1911).

years later when the bishop informed the Society for the Propagation of the Faith in France:

> It has sent forth, inside of eight years, over twenty-five priests, some of them belonging to the country. Their studies were pursued in some cases, entirely, in others, in part, in this seminary. The community consists, at the present time, of about fifty individuals, of whom five are priests, twelve ecclesiastics, ten brothers, and the others are pupils.[10]

Yet the situation at the Barrens was not a happy one, and the majority of the Vincentians were so discontent with having to conduct both a seminary and a school for lay boys that they complained to their superiors in Paris. In consequence of their remonstrances the congregation's general assembly in 1835 decreed that the boys' school should be closed, and that only those candidates for the diocesan priesthood should be admitted to the seminary for whom the bishop was willing to pay the equivalent of an annual fee amounting to about $120. For the better part of the next two years the issue was in dispute between the Vincentians of Missouri and Paris on the one side and the Bishop of Saint Louis on the other. The latter felt that closing the so-called college would have a ruinous effect on his diocesan interests, and when he saw that he was not likely to prevail on his own, he invoked the aid of the Congregation de Propaganda Fide at Rome. It proved to be a successful tactic and in the spring of 1837 the superior general of the Vincentians agreed to revoke his directive about the school for boys on these conditions: that seminarians who did not wish to teach should not be asked to do so; that diocesan students supported by the seminary should be held to a reasonable num-

---

[10] Rosati to the Abbé Perreau [sic], New Orleans, June 7, 1827, "Letters Concerning Some Missions of the Mississippi Valley, 1818-1827," *Records of the American Catholic Historical Society of Philadephia*, XIV (1903), 202.

ber; and that the seminarians be kept as much apart from the lay students as possible.[11] Thus the seminary continued at the Barrens until it was moved into the see city in 1843 when there were fifteen students—one Italian, two Frenchmen, eleven Irish, and a single American who had been born in Kentucky.

During the years under consideration in none of the thirty-three dioceses constituting the Middle West as defined above was there anything even approaching a state of affluence, among the Catholic people. True, the Church in Saint Louis had benefitted handsomely from the generosity of the first Catholic philanthropist of that region of the country, John Mullanphy, who before he died in 1833 had established a convent of the Religious of the Sacred Heart and a hospital of the Sisters of Charity in Saint Louis, as well as a foundation of the Sisters of Loretto and a church and novitiate for the Jesuits at Florissant, Missouri. There were, indeed, a few princely gifts a generation later, such as those of Boston's leading Catholic philanthropist, Andrew Carney; but not until the final decade of the century did a Catholic seminary become the beneficiary of the kind of donations

---

[11] The Rosati-Vincentian differences are treated in Trisco, *op. cit.*, pp. 290-296, on the basis of hitherto unpublished documents from the archives of the Congregation de Propaganda Fide. In January, 1875, Canon Peter Benoit, President of Saint Joseph's College, Mill Hill, London, arrived in the United States. On a visit to Richmond, Virginia, he noted the large boys' school erected by Bishop James Gibbons which had three seminarians and some laymen as teachers. Benoit stated: "These Seminarians study Philosophy a little. After 2 years they return to the seminary, more manly, the Bp thinks, more tried & with a fresh relish for their higher studies. His diocese, like many others, has suffered much from discarded European Priests, coming & causing scandal. He is educating youths born here. But he speaks in the highest terms of the Belgian & Dutch Priests. He wants well-educated & zealous Priests. These are sure to be much respected. . . ." "Hasty Notes of a Journey to America . . .," p. 108, photostat. Archives of the Society of Saint Joseph, Baltimore. The writer is greateful to his friend, the Reverend Peter E. Hogan, S.S.J., archivist, for permission to quote this manuscript.

that the Methodists received from Daniel Drew or the Epis-
copalians from Cornelius Vanderbilt.[12]

For Catholic seminaries in general, therefore, it was not
philanthropic gifts that constituted the main support, but
rather the donations of the immigrant aid societies of Europe,
viz., the Society for the Propagation of the Faith of Lyons-
Paris, the Leopoldinen-Stiftung of Vienna, and the Ludwig-
Missionsverein of Munich, plus the free will offerings of the
Catholic laity, with the former by far the more important in
the first half of the century. For example, the infant Diocese
of Milwaukee received during its first three critical years
(1844-1846) a total of $14,320 from the immigrant aid
groups named above. This money enabled Bishop John Martin Henni in the spring of 1845 to inaugurate a seminary in
a frame structure near his own residence, with the initial
student body composed of three seminarians, a German, an
Italian, and an Irishman. And through the following nine
years while the seminary was located in the city, the chief
support derived from the same source, a period, incidentally,
during which the seminary did not have a single American-
born student. The Milwaukee school was fortunate in another
way in being the object of the extraordinary zeal of the Aus-
trian-born priest, Joseph Salzmann. Not only did he travel
to Europe to recruit students, gather books to form a library,
and make the institution widely known in Catholic circles

---

12 When the Archdiocese of Saint Paul was given $500,000 in 1890 for the
building of a theological seminary, it was from the non-Catholic President
of the Great Northern Railroad, James J. Hill. In Hill's judgment the
Catholic Church was the most powerful influence in shaping the future
of the thousands of immigrants then pouring into the United States. This
being true, it was his belief that support should be furnished to those
who were referred to as "the anointed agents of the only authority that
it [the immigrant body] understands or will obey." To the railroad mag-
nate it was a practical matter. As his biographer paraphrased Hill's
sentiments, "This is as much a matter of good business as is the improvement of farm stock or the construction of a faultless railroad bed."
Joseph Gilpin Pile, The Life of James J. Hill (New York: Doubleday,
Page & Company, Inc. 1917), I, 64.

by his speeches and correspondence, but during the twenty years that followed the seminary's move in 1854 to Saint Francis, Salzmann collected over $100,000 for the institution's maintenance and development.[13] Financial help from whatever source was welcome, needless to say, in a diocese whose see city's 1,712 inhabitants of 1840 had multiplied to 45,246 by the year before the Civil War, with Wisconsin's estimated 20,000 Catholics of 1845 having in fifteen years increased to 180,000.

Nor was the financial assistance given by the French, Austrian, and Bavarian societies confined to seminaries of their own language groups in this country. The sources for the history of nineteenth-century Catholicism in every part of the United States contain repeated references to the debt owed to the European aid societies, and in no category outside that of parish churches and parochial schools were the benefactions more notable than to the struggling seminaries.[14] While a good many German-speaking Catholic im-

---

[13] Peter Leo Johnson, *Halycon Days, Story of St. Francis Seminary, Milwaukee, 1856-1956* (Milwaukee: Bruce Publishing Company. 1956), p. 58. From 1856, the year in which the Milwaukee seminary was dedicated at its present site, until 1889 a total of 813 priests had finished their studies there and were ordained (*ibid.*, p. 397).

[14] For example, it was a gift from the Leopoldinen-Stiftung of Vienna in May, 1832, that provided the necessary means for Bishop Francis Patrick Kenrick of Philadelphia to receive during the next year and a half six students into his own residence, four of whom, as he told his people in a pastoral letter of January 29, 1834, appealing for funds, "are now employed in the study of divinity." *Catholic Herald* (Philadelphia), February 6, 1834, quoted by George E. O'Donnell, "Rev. Francis X. Guth and the Founding of St. Charles Seminary, Philadelphia," *Records of the American Catholic Historical Society of Philadelphia*, LXXIV (December, 1963), 231. For the history of this institution, see the same author's *St. Charles Seminary, Philadelphia* (Philadelphia: American Catholic Historical Society of Philadelphia. 1964). Practically every bishop in the United States in these years bore witness to the generosity of the European immigrant aid societies to their hard pressed seminaries. John England, first Bishop of Charleston, emphasized that fact in a report of his diocese which he wrote while at Rome in 1833 for Carlo Cardinal Pedicini, Prefect of the Congregation de Propaganda Fide. Having described the scarcity of native vocations, his travels in Europe

migrants settled in southern Indiana in the years after 1830, no more than in a number of other places were they so numerous as to constitute an area of special concern for Vienna and Munich's immigrant aid societies, in the sense that was soon to be true of dioceses like Milwaukee and Cincinnati. Yet from the outset the Diocese of Vincennes received generous sums, a fact that the French-born first bishop, Simon Bruté, did not fail to note in a letter to the Archbishop of Vienna written on the eve of his sailing from Le Havre for home in May, 1836. He told Vinzenz E. Milde that he could not depart without assuring him of his heart-felt gratitude for what he termed "such an abundance of kindness and assistance given me during my stay in Vienna." By virtue of the Leopoldinen-Stiftung's benevolence, he said, eleven priests, two deacons, two subdeacons, three men in minor orders, and two promising students were accompanying him to his frontier diocese.[15]

Other mid-western prelates had a similar story to that of Bishop Bruté. In Saint Louis, for example, it was a gift of $8,600 from the Society for the Propagation of the Faith that permitted Archbishop Peter Richard Kenrick in 1848 to

---

to recruit seminarians, and the fact that up to that time he had thus succeeded in producing twenty priests for the diocese, England stated: "The aid which came to me from France has almost extinguished the debt of my poor little seminary, and has relieved me of an embarrassment which for a long time kept me in a state of painful suspence." "Papers Relating to the Church in America from the Portfolios of the Irish College at Rome," *Records of the American Catholic Historical Society of Philadelphia*, VIII (1897), 322.

15 Bruté to Milde, Rouen, May 30, 1836, Mary Salesia Godecker, O.S.B., *Simon Bruté de Rémur, First Bishop of Vincennes* (Saint Meinrad: Saint Meinrad Historical Essays. 1931), p. 274. As it turned out, Vincennes received from Vienna the largest sum of any American diocese, $28,400 over a period of about thirty years. The French Society for the Propagation of the Faith gave the Diocese of Vincennes a total of $238,000 up to 1869, and the Ludwig-Missionsverein of Munich contributed an additional $2,040. For these figures, see Theodore Roemer, O.F.M.Cap., *Ten Decades of Alms* (Saint Louis: B. Herder Book Company. 1942), pp. 85, 94, n. 10, 148, n. 14.

move his theological school from the see city to Carondelet where it was conducted by the diocesan clergy. The average annual sum of $2,100 over the next four years from the same source was of paramount importance, and when the French society informed Kenrick in 1852 that no further aid would be forthcoming, he made a strong appeal to his people in a pastoral letter, acknowledging that while he recognized the reasonableness of the society's action, he could not, he said, "but feel the withdrawal of a resource which, hitherto, has principally enabled us to support the Theological Seminary of this Diocese."[16]

Archbishop Kenrick's neighbor to the north was the French-born prelate, Mathias Loras, first Bishop of Dubuque, who had come to this country in 1830. From his consecration in December, 1837, he was at pains to keep Lyons closely informed of developments in the Catholic life of Iowa, Wisconsin, and Minnesota, mentioning again and again his seminary needs. In October, 1856, for example, he informed the Society's directors that he had assembled a choice group of twelve young men, "nearly all of them Americans," who said Loras, "are the hope of the church of Iowa."[17] His appeals met with a good response that began in 1838 and continued to 1866 to the total of $119,000.[18] Loras' friend, Joseph Cretin, first Bishop of Saint Paul, had a similar goal for a seminary after the erection of his see in 1850 separated Minnesota from the ecclesiastical jurisdiction of Dubuque. But both Cretin and his successor, Thomas L. Grace, O.P., had to content themselves with improvisations, for the nearly $100,000 received from France, the $41,798 from the Ludwig-Missionsverein, and the $2,600 contributed

---

[16] Pastoral letter of 1852, John Rothensteiner, *History of the Archdiocese of St. Louis* (Saint Louis: The Author. 1928), I, 841.
[17] Loras to the Society for the Propagation of the Faith, Lyons, Table Mound, October, 1856, Matthias M. Hoffmann, *The Church Founders of the Northwest* (Milwaukee: Bruce Publishing Company. 1937), p. 324.
[18] Roemer, *op. cit.*, p. 88.

by Vienna were quickly absorbed in more urgent diocesan
needs.[19] Although as late as November, 1881, Bishop Grace
acknowledged in a pastoral letter that a seminary was "the
most essential (of several diocesan works)," the establishment of which he maintained he had at heart for many
years, it was something which, he confessed, "we are obliged
still to postpone, in view of the inadequacy of the means to
insure success and permanency for the undertaking."[20]

The reception of financial assistance for the various enterprises of these pioneer dioceses was conditioned not only by
the judgment of the European societies as to the date when
an American jurisdiction might be expected to stand on its
own feet, but, too, by the political and economic fortunes of
their own home countries. Thus when Napoleon III was
defeated by Prussia in 1870 and in the ensuing chaos the
Commune seized power in Paris, funds from the immigrant
aid society's headquarters were cut off, a fact that was keenly felt by many American dioceses. The Cistercian Vicar
Apostolic of Nebraska, James M. O'Gorman, had never had
either sufficient men or means to maintain even so much as
a house seminary; but it was the money from the Society for
the Propagation of the Faith that had enabled him to pay
the expenses of a number of candidates who were studying
for his vicariate. As a result of the situation in France, Bishop
O'Gorman addressed his first appeal for money to his own
people for this cause in May, 1871. He remarked in his pastoral letter that many Catholics did not realize the difficulties involved in supplying good priests to the missions. "They
are not aware," he said,

> that even after he has sent a young candidate to a Theological
> Seminary, he must frequently wait four or five or even more

---

[19] *Ibid.*, pp. 116, 148, n. 14, 154, n. 16.
[20] *Northwestern Chronicle*, November 26, 1881, James Michael Reardon,
The Catholic Church in the Diocese of St. Paul (Saint Paul: North Central Publishing Company. 1952), p. 191.

years, before he can be ordained and appointed to exercise the duties of the sacred ministry. The expenses during all these years in very many cases devolve entirely upon the Bishop. They are very considerable, and either he has to meet them or otherwise permit souls to perish which have been committed to his charge. The rapid increase of population in this Vicariate, and particularly in Nebraska, obliges us to use every effort to supply the wants as they arise, but this we can no longer do without appealing to you and imploring your aid.[21]

By mid-century the nine dioceses established at that time within the geographical area previously defined had, according to the admittedly uncertain statistics of the *Metropolitan Catholic Almanac*, 476 priests who were serving an estimated Catholic population of around 500,000 souls scattered through eight states and five territories comprising a total of 805,935 square miles.[22] Enough has been said of the general ecclesiastical conditions to appreciate the difficulties involved in trying to furnish a reasonably well-educated ministry for the rapidly expanding Catholic community of the Middle West. One solution that recommended itself to a number of bishops was to have their students trained in

---

[21] Pastoral letter of James M. O'Gorman, O.C.S.O., Omaha, May 5, 1871, Henry W. Casper, S.J., *History of the Catholic Church in Nebraska. The Church on the Northern Plains, 1838-1874* (Milwaukee: Bruce Press. 1960), p. 295. Two years later Bishop Borgess of Detroit held a diocesan synod in which the need for a theological seminary was expressed. In 1874 Borgess issued the first report on the diocesan seminary project, reminded priests and people of their obligation to give to that end, and noted the small sum received to date. As a result of the 1874 appeal $4,705.94 was collected, and two years later Borgess once again emphasized this need in a pastoral letter of August, 1876. At the time there were fifty theological students being supported in various seminaries of whom twenty-eight later served as priests in the diocese. [Paré, *op. cit.*, pp. 553-554].

[22] *Metropolitan Catholic Almanac and Laity's Directory for the Year of Our Lord 1851* (Baltimore: Fielding Lucas Jr. 1850), pp. 224-225. Since the preface was dated December 1, 1850, the figures were obviously of that year. The volume of this *Directory* for the previous year had listed a total of eighty-one major seminarians studying for the ten dioceses of the Middle West.

one or other of the scholasticates of the religious congregations along with the congregation's own subjects. As we have
seen, as early as 1818 the Vincentians had begun to educate
candidates for the diocesan clergy at the little seminary of
Saint Mary of the Barrens south of Saint Louis. From the
foundation of their congregation by Saint Vincent de Paul in
1625, this had been one of the principal works of the Vincentians or Lazarists, and it was not surprising, therefore,
that soon after his consecration at Rome in 1815 Bishop
Dubourg should have sought them out and invited them to
his diocese for this purpose. Training future priests was likewise the objective of the Sulpicians whose Baltimore seminary had become by mid-century the Catholics' nearest approach to a national school of theology with a considerable
number of candidates for mid-western dioceses enrolled in its
student body. But aside from a few individual Sulpicians
like Bishops Flaget and David in Kentucky and Father
Gabriel Richard at Detroit, the followers of Olier had no
corporate life in the Middle West until Saint John's Seminary
opened at Plymouth, Michigan, in 1949.

Another group of religious who played a leading role in
mid-western clerical education were the Benedictines. The
black monks first established a house in this country at Saint
Vincent's which was located about forty miles east of Pittsburgh. There Boniface Wimmer, O.S.B., and his confrères
settled in 1846 and within two years they were training men
for the priesthood. They were especially interested in German-speaking students intended for the multiplying German
immigrant congregations, but in 1852 English-speaking seminarians were also accepted. It was from this pioneer foundation that the Middle West received its first contingent of
Benedictines when five monks arrived in Minnesota in May,
1856, to lay the foundations for the present large and widely
influential Saint John's Abbey at what is today called Collegeville. It was as a seminary that Saint John's educational

program was inaugurated in 1857, although candidates for the diocesan priesthood were not admitted until 1868. Since the nearest Catholic theological school to the east and south was Saint Francis near Milwaukee, with nothing excepting California, between Saint John's and the Pacific Coast until a group of Swiss Benedictines opened Mount Angel Seminary south of Portland, Oregon, in 1889, it was to be expected that certain mid-western dioceses would have availed themselves of Saint John's facilities for their students. And that the monks in Minnesota gave satisfaction would seem to be evident from the 1,206 diocesan priests who were educated at Saint John's between 1868 and 1956.[23]

---

[23] Colman J. Barry, O.S.B., *Worship and Work. Saint John's Abbey and University, 1856-1956* (Collegeville: Saint John's Abbey. 1956), p. 112. There were 472 Benedictine priests ordained during the same period. Although of no direct service to the Middle West, mention may be made of two California seminaries which existed between 1842 and 1866. The first was housed at Santa Barbara Mission when Bishop Francisco Garcia Diego, O.F.M., arrived there in January, 1842, with six Mexican-born seminarians whom he placed under the direction of his fellow friars. In May, 1844, the seminary was transferred to Mission Santa Ines. The bishop ordained three students in January, 1846, but thereafter the institution became more a minor seminary and school for lay boys until finally closed in 1882. The theological seminary passed through several administrations, among which was that of Eugene O'Connell, an Irish-born priest whom Joseph S. Alemany, O.P., Archbishop of San Francisco, induced to come to California from All Hallows College. In September, 1853, O'Connell's rectorship at Santa Ines was brought to an end when he was recalled to the see city, made pastor of Mission Dolores, and Rector of Saint Thomas Aquinas Seminary which was located nearby and which lasted until 1866. Meanwhile in southern California the newly consecrated Bishop of Monterey, Thaddeus Amat, C.M., arrived in November, 1855, with several Spanish-born seminarians and the Spanish Vincentian, Blasius Raho. Rather than attempt to revive the theological school at Santa Ines, Amat made Raho superior of a seminary which he established in his own residence, and on March 19, 1856, the bishop ordained five men to the priesthood. For these California institutions, see the unpublished thesis for the Ed. D. degree of Finbar Kenneally, O.F.M., "The Catholic Seminaries of California as Educational Institutions, 1840-1950," University of Toronto (1956); Francis J. Weber, *California's Reluctant Prelate. The Life and Times of Right Reverend Thaddeus Amat, C.M., 1811-1878* (Los Angeles: Dawson Book Shop. 1964), pp. 42-43; Maynard Geiger, O.F.M., *Mission Santa Barbara,*

What Saint John's was to the Church in the upper Mississippi Valley, Saint Meinrad's, a foundation made in southern
Indiana in March, 1854, by monks from the Abbey of Ein-
siedeln in Switzerland, was to that part of the Middle West.
Beginning very modestly with a boys' school, they next advanced to a minor seminary, and slowly there emerged a
major seminary, in which the prior reported three theological
students in November, 1861, who, he said, would be ready
for ordination to the priesthood the following year.[24] Some
of the candidates for the Diocese of Vincennes were sent to
Saint Meinrad's, and on June 21, 1867, Bishop Maurice de
Saint Palais ordained four theologians which marked the
seminary's first ordination of diocesan priests. This was a
significant step in the institution's history, to be sure, but
not as noteworthy as the day in September, 1868, when de
Saint Palais ordained eight men, six for the diocesan priesthood and two Benedictines.[25] But the monks' success in Minnesota and Indiana was not repeated when it was tried in
Kansas. Louis M. Fink, O.S.B., Bishop of Leavenworth, prevailed on Saint Benedict's Abbey at Atchison to open a
seminary in 1882 to which he sent six students. "But the
experiment was discontinued after one year," said the historian of the abbey, "because the faculty found teaching in
both college and seminary too strenuous, and adequate space
was not available."[26]

1782-1965 (Santa Barbara: [Old Mission]. 1965), pp. 126-131; John B.
McGloin, S.J., *California's Pioneer Archbishop. The Life of Joseph S.
Alemany, O.P., 1814-1888* (New York: Herder and Herder. 1966), Chapter VII, "The See of Monterey, 1850-1853," and Chapter VIII, 'Archbishop Alemany's First Decade in the See of San Francisco, 1853-1863."

[24] Martin Marty, O.S.B., to Abbot Henry IV Schmid von Baar, O.S.B.,
Saint Meinrad, November 11, 1861, Albert Kleber, O.S.B., *History of
St. Meinrad Archabbey, 1854-1954* (Saint Meinrad: A Grail Publication.
1954), pp. 152-153.

[25] *Ibid.*, pp. 180, 182

[26] Peter Beckman, O.S.B., *Kansas Monks. A History of St. Benedict's Abbey*
(Atchison: Abbey Student Press. 1957), p. 253. Conducting seminaries
for American candidates for the diocesan priesthood at times created

In addition to those who received their theological education in mid-western seminaries, a certain number of students
were sent from this region to Rome's Urban College of the
Propaganda, a seminary founded in 1627 for the express
purpose of training priests for missionary lands. The limited
number of places available were at times at a premium, but
in 1830 the Diocese of Bardstown was successful in gaining
admittance for two students, James M. Lancaster and Martin J. Spalding, who was destined to die as Archbishop of
Baltimore, and two years later Spalding's younger brother,
Benedict, joined them at Rome. Likewise in 1832 two candidates of the Diocese of Saint Louis were accepted at the
Urban College, as were two youths of the Ottawa Indian
tribe who were sent by Bishop Edward Fenwick of Cincinnati. Although the latter two did not persist, two other
candidates for Cincinnati remained and were ordained, the

---

problems of adaptation of the Benedictine rule and customs which did
not meet with favor on the part of certain of the monks' European
confrères. For example, after Martin Marty's election as Abbot of Saint
Meinrad in January, 1871, he changed from the Benedictine to the
Roman breviary on the score that the latter was not burdened with
special feasts that were not relevant for diocesan seminarians and diocesan priests sent to the abbey by their bishops for disciplinary reasons.
Placidus Wolter, O.S.B., of Beuron for one was shocked. He told his
friend, Frowin Conrad, O.S.B., a monk of Engelberg who later became
Abbot of Conception Abbey in Missouri:

> It was with complete astonishment that I received the information
> that St. Meinrad is seriously considering the substitution of the
> Roman Office for our Benedictine Office! I was especially amazed
> at the reasons offered to justify this change — that the common
> recitation of the Divine Office would thus be made easier for the
> seminarians. I was tempted to think that the monastery tailor could
> be able to say with equal justice, that it would be easier for him if
> all the monks would give up wearing the monastic cowl and would
> wear a soutane. But how in the world can a true son of St. Benedict
> deliberately set aside the twelfth chapter of the Holy Rule, and on
> his own initiative abandon a form of prayer which our Holy Father
> used and sanctified?

[Wolter to Conrad, Beuron, April 17, 1874, Edward E. Malone,
O.S.B. (Trans. and Ed.), "Documents: Placidus Wolter and American Benedictines," *American Benedictine Review*, XVI (June, 1965),
315-316.]

Irish-born Joseph O'Mealy and the convert, James F. Wood, a future Archbishop of Philadelphia. Other bishops of the Middle West like Loras of Dubuque, Kenrick of Saint Louis, and Quarter of Chicago, attempted to send students to the Roman seminary, but their requests were declined on the score of lack of accommodations.[27]

Two other developments in the theological training of priests of the American Church in general, and the Middle West in particular, that took place around the mid-century should be mentioned, namely, the establishment of seminaries at Louvain in Belgium and in Rome. In the first instance the impetus was owed to a prelate of the Middle West, Martin J. Spalding, Bishop of Louisville, who on a visit to Belgium in January, 1853, conceived the idea of a seminary for the training of priests for the American missions in connection with the Catholic University of Louvain. Spalding had a more than ordinarily high intellectual ideal for the priesthood and his naturally enthusiastic nature quickened at the prospect. "A hundred young men educated at Louvain for the American missions!", he exclaimed to Archbishop Kenrick of Baltimore on the very day that he had proposed the idea to Engelbert Cardinal Sterckx, Archbishop of Malines. "Is not the thought enlivening?" he asked. Two months later while at Florence in Italy the matter was still on his mind as he ruminated about how an American seminary at Louvain might enhance the standards of theological

---

[27] A half century later this situation still obtained at the Urban College. Bernard Smith, O.S.B., who acted as Roman agent for many English-speaking bishops, informed Roger Vaughan, Archbishop of Sydney, in the summer of 1880 that his appeal for a student had failed. He said:

> With regard to the student in the Propaganda, the petition came too late. I would advise you to write a letter to the Cardinal [Prefect] and ask him to grant you a place for a student in the College of the Propaganda. But the petition should be made six months before the time.

[Smith to Vaughan, Rome, August 7, 1880, copy, Archives of the Archdiocese of Sydney. The writer is grateful to Columba E. Halsey for permitting him to see the copy of this letter].

education among the Catholic clergy of the United States. In a later letter to the Archbishop of Baltimore before leaving Europe Spalding remarked:

> Our studies in America are woefully below the European standard, and a few good missionaries educated in Belgium scattered through our various Dioceses would leaven the whole mass.[28]

It is not necessary to recount here the full story of the frustrations and disappointments encountered by Spalding and the institution's other sponsors. Suffice it to say, opposition arose in various forms, ranging from the indifference of some churchmen to the open hostility of others, to neither of which, be it said, were the bishops of the Middle West immune. John B. Purcell, Archbishop of Cincinnati, and Peter Richard Kenrick, Archbishop of Saint Louis, were, perhaps, the two most formidable foes, although the latter mellowed toward the college as time passed. Yet in spite of all the obstacles, Spalding and his associates triumphed in the end and Louvain's American College was formally inaugurated on March 19, 1857, thanks in the main to two bishops of this region, Spalding of Louisville and Lefevere of Detroit. During most of the first half century the students

---

[28] Spalding to Kenrick, Florence, March 6, 1853, John D. Sauter, *The American College of Louvain, 1857-1898* (Louvain: Bibliothèque de l'Université. Bureaux du Recueil. 1959), p. 19. If Purcell of Cincinnati had been correctly informed, the first suggestion of an American seminary in Europe for the training of missionaries came from Andreas Räss, Coadjutor Bishop of Strasbourg, [Purcell to John Hughes, Cincinnati, January 24, 1842, Archives of the Archdiocese of New York, microfilm, Manuscript Collections, The Catholic University of America]. During the work on this article the author incurred a deep debt of gratitude to his former student and friend, the Reverend John P. Marschall, C.S.V., who not only was ever willing to verify certain references not available to the writer, but who also was most generous in supplying items from his own research pertaining to seminary training in this period. For that singular service he wishes to thank Father Marschall, especially for the letter of Purcell to Hughes cited above, for the Kenrick to Kenrick letter in Note 62, and likewise for the letters in Notes 69 and 72.

were recruited in good measure from European countries
with the largest number coming from the German states,
especially Prussia, followed by Belgium, Holland, and Ireland in that order, with even a few students from Canada.
For many years the American-born seminarians were a mere
handful, although among the earliest arrivals from the
United States was Spalding's nephew, John Lancaster Spalding, of Lebanon, Kentucky, who was sent there by his uncle
in 1859 and who eighteen years later became the first American-born alumnus to be made a bishop. Between 1860 and
1890 the college trained, either in whole or in part, 329
priests many of whom served in mid-western dioceses, and
of these nine—six born in Belgium, and one each in Germany,
Canada, and the United States—were raised to the hierarchy,
three of them governing dioceses of the Middle West.[29]

If the proposal of a seminary to train at Louvain future
priests for the American missions incurred opposition in the
hierarchy of the United States, it took almost a command
from Pope Pius IX to win anything like general support for
a seminary at Rome. The idea originated with Gaetano
Bedini, titular Archbishop of Thebes and Apotolic Nuncio to
Brazil, who came to the United States in June, 1853, and
remained for eight months. Upon his return home he submitted a detailed report of his observations concerning the
American Church to Filippo Cardinal Fransoni, Prefect of
the Congregation de Propaganda Fide.[30] Among Bedini's
recommendations was one that stated his strong belief that
a seminary for the education of American priests should be
established in the Eternal City. His suggestion was prompted
by his conviction that in Rome the students would get what

---

[29] *Ibid.*, p. 114.
[30] The report was signed at Rome on July 12, 1854, and the full text is contained in James F. Connelly, *The Visit of Archbishop Gaetano Bedini to
the United States of America, June, 1853-February, 1854* (Roma:
Libreria Editrice dell' Università Gregoriana. 1960), pp. 193-287.

he termed "a wider, more complete and more solid education" than they were receiving in their own country. He
had been present at a number of examinations and scholastic
exercises in American seminaries and, he remarked, "I was
not at all satisfied with the results." According to Bedini,
once the young priest was ordained in the United States, the
numerous duties of the ministry left him no time to continue
his studies. Moreover, the incentive and encouragement to
further his intellectual life were lacking since, he said, "the
most outstanding priest is the one that has built the most
churches and begun the most institutions."[31]

Pio Nono took readily to Bedini's idea and made it his
own, letting his wish be known in a letter to the bishops of
the Province of New York in January, 1855. From the outset
the two most enthusiastic and consistent American promoters
were Archbishop Francis Patrick Kenrick and Bishop Michael O'Connor of Pittsburgh, both of whom were alumni of
Rome's Urban College of Propaganda. Among the hierarchy
in general, however, the suggestion met with what the college historian termed an "uncertain response." Initially John
Hughes, Archbishop of New York, had been clearly opposed
to an institution of this kind, although he made a fairly
rapid *volte face* once Pius IX had spoken. When the bishops
of the Province of Cincinnati met in their First Provincial
Council in mid-May of 1855 the six prelates—one was ab-
sent because of illness—were unanimous in declaring the
idea a fine one in theory, but they felt it was not an opportune time to launch the project. First, said the bishops, there
was no need for a college in Rome, secondly, it would syphon
off money that was badly needed to finance the seminaries
in the United States, and, finally, Americans establishing an
institution such as the one proposed would furnish the Know-
Nothings with plausible evidence of the 'foreignism' of the
Catholic Church. The unanimous opinion of the six bishops

---

[31] *Ibid.*, p. 244.

who attended the First Provincial Council of the Province of Saint Louis the following October, was practically the same as that of their colleagues in Cincinnati. While the reaction from the Provinces of San Francisco and New Orleans was more postitive, the widespread poverty in material means and the scarcity of Catholic laity in these provinces in no way made up for the negative replies from the two more prosperous and populous provinces of the Middle West.

The lack of enthusiasm in the United States for a seminary in Rome in no way prevented the project from being carried out, for as the historian of the college stated, it had become clear that Pius IX fully intended to establish an American college in Rome, "regardless of how great or how slight assistance the bishops of the United States might give him."[32] Suffice it to say, the plans went forward and on December 8, 1859, the American College was formally opened with an initial student body of twelve men of whom three were from mid-western dioceses, two from Chicago and one from the Diocese of Alton, Illinois. Whereas, as we have seen, Louvain's American College was, insofar as personnel was concerned, for many years a missionary seminary 'for' rather than 'of' the Church in the United States—of the six men who headed the institution in the first half century, four were Belgian-born and two were born in The Netherlands—it was otherwise at Rome. In the latter case it is true that for the first three months the college was governed by an Irish Benedictine, Bernard Smith, as pro-rector, but in March, 1860, he was succeeded by the Brooklyn-born priest, William G. McCloskey. And of the eleven men who headed the institution after McCloskey's resignation in 1868—ten rectors and one pro-rector—all but one were native Americans. While the Middle West showed little enthusiasm for the Roman seminary in its initial stages, as time passed this area

---

[32] Robert F. McNamara, *The American College in Rome, 1855-1955* (Rochester: Christopher Press, Inc. 1956), p. 28.

supported it as well as other parts of the country. Many priests whose ministry was exercised in this region owed all or part of their theological training to Rome's Urban College of Propaganda while in residence at the American College.

Although Archbishop Bedini was doubtless right in observing that theological instruction in Rome was of a higher quality than in some of the seminaries he had visited in the United States, the Roman system likewise had its critics. John Henry Newman was a student at the Urban College of Propaganda in 1846-1847, and he told a friend that he had been informed that he would find, as he expressed it, "very little theology here, and a talk we had yesterday with one of the Jesuit fathers here shows we shall find little philosophy."[33] A generation later one of Newman's countrymen, Wilfrid Ward, in speaking of the intellectual aspects of the training he had received during his brief time in Rome in 1877-1878, remarked, "I did not find this at all inspiring—but on the contrary very trying." What upset Ward most was the emphasis on sheer memory, the closed mind of many professors to an opponent's arguments, and what he said was "set forth in the system as 'faith' [but which] may intelligibly be objected to as the bolstering up of prejudices inculcated by authority with no real appeal to the reason of man."[34]

Meanwhile what were probably the deepest and most widespread personal influences at work in shaping the seminaries of the United States, namely, the Vincentians, Sulpicians, and the diocesan priest-professors educated in Ireland, were not likely to develop a pattern basically different from that of which Newman and Ward had complained dur-

---

[33] Newman to John D. Dalgairns, Rome, November 22, 1846, Charles Stephen Dessain (Ed.), *The Letters and Diaries of John Henry Newman* (London: Thomas Nelson and Sons Ltd. 1961), XI, 279. For other observations of Newman on theological education in Rome, see, e.g., *ibid.*, XI, 291-297; XII, 47-49; 88-90.

[34] Manuscript memoirs of Ward written in 1913, Maisie Ward, *The Wilfrid Wards and the Transition* (New York: Sheed & Ward. 1934), pp. 65-66.

ing their time in Rome. One could scarcely expect an emphasis on superior intellectual achievement and the use of the most up to date pedagogical methods in seminaries conducted by the Vincentians and Sulpicians, if these men were to be true to the spirit of their respective founders. Neither Vincent de Paul nor Jean-Jacques Olier encouraged their followers in a pursuit of knowledge beyond what was necessary for the *scientia competens* of their ministry. Thus when a Vincentian missionary at Genoa asked Saint Vincent's advice in 1659 about how he could best combine knowledge with virtue in order to improve his service to souls, the latter replied:

> The desire to learn is good, provided that it be moderated. Virtue always has two vices at its side, and this love for knowledge is capable of being defective either by want or by excess. Yours, thanks to God, is not the first; and in order that it not be the second, remember the advice of Saint Paul who recommends us to be temperate in knowledge. A moderate competence suffices, and that which one wishes to have beyond that is rather to be feared than to be desired by workers of the Gospel, because it is dangerous: it inflates, it tends to show off, to make believe, and in the end to avoid humble tasks, simple and familiar, that are able to be the most useful. That is why our Lord took disciples who were not capable of making something of them beyond this.[35]

Father Olier, like his friend, placed the greatest stress on the virtues of humility and obedience, the latter of which he described as, "the life of the children of the Church, the compendium of all virtues. . . ." To the Sulpician founder study was but another way of advancing in holiness and in the love of God. "If you study from any other motive than that of piety," he said

---

[35] Vincent de Paul to Gaspard Stelle, Paris, July 18, 1659, Pierre Coste, C.M., (Ed.), *Saint Vincent de Paul: Correspondance, Entretiens, Documents* (Paris: Librairie Lecoffre. J. Gabalda. 1923), VIII, 32-33.

all your knowledge will serve only to make you more vain,
more full of yourselves, more self-opinionated and attached to
your own private judgment; in a word, the more learned you
become, the drier will be your devotion. To be learned without being puffed up is a miracle: *'Scientia inflat.'*[36]

Maxims of this kind remained the accepted tradition of both
religious societies, as was illustrated by one of Olier's sons
nearly two centuries later when Ambrose Maréchal, S.S.,
third Archbishop of Baltimore, counseled an American convert priest who was making his Sulpician solitude (novitiate)
in Paris that his principal object should be that of penetrating himself with the spirit of Saint Sulpice, to which he
added

> & be well persuaded, my dear friend, that if you come here
> having imbibed all of that, this immense advantage will be for
> you & for the Church in the United States, infinitely prefer-
> able to all the knowledge that you can acquire during your
> sojourn in Europe. . . .[37]

As a contemporary writer has stated regarding Vincent de
Paul and Olier, since these two men exercised such a profound influence on the entire French seminary system and
that of the United States as well, "it was inevitable that
many of these characteristics should appear in the American
diocesan seminary."[38]

In the case of what was one of the largest and undoubtedly most influential groups among the priests of the American
Church, the Irish, the majority had finished their theological

---

[36] Quoted in Edward Healy Thompson, *The Life of Jean-Jacques Olier,
Founder of the Seminary of St. Sulpice.* New and enlarged edition (London: Burns and Oates. 1886), pp. 462-463.

[37] Maréchal to Samuel Eccleston, Baltimore, February 12, 1826, Columba
E. Halsey, O.S.B., "The Life of Samuel Eccleston, S.S., Fifth Archbishop
of Baltimore, 1801-1851," unpublished master's thesis, The Catholic
University of America (1963), pp. 19-20.

[38] Stafford Poole, C.M., *Seminary in Crisis* (New York: Herder and Herder.
1965), p. 49.

education by the time they arrived in the United States. They had come from various institutions—Saint Patrick's College, Maynooth, and All Hallows College, Dublin, as well as from less well known seminaries such as those in Carlow, Thurles, and Kilkenny. All these schools, however, were dominated by a narrow and rigorous spirit which naturally left a lasting imprint on most Irish priests, and those appointed to the faculties of American seminaries were often of this mind. Nor was the national seminary of the Irish Church an exception. For example, when Henry F. Neville, Rector of the Catholic University of Ireland, stated in 1879 that in the early years the teaching at Maynooth had been characterized by a strong strain of Gallicanism which the professors had imbibed in the French schools they had attended,[39] there was a quick and vigorous dissent from Maynooth's vice president, William J. Walsh. The latter did not deny, however, that an austere and anti-probabilist school of thought had long continued to set the tone in the courses in moral theology.[40] According to Walsh, the principal cause for this rigor lay outside Ireland, namely, in the directives from the Congregation de Propaganda Fide at Rome. As an example he cited the letter of July, 1796, in which Propaganda had warned the Irish bishops about the dangers of liberalism and cautioned against dissociating, as it was said, "the mildness and suavity of Evangelical charity," from what was described as *that salutary severity which is characteristic of Christian teaching.*"[41] To Walsh a further indication that the Holy See had been the source of inspiration for much of the ultra-conservatism at Maynooth was the action of Hyacinth Cardinal Gerdil, Prefect of Propaganda,

---

[39] Henry F. Neville, "Theology, Past and Present, at Maynooth," *Dublin Review*, 3rd Series, XXXIII (October, 1879), 449-464.
[40] William J. Walsh, "The Alleged Gallicanism of Maynooth and of the Irish Clergy," *Dublin Review*, 3rd Series, XXXIV (April, 1880), 242.
[41] *Ibid.*, p. 247.

in sending to Ireland shortly after Maynooth opened in 1795 a large supply of copies of the moral theology of Paul Gabriel Antoine, S.J. (1677-1743). Antoine's book was an exceedingly rigorous work which had appeared first in 1726, and which was more or less imposed on the faculty of the new Irish seminary seventy years later; moreover, the Maynooth official added, it continued to be used at Rome's Urban College of Propaganda until 1830 and perhaps later.[42]

As it is idle to suppose that any man can divest himself of the ethnic element in his life, given that by the mid-century the American Catholic community was largely immigrant in character, it would be unreal to expect that the early seminaries should have been devoid of a nationalist coloring of one kind or another. From the outset this situation existed at the mother seminary, Saint Mary's in Baltimore, where, indeed, the French predominance lasted into the present century. It was chiefly that fact that prompted Bishop England to open his own seminary in Charleston in January, 1822, rather than have his students subjected to the French influence at Baltimore. England maintained that while the Irish were easily assimilated in this country, the French, as he told Michael O'Connor, future first Bishop of Pittsburgh, "never can become American." He acknowledged that the French clergy were generally good men who had at heart the best interests of religion, but, he said, "they make the Catholic Religion. . . . appear as exotic, and cannot understand why it should be made to appear assimilated to American principles. . . ."[43]

As for the Irish, most of their numerous missionaries in the American Church had finished their theology in Ireland before they came out to the new world, and through the

---

[42] *Ibid.*, p. 248.

[43] England to O'Connor, Charleston, February 25, 1835, Peter Guilday, *The Life and Times of John England, First Bishop of Charleston, 1786-1842* (New York: America Press. 1927), I, 481-482.

remainder of their lives they generally adhered to the conservative spirit in which they had been nurtured in the
Irish seminaries, whether they were engaged in parochial
work or in teaching lay students or seminarians. Insofar as
the Germans were concerned, their principal seminary in
the Middle West, Saint Francis in Milwaukee, continued to
be strongly German in personnel and atmosphere through
most of the century. And in 1858 when the seminary of the
Archdiocese of Saint Louis was closed, the majority of the
students were thereafter sent to Milwaukee.[44] A bond was
thus forged between the priests of the two dioceses which
showed itself in a practical way at the time of the founding
at Chicago in February, 1887, of the Deutsch-Amerikaner
Priester-Verein, an organization intended as an instrument
for breaking the Irish monopoly of the posts of authority in
the American Church.

Whether their founders were French, Irish, or German
in origin and spirit, therefore, the seminaries of the Middle
West—and of the country in general—during this period were
not conspicuous as Americanizing institutions. The same
could be said for the religious orders' seminaries which enrolled candidates for the diocesan priesthood, such as Saint
John's in Minnesota and Saint Meinrad's in Indiana, which
were predominantly German in tone through the early
decades of their history. And since there was no real graduate training in Catholic theology in this country before the
1890's, the seminary faculties were usually composed of
men born and educated abroad with a minority of American-
born priests who had been sent to Europe for their education. These national patterns in the mid-western seminaries
were likewise reflected in the bishops of the region. For
example, the sixteen prelates of the Middle West who attended the Second Plenary Council in October, 1866, had as

[44] John Rothensteiner, *History of the Archdiocese of St. Louis* (Saint
Louis: The Author. 1928), I, 844.

their countries of birth: France, five; Ireland, five; United States, three; and one each, Austria, Germany, and Switzerland. These same bishops had been educated as follows: exclusively in the United States, four; in the United States and Rome, three; in France and the United States, two; in Ireland and the United States, two; exclusively in France, two; exclusively in Ireland, two; and exclusively in Austria, one.

It is a relatively simple task for the historian to record external facts about a seminary's foundation, such as the persons and circumstances to which its foundation was owed, the growth of its student body, and the expansion of its physical plant. It is quite another thing to recapture an institution's prevading spiritual and intellectual atmosphere, to trace the origin of its academic policies and patterns, and to account for features of its life like the faculty's general philosophy of education, the textbooks they selected and how they recommended that the students use them, the methods of instruction they followed in regard to course materials being analyzed or memorized, the amount of student freedom of thought and expression that they fostered and allowed, and the students' own careers after they had left the seminary. Even if scholarly histories of all the midwestern nineteenth-century seminaries were available—and such is the exception, not the rule—some of these points would still be difficult to determine with precision and accuracy.

One Catholic theological institution of the Middle West, however, that had this service rendered it with more than ordinary success was Saint Francis Seminary in Milwaukee. For our present purpose Saint Francis had the added advantage of having been founded and developed under auspices other than Vincentian, Sulpician, or Irish. From 1845 when a beginning was made in the home of Bishop Henni, responsibility for theological instruction in the Diocese of

Milwaukee, as we have seen, was largely in the hands of German-speaking clergy whose uppermost thought was to furnish priests for Wisconsin's expanding German Catholic communities, although at no time was the seminary intended exclusively for students of German birth or ancestry. In any case, by reason of the number of its prominent professors who had received their training at Innsbruck and Linz—men like Joseph Salzmann, Fredrick Katzer, Joseph Rainer *et al.*—theological education at Saint Francis followed along the lines of these Austrain seminaries. From the outset the textbooks were mainly by Jesuit authors, two of the leading ones being by professors of the Roman College, namely, Giovanni Perrone's *Compendium Dogmaticae Theologiae* and the *Compendium Theologiae Moralis* by Jean-Pierre Gury which was in use after 1850.[45]

Needless to say, it takes more than a knowledge of what textbooks were used to determine the type and quality of instruction imparted by any educational institution; far more important in the students' intellectual formation is the attitude that the professors take toward the textbooks and how they direct them to be used, information that is not at all easy for the historian to uncover. Yet the presence of Gury and Perrone at Milwaukee, as well as in a number of other American seminaries, suggests the traditional pattern maintained in these institutions in the days before the thomistic revival, a movement that would displace authors like Gury and Perrone. In fact, the only exception to the employment of manuals written by European Catholic theologians in the United States were the works of Francis Patrick Kenrick, and even Kenrick confessed that while his books had been recommended at the Fifth Provincial Council of the hierarchy in May, 1843, six months later the Archbishop of Baltimore, Samuel Eccleston, S.S., had not yet issued the recommendation. He told his brother:

---

[45] Johnson, *op. cit.*, pp. 222-226.

The commendation to adopt the Theology [text books] which are my work, has not yet been issued by the Archbishop of Baltimore, and they at the Mountain [Mount Saint Mary's, Emmitsburg] are hesitating lest they appear to hurt the majesty of the city [Rome] by introducing the work of a stranger.

Many copies of his manuals, Kenrick added, had been sold at Saint Mary's in Baltimore, a fact that prompted him to believe it was "an indication that they are not averse to using them."[46] But formal adoption of the Kenrick volumes as the approved textbooks was apparently another thing.

A quarter century later Canon Peter Benoit, President of Saint Joseph's College, Mill Hill, London, made an extensive tour of the United States during which he stopped at a number of seminaries. At Baltimore in late January, 1875, he found the Sulpicians using the *Institutiones Theologicae* of Jean-Baptiste Bouvier, a moral theology used extensively in France, Canada, and the United States. But, Benoit noted, at Saint Mary's, "They have no ecclesiastical history. This seems to me a great defect."[47] Three months later at Bishop William G. McCloskey's short-lived seminary near Louisville, he found that the moral theology text was Gury while Perrone was used for dogmatic theology. His added comment offered some insight into the instructional methods of the period:

> The professors lecture & the students take notes. They follow Pabish's Alzog & intend to finish it in 3 years [Johann B. Alzog, *Manual of Church History* translated by Francis J. Pabish and Thomas S. Byrne]. But they skip the dogmatical parts. The professor simply lectures on history, abridging some parts & enlarging on others, without any notes being taken by the students.[48]

---

46 Kenrick to Kenrick, n.p., December 4, 1843, F.E.T. [Francis E. Tourscher, O.S.A.] (Trans. and Ed.), *The Kenrick-Frenaye Correspondence . . . 1830-1862* (Philadelphia: The Editor. 1920), pp. 179-180.
47 Benoit, *op. cit.*, p. 40.
48 *Ibid.*, p. 256.

In early May the English priest had a personal meeting at
Mount Saint Mary's of the West in Cincinnati with Pabish
whose observations he summarized as follows:

> He considers [Joseph E.] Darras a pleasant history to read in
> the refectory; but is not always accurate & what is perhaps
> worse states no authorities which is as bad as a judge deciding
> on a case without weighing the truth & worthiness of the wit-
> nesses. He considers, on that account Alzog as a good text
> book, because he gives the value of each author. He has two
> lessons a week of three quarters each, & the students prepare
> 12 pages each time. He contents himself with the summary
> about the Gnostics, on acc't of that sect being too complicated
> in its ramifications.[49]

Benoit's final seminary call was at the Paulist house of
theology in New York shortly before he sailed for home.
There he chatted with Augustine Hewit who was then teaching dogmatic theology and philosophy. Hewit told him he
had discarded Perrone as "being antiquated" and had adopted a new six-volume work of a Sulpician who was "not a
strict Thomist." In referring to the tract *De gratia*, Hewit
said he had asked Dr. Lynch [Patrick N. Lynch, Bishop of
Charleston?] about it, but the latter had told him he had
studied that treatise for six months "under a learned teacher
& had given it up in despair & he exhorted him not to begin
at it."[50]

---

[49] *Ibid.*, p. 291. Scholasticism was in vogue among the Catholics of the
United States in 1846. For example, a foreign visitor wrote:
> You must know that the scholastic form of doctrine is that which
> is in vogue here, and nothing but that. Petavius, whom I mentioned,
> seemed to have but little favour in their eyes. They take their faith
> as they find it in the scholastics but of the early Fathers I sh[d] im-
> agine they knew, many of them, but little.

Thomas F. Knox to John Henry Newman, Boston, September 22, 1846,
photostat, Archives of the Brompton Oratory, London [furnished by C.
Stephen Dessain of The Oratory, Birmingham].

[50] *Ibid.*, pp. 316-317. Benoit also visited the Vincentians' seminary near
Niagara Falls about which his remarks were confined to the scenery, the
hospitality of the faculty, and to the procurator, P. V. Kavanagh, C.M.,

Throughout the Catholic world in general, however, there was practically no theological progress until the 1880's. So much did the siege mentality govern the Holy See's attitude early in the century that Luigi Taparelli d'Azeglio, S.J., was removed from his post as Rector of the Roman College in 1828 for having introduced thomistic philosophy into the courses of that institution. Indicative of this all but universal ultra-conservatism and decadent outlook in Catholic circles were the canons pertaining to theology and philosophy enacted by the American bishops in the Second Plenary Council of Baltimore in October, 1866. Under the heading of major seminaries little was said beyond recommending that in provincial seminaries Scripture should be treated in a more ample and distinguished way than in diocesan seminaries, with a year of Hebrew prescribed for Scripture students; while in philosophy the various systems of thought, especially the more recent, should be explained, it was said, in a manner that would easily enable the students to refute [*facile refellantur*] the difficulties raised by attacks on the authority of canon law or on the doctrine of the Church.[51]

With the death of Pius IX and the election of Leo XIII in February, 1878, however, there came an improvement in the official attitude toward intellectual affairs which, in turn, ultimately produced a change for the better in the seminaries. During the thirty-two years that he had served as Bishop of Perugia (1846-1878), the new pontiff had taken a particular interest in his seminary where he fostered the study of thomism. Men with special competence in thomis-

---

who had driven him "in his buggy to Darwin's hotel." Kavanagh cultivated a large farm and had fifteen horses which were more a convenience than a source of income, to which was added the comment, "Tho' he has a number of pigs, they eat little or no pork. They kill some cattle, but get their meat mainly from the butcher. The meat is cheap, but tough. . . ." (pp. 301-302).

51 *Concilli Plenarii Baltimorensis II. . . . Acta et Decreta* (Baltimore: John Murphy Company. 1868), No. 178, p. 108.

tic studies were brought to Perugia such as the future pope's own brother, Giuseppe Pecci, and Francesco Satolli, both of whom assisted him in the same cause later at Rome; and while at Perugia he had likewise established an Academy of Saint Thomas Aquinas to stimulate thought and discussion among the seminarians and younger priests.[52] Early in the new reign there was published the encyclical, *Aeterni Patris* (August 4, 1879) which exhorted the bishops of the world "in all earnestness" to restore the study of Saint Thomas.[53] This emphasis on Aquinas was, indeed, an improvement on the stagnant condition of theological and philosophical studies before Leo XIII, although certain guidelines in the encyclical, and in the apostolic letter, *Cum hoc sit* which a year later (August 4, 1880) made the pope's desires about the teaching of thomism in the seminaries more explicit, would scarcely conform to the openness of mind and approach that the academic world both then and now would associate with intellectual inquiry. For instance, in *Aeterni Patris* the bishops were counseled in selecting teachers to be careful to choose men who would "implant the doctrine of Thomas Aquinas in the minds of the students," as well as to see to it that in their present diocesan institutions and in those they would establish in the future, the professors would "illustrate and defend this doctrine, and use it for the refutation of prevailing errors."[54]

---

[52] Eduardo Soderini, *The Pontificate of Leo XIII*. Translated by Barbara Barclay Carter (London: Burns Oates & Washbourne Ltd. 1934), I. 70-72.

[53] John J. Wynne, S.J. (Ed.), *The Great Encyclical Letters of Pope Leo XIII* (New York: Benziger Brothers. 1903), p. 56.

[54] *Ibid.* For a detailed and judicious critique of the thomistic revival inaugurated by Leo XIII, see Roger Aubert, "Aspects divers du Néo-Thomisme sous le Pontificat de Léon XIII," Giuseppe Rossini (Ed.), *Aspetti della Cultura Cattollica nell' età di Leone XIII. Atti del Convegno tenuto a Bologna il 27-28-29 Dicembre 1960* (Roma: Edizioni Cinque Lune. 1961), pp. 133-227.

When the American bishops assembled in Baltimore for their plenary council in November, 1884, therefore, they had the clear mandate of the pope before them. By reason of these papal documents, the seminary decrees on this occasion were a good deal more specific than those of 1866. All American professors of theology and philosophy were now told to comply strictly with the wishes of Leo XIII by following faithfully in the footseps of Aquinas.[55] At the same time the course in the major seminaries was lengthened to six years as an official policy with, as has been said, two years devoted to philosophy and four to theology. The decree permitted an exception if necessity demanded it in particular cases, a point inserted to meet the objections of western bishops like Joseph S. Alemany of San Francisco and his coadjutor, Patrick W. Riordan, and James O'Connor, the Vicar Apostolic of Nebraska, who contended that certain regions of the West were too greatly in need of priests to adopt the six-year ruling as an unalterable policy.[56]

It is probably a compliment to the churchmen of the period to say that the extant evidence reveals little by way of complacency about theological education in Catholic circles on either side of the Atlantic. John England, first Bishop of Charleston, for example, had been highly critical almost from the time of his arrival in the United States in 1820 of the Sulpicians' seminary in Baltimore, and for a time he worked for a national seminary as a possible remedy. The proposal was discussed in the First Provincial Council of Baltimore in October, 1829, after having been raised by Benedict Fenwick, Bishop of Boston; but it failed to win approval at this time as it did four years later in the next

---

[55] *Acta et Decreta Concilii Plenarii Baltimorensis Tertii* (Baltimore: John Murphy Company. 1886), No. 168, pp. 86-87.
[56] Francis P. Cassidy, "Catholic Education in the Third Plenary Council of Baltimore," *Catholic Historical Review*, XXXIV (October, 1948), 285-286. Major seminaries are treated here, pp. 281-288.

conciliar gathering. And one of the stoutest opponents was a bishop from the Middle West, Flaget of Bardstown, who felt that a national seminary in Baltimore would be too distant and to expensive for his students to warrant his support.[57] Reflecting what might have been a disappointment over the hierarchy's failure to act in this regard, some months after the council of 1833, John Hughes, the man who in less than four years would be consecrated as coadjutor to John Dubois for the See of New York, remarked to his former professor of theology, Simon Bruté:

> With regard to any thing being done for the Education of Clergymen, I despair of it, until the Bishops & Colleges or college shall understand each other, and themselves better. It is a subject on which there is too great a variety of opinion — and on which each Superior looks only to the boundaries of his own jurisdiction.[58]

[57] Guilday, *op. cit.*, "The Diocesan Seminary of Charleston, 1822-1832," I, 474-516. See also Lloyd P. McDonald, S.S., *The Seminary Movement in the United States: Projects, Foundations and Early Development, 1784-1833* (Washington: The Catholic University of America. 1927), pp. 60-63, where there is sketched the renewed discussion of a central or national seminary at the Second Provincial Council in October, 1833. Once again the lack of financial endowment and the differences among the bishops over the idea prevented any effective action being taken. Regarding England's criticism of the Sulpician method of conducting seminaries, nearly twenty years later Newman revealed an unsympathetic attitude toward the Sulpicians. While acknowledging that they were excellent priests, he alluded to their Gallican views that had incurred the displeasure of the Holy See in several instances, and to what he heard of "the stiffness and dryness of the text books in use" at the Sulpicians' seminary at Issy outside Paris. "Besides," added Newman to Thomas F. Knox, a convert to Catholicism who had consulted him about whether or not he ought to remain on at Issy for theology, "it is not a place for those who like you or ourselves have been forced to exercise the intellect so carefully in the English Universities—so long a course of slow reading is utterly unfit for us and a mere waste of time, keeping you from important duties when you are intellectually fit for them." [Newman to Knox, Rome, July 17, 1847, Dessain, *op. cit.*, XII, 97; see same to same, Rome, September 10, 1847, XII, 112-113].

[58] Hughes to Bruté, n.p., June 10, 1834, John G. R. Hassard, *Life of the Most Reverend John Hughes* (New York: D. Appleton and Company. 1866), p. 149.

The provincialism which Hughes deplored was not, of course, peculiar to his time, for long after he had passed from the scene it continued to be a major stumbling block to the improvement of theological education.

Relatively few dioceses of the Middle West either then or during the remainder of the century could afford the luxury of their own seminary, either from the scarcity of funds to maintain the institution or of men trained to teach. In this regard developments in the Archdiocese of Saint Louis were more or less typical. One can readily imagine the problems created for the intellectually gifted seminarian—to say nothing for a conscientious professor with scholarly instincts on whom the demands might be made—when one is told that the rector and an assistant professor of Saint Louis' theological seminary in the 1850's taught logic, metaphysics, ethics, dogmatic theology, moral theology, and liturgy, and that the archbishop himself lectured on natural philosophy, science, Scripture, and canon law! Father John O'Hanlon was appointed to the faculty in September, 1851, and in his memoirs written many years later he included an account that would leave a lasting impression on the mind of any reader who placed a high premium on academic standards. He was asked to leave his post as assistant pastor of Saint John's Church in the see city and to move to the seminary in Carondelet where, he said

> I became Prefect of Studies, and in addition to my English classes, I had those of Logic, Metaphysics, and Ethics, as also those of Sacred Ceremonies and Ritual, with Sacred Scripture. Besides, I had to discharge the duties of Chaplain for the Sisters of St. Joseph, at their Convent in the town; celebrate Mass for them each morning in their chapel; as likewise to give catechetical instruction, to the young ladies educated there, once in each week. All this work, left me hardly any spare time to study for my various classes; and, for necessary relaxation or exercise, there was little or no leisure. Occasionally on Sundays, I went into the city at the Archbishop's request to preach

in the Cathedral, but seldom otherwise; for, our city friends were frequent visitors to our Seminary, while our servant and van-driver supplied us with necessaries for the house or conveyed messages.[59]

Under circumstances such as these it was hardly surprising that Archbishop Kenrick should have thought of abandoning the seminary. But when he proposed the idea to his brother, Francis Patrick, Archbishop of Baltimore, the latter replied. "The thought of giving up your Seminary does not please me. A metropolitan see needs such a support to which the other sees [of the province] may come [send students]."[60] The following spring the American hierarchy held its First Plenary Council in Baltimore where they enacted a decree exhorting each bishop who did not have his own seminary to consult with the bishops of his province so that there might be at least one seminary in every ecclesiastical province.[61] Being the metropolitan of the Province of Saint Louis, Peter Richard Kenrick may have felt a further obligation to continue his seminary at Carondolet in consequence of this legislation. In any case, three months later he turned once more to his brother in Baltimore to inquire if he knew of any religious congregation whom he might engage to staff the seminary. Francis Patrick confessed that he knew of no available religious community for this purpose, and he added that it would be useless to apply to the Sulpicians since they

---

[59] John O'Hanlon, *Life and Scenery in Missouri. Reiminiscences of a Missionary Priest* (Dublin: J. Duffy & Company, Ltd. 1890), pp. 228-229.

[60] Kenrick to Kenrick, Baltimore, November 24, 1851, *The Kenrick-Frenaye Correspondence*, p. 328.

[61] *Concilium Plenarium Totius Americae Septentrionalis Foederatae, Baltimori habitum Anno 1852* (Baltimore: John Murphy Company. 1853), p. 47. Much the same legislation was enacted at the Second Plenary Council in October, 1866, in the twelve decrees of Chapter VII, "De Seminariis Ecclesiasticis Constituendis et Ordinandis," *Concilii Plenarii Baltimorensis II. . . .*, pp. 105-110.

had declined to take any further assignments of this kind.[62] As it turned out, the Archbishop of Saint Louis carried on for six more years and then closed the archdiocesan theological seminary, and for the next thirty-four years candidates were sent to seminaries in Milwaukee, Baltimore, and other places until the opening of Kenrick Seminary in December, 1892.

A situation such as that described by O'Hanlon at Saint Louis in the 1850's would, indeed, preclude the possibility of proper preparation of daily classes, not to speak of the enrichment of mind that any teacher may derive from leisurely reading. But the Saint Louis seminary was not unique in this regard, for the historian of Saint Francis in Milwaukee stated that faculty members there were responsible for several fields which, as he said, "left them little or no time to pursue specialities or indulge in writing."[63] And this was to say nothing of the disadvantage which the students experienced from instruction at the hands of ill prepared professors, or from the excessive number of classes for which they were held responsible by the accumulating curricular demands of the Holy See, of the American plenary and provincial councils, or of the individual bishop or seminary faculty. Even in the best seminaries—and that very late in the century—students' class loads were far too heavy for effective education, with averages of twenty-one hours a week at Saint Francis in Milwaukee and of nineteen hours a week at Saint John's in Brighton, Massachusets, the major seminary of the Archdiocese of Boston.[64]

---

[62] Kenrick to Kenrick, Saint Louis, Feast of Saint Mary of the Snows [August 5], 1852, Archives of the Archdiocese of Baltimore, 29-R-46. The reply of Francis Patrick to his brother was dated Baltimore, August 9, 1852, Tourcher, *op. cit.*, p. 332.

[63] Johnson, *op. cit.*, p. 225.

[64] John E. Sexton and Arthur J. Riley, *History of Saint John's Seminary, Brighton* (Boston: Roman Catholic Archbishop of Boston. 1945), p. 75.

It was due to a combination of discouraging factors of this kind, plus the blight that fell over all Catholic scholarly endeavor as a consequence of the fear and suspicion engendered by the phantom heresy of Americanism, as well as the sometimes frantic search in seminary faculties for modernists that followed the uncovering of that very real heresy, that would account for so few men of distinction emerging from the Catholic seminary world of the Middle West and other parts of the country. For the man who had the courage to withstand these powerful pressures often emanating from official circles, was, indeed, the rare exception. Father John B. Hogan, S.S., first Rector of Saint John's Seminary in Brighton, was such a man. Shortly after his death Hogan was paid a remarkable tribute by a former student, Austin Dowling, a future Archbishop of Saint Paul, who described him as one who "had the rare gift of filling the student's mind with the unrest of inquiry." Dowling then added:

> Often he would seem to go the very limit of daring in the vigor with which he plied us with objections, annihilated all our arguments and then walked off without vouchsafing an answer to our difficulties.
>
> But, sure of his own faith, he had no fear of ours, while he did fear the vicious effect of the smug satisfaction which a boy may feel — and never afterwards lose — in dealing flippantly with the grave problem of thought.[65]

There were probably other seminary men in the Middle West and elsewhere in these years whose keenness of intellect left a lasting impression of this kind in the classroom, the while their priestly conduct was an inspiration to students' spiritual lives. To name one instance where a real

---

[65] *A Garland of Affectionate Tributes to the Memory of the Very Rev. John Baptist Hogan, D.D., S.S.* (Boston: Alumni St. John's Seminary. 1906), p. 33. Hogan had died on September 30, 1901, and the memorial meeting was held on February 4, 1902.

measure of success was achieved in this regard, Archbishop Ireland strove energetically to bring about this happy combination in Saint Thomas Seminary and its successor, the Saint Paul Seminary, which opened in September, 1894. And one of the principal means he used to gain his end was to assemble a good library. When the distinguished English Benedictine and later cardinal, Francis Aidan Gasquet, visited the institution in the autumn of 1904 he was struck by this fact. He said:

> It was a source of wonder to me to find already on the shelves almost every book of any value for the purpose he [Ireland] had in view. I tested the collection in various ways, by looking for works I hardly supposed could be found there, but in most instances they were in their places.[66]

Insofar as the factors influencing the content, spirit, and method of Catholic theological education in the Middle West were concerned, there was never the marked influence of the older institutions and traditional thought patterns of the East that was true, for example, of New England's influence on the Protestant colleges and seminaries of this region.[67] To be sure, a number of Catholic bishops and seminary men in the western dioceses had their first extended experience in eastern seminaries, as was the case with Archbishop Purcell, founder of Cincinnati's Mount Saint Mary's

---

[66] F. A. Gasquet, O.S.B., "Some Impressions of Catholic America," *Dublin Review*, CXXXVIII (April, 1906), 87. Gasquet also visited Saint Bernard's Seminary in Rochester, New York, which had been founded by Bishop Bernard J. McQuaid and dedicated on August 20, 1893. The English visitor spoke of the "undoubted success" of Saint Bernard's and attributed it in part to the fact that McQuaid recognized, as Gasquet put it, "that the first essential in a seminary, of course after good discipline, was excellence of teaching. He consequently from the first has obtained the services of the best professors, and he has spent money lavishly in educating students likely to make good teachers in the best schools of France, Germany and Italy." (p. 95).

[67] See, for example, E. Kidd Lockard, "The Influence of New England in Denominational Colleges in the Northwest, 1830-1860," *Ohio State Archeological and Historical Quarterly*, LIII (January-March, 1944), 1-13.

of the West Seminary whose very name was taken from Purcell's alma mater at Emmitsburg, Maryland. Similarly Archbishop Kenrick of Saint Louis was rector for nearly three years of Saint Charles Seminary in Philadelphia before he went to the West, and Bishop Bruté's American experience had been largely lived around Mount Saint Mary's in Emmitsburg before he assumed charge of the new see of Vincennes. Moreover, one of the most widely used series of theological textbooks, those of Francis Patrick Kenrick, were for the most part written between 1830 and 1863 while the author was governing the sees of Philadelphia and Baltimore. Yet the same Kenrick whose manuals were used in the seminaries of Bardstown, Cincinnati, and Saint Louis, served his apprenticeship, so to speak, during the first five years of his life in the United States (1821-1826) at Saint Joseph's Seminary in Bardstown.[68]

For anyone who reads fairly extensively in the sources and literature on American Catholicism in the last century, it is not difficult to gain the impression that seminary education was a subject of almost constant interest in clerical circles, if not of constant complaint, and that in all sections of the country. For example, George A. Carrell, S.J., first Bishop of Covington, felt something was awry with the way in which the Catholic clergy were being trained. In November, 1855, he told Father Francis Lhomme, S.S., Superior of Saint Mary's Seminary in Baltimore, that he had learned from one of the priests of his cathedral [Thomas R. Butler] that in what was described as "the neighboring diocese" [Cincinnati ?], one priest ordained only three or four years had bought a brick house, another a farm, and still others were credited with having "lots of money." "*Money & drink*," said Carrell, "seem to be the mania of many priests," and he then concluded:

---

[68] Hugh J. Nolan, *The Most Reverend Francis Patrick Kenrick, Third Bishop of Philadelphia, 1830-1851* (Washington: The Catholic University of America Press. 1948), p. 244.

The greatest want of our country is a clergy trained from early boyhood. We stand in need of 'small seminaries' well endowed, conducted by men of trained virtue. All this will come in God's good time.[69]

The suggestion of minor seminaries was one with which Father Lhomme would have heartily agreed, for only the previous year he had prevailed on the Archbishop of Baltimore to invite the American bishops generally to send students to the new Sulpician minor seminary, Saint Charles College at Ellicott Mills, Maryland, where in 1853 ninety per cent of the eighty-one students were Baltimoreans. The appeal was effective insofar as the East was concerned, as the next year showed a marked increase of students from New England and the middle Atlantic states, but the Middle West was too far removed to enable bishops with limited means to send their students to Saint Charles in any number. There were mid-westerners, however, who agreed that this was the way to attract native vocations and to strengthen priestly training. In fact, an unnamed writer in the short-lived journal of Chicago's University of Saint Mary of the Lake, declared preparatory seminaries to be "our greatest want," and he maintained that it was not any defect in American Catholic youth that caused a scarcity of vocations to the priesthood, but rather what were described as "the scanty facilities which are afforded them of preparing themselves for the ministry."[70]

---

69 Carrell to Lhomme, Covington, November 11, 1855, Lhomme Papers, Archives of the Society of Saint Sulpice, Roland Park, Baltimore.

70 "Clerical Seminaries," *The Monthly*, I (June, 1865), 412. The writer is grateful to the Reverend George J. Dyer, Librarian of the Feehan Memorial Library, Saint Mary of the Lake Seminary, Mundelein, Illinois, for providing a photostat copy of the article from this rare journal. Five years previous to *The Monthly's* treatment of this question, Father Jeremiah W. Cummings, Pastor of Saint Stephen's Church, New York, wrote a forceful essay along the same lines in which he deplored the importing of more foreign priests, urged the establishment in this country of minor seminaries, and grew quite defensive about the lack of native vocations. "No vocations!" exclaimed Cummings, "There must be

In the judgment of a number of Catholic churchmen of
the period a remedy for the faulty theological instruction was
not to be found in importing more foreign-born priests, or in
the opinion of others, even in sending American youths
abroad to study. It was rather in developing strong seminaries at home. Such was the prevailing view in the Province
of Cincinnati, one of the more prosperous areas of the
Church in the Middle West, where in spite of its relative
affluence serious difficulties were encountered in trying to
finance the principal major seminary. Archbishop Purcell
made the fact known in April, 1855, through the pages of the
Catholic Telegraph when he appealed to his clergy and laity.
for a more generous support of Mount Saint Mary's Seminary
of the West. In the following month the same motive was in
part behind his offer of the institution as a provincial seminary to his suffragan bishops in the First Provincial Council
of Cincinnati. With a further view to improving the quality
of instruction and of increasing its prestige, in the same
council Purcell and his six suffragans unanimously requested
the Holy See to permit Mount Saint Mary's to confer theological and philosophical degrees. But the Cincinnati prelates' petition ran counter to the idea then uppermost in the
mind of Pius IX for an American seminary in the Eternal
City and it was not, therefore, granted.[71] We have already

---

vocations to the priesthood wherever there are vocations to the faith."
"Vocations to the Priesthood, *"Brownson's Quarterly Review* [Third New
York Series], I (October, 1860), 498. A decade later the new Bishop
of Louisville, William G. McCloskey, painted a very dismal picture of
the state of the 'small seminary' of his diocese as he found it when he
came on the scene. McCloskey's report was submitted to the Congregation de Propaganda Fide with a covering letter dated August 2,
1870; the writer wishes to thank Columba E. Halsey for providing him
with a copy of the section dealing with the seminary.
71 Martin J. Kelly and James M. Kirwin, *History of Mt. St. Mary's Seminary of the West, Cincinnati, Ohio* (Cincinnati: Keating & Company.
1894), pp. 78-79. The pertinent decrees of the council of May, 1855,
are given here (pp. 79-80). Kelly and Kirwin also included the text of
Purcell's pastoral letter of February, 1856, on the seminary in which he

seen the mid-western opposition to the proposal of an American seminary in Rome, and further light on the cause of that opposition may well have been provided by the papal consul general who resided in New York and who early in 1857 told the Cardinal Prefect of Propaganda:

> There is an opinion among several eminent ecclesiastics that the education which is given in Rome does not impart the *true ecclesiastical spirit.* Excellence in this regard has not been noticed in those among us who have been students at Rome & the result of the comparison is that by contrast there is found a superiority in the students of the Sulpicians, whose system tends to give a true ecclesiastical spirit well adapted & very necessary in the present circumstances of this country.[72]

thanked the clergy and laity for their previous donations, but regretted that the result was, he said, "far from having met the wants of the Seminary, or our anticipations." As a consequence the archbishop felt compelled to adopt a plan for an annual collection for the seminary (p. 83). The most recent historian of the Cincinnati seminaries, however, would not agree that lack of money was the real problem. Francis J. Miller stated: "My research would tend to indicate that Purcell's problems were mainly with personnel and a mis-management of money. I would, therefore, say that the Bishops of Cincinnati were never seriously concerned with the financial support of the seminary." [Miller to the writer, Hamilton, Ohio, August 20, 1965]. See Father Miller's unpublished doctoral dissertation, University of Cincinnati (1964), 'A History of the Athenaeum of Ohio, 1829-1960' (Ann Arbor: University Microfilms, Inc. 1965). A German-born priest, Ferdinand Kühr, who held the rectorship of the Cincinnati seminary for a few months in 1837, was shocked by the lack of discipline among the students, the poor quality of instruction, and the ignorance of the faculty. Kühr said the rector and professor at the time of his writing were not able "to speak two words in Latin. . . ." [Kühr to the Prefect of Propaganda, Canton, Ohio, December 10, 1837, Trisco, *op. cit.,* p. 222, n. 221].

[72] Louis B. Binsse to Alessandro Cardinal Barnabò, New York, February 2, 1857, Archives of the Congregation de Propaganda Fide, Scr. orig. Vol. 983, fol. 641a-641v. Recent research would tend to support the papal consul's report. Under the heading, "The Propaganda's Alumni," Father Trisco examined the careers of a half dozen or more priests of dioceses in the Middle West up to 1850 which led him to remark "how unstable many of them proved to be." (*op. cit.,* p. 218). In conclusion Trisco stated: "If a general opinion based on the performances of the Propaganda's alumni in the West may be ventured on the quality of the education imparted at the Urban College, it would seem that that education,

If what was called the 'true ecclesiastical spirit' could not be had in the Roman seminaries devoted to the training of the diocesan clergy, neither were these institutions noted for the intellectual stimulation one might rightly expect to find in the Church's principal theological schools. We have already seen the opinion of Newman and Ward on Roman ecclesiastical education in the late 1840's and late 1870's. In 1863 there arrived in the Eternal City Johannes Janssen, the famous German historian, who was at the same time a devout priest who had a deep respect for the Holy See. He was spiritually uplifted by an audience of Pius IX and by his visits to the various churches and shrines, but he was scandalized at the Romans' neglect of their archival riches, by the defective organization of the libraries, and by the ecclesiastical authorities' lack of interest in higher learning and in scientific and scholarly endeavor.[73] If there was to be a reform in American Catholic theological education, then, it would seem the inspiration would have to come from somewhere else than Rome. In the end those in search of higher academic standards felt more rewarded by what they found in the secular institutions of the United States than they did in Catholic circles with the exception, of course, of the Catholic University of Louvain.

There was one bishop of the Middle West in these years who had vision and courage enough to make at least an heroic attempt to launch something beyond a conventional seminary. After a very brief stay at Maynooth, William Quarter, Irish-born first Bishop of Chicago, had come to this country where he enrolled at Mount Saint Mary's in Emmitsburg and was ordained in 1829. Before his untimely death in

---

however excellent it may have been in itself, had to be adapted to the peculiar exigencies of the local missions. The ability to effect such an adaptation depended on the intelligence and temperament of the individual priests; some, like Martin Spalding, were quite capable of doing so; others appeared too inflexible." (p. 224).

[73] Aubert, *Le Pontificat de Pie IX, 1846-1878*, p. 185.

April, 1848, at the age of forty-three, Quarter had seen the beginnings of his University of Saint Mary of the Lake of which a major seminary, opened in May, 1844, served as the school of theology. In the following September a German missionary, Father Adelbert Inama, O.Praem., visited Chicago and later wrote a description of the institution which was anything but complimentary. Calling the school a university was to Inama an example of "Celtic magnification," and he was astonished to learn that "a Protestant government," as he called the Illinois legislature, should have granted the power to confer degrees to this Catholic institution which was referred to as "the Irish University of Chicago."[74] Inama was highly censorious of classrooms created by putting up partitions in an old board chapel, and even more of the pretentious titles of president and vice president borne by two recently ordained priests who constituted the faculty and gave instruction "in all courses and many languages" while taking care of a parish. On a second visit in late October, Inama found eleven students among whom was a single theologian who, he stated, "was without a professor." The university's funds, he added, "register zero," a point that he mentioned only to make it doubly clear that if an Irish bishop had attempted an institution of this kind on his own and had failed, "the Germans surely would need aid from abroad in a similar undertaking."[75]

'University' was, indeed, an exaggerated term to give to Bishop Quarter's institution, but Saint Mary of the Lake was not quite the failure that Inama believed it to be. It continued on after its founder's death and by 1863 there

---

[74] Inama wrote this letter from Salina, New York, February 28, 1845, probably to the superior of the monastery at Wilten, Tyrol. *Letters of the Reverend Adelbert Inama, O. Praem.* Translated from the German. (Madison: State Historical Society of Wisconsin, n.d.), pp. 75-76. This work was a reprint from the *Wisconsin Magazine of History*, XI-XII (1927-1928).

[75] *Ibid.*, p. 76.

were schools of medicine and law, along with theology and liberal arts, which though small in numbers were in relatively good condition. Yet Chicago's third bishop, James Duggan, suddenly closed the University in January, 1866, an action which becomes intelligible when it is known that he had already begun to show signs of the mental abberation that ultimately caused the unfortunate man to spend the last thirty years of his life in an insane asylum. The school of theology held on for two more years, but then just as suddenly it was closed by Duggan in August, 1868, upon his return from Carlsbad, Germany. The four professors were dismissed from the diocese and the twenty-eight students were dispatched to Saint Francis Seminary in Milwaukee.[76] Thus there came to an inglorious end the mid-western Catholics' only viable effort during the last century to make theological training for the diocesan clergy an integral part of university education.

Actually, Americans in general showed little understanding of any phase of higher education until well into the second half of the century. As one writer has said:

> The American college did not find the answers to the questions raised by the rising tide of democracy until after the Civil War. Nor did it, until then, begin effectively to grapple with the question of quality, of standards, of excellence.[77]

We have already noted the fact that Catholics made very slight distinction between the so-called colleges and the seminaries, except that frequently students in the latter acted as teachers in the former, with the two groups usually housed in separate buildings. In itself a situation of this kind re-

---

[76] Harry C. Koenig, "History of Saint Mary of the Lake Seminary, Mundelein, Illinois," pp. 39-40. The writer wishes to thank his friend, Monsignor Koenig, Pastor of Saint Joseph's Church, Libertyville, Illinois, for the loan of this manuscript.

[77] Frederick Rudolph, *The American College and University. A History* (New York: Alfred A. Knopf. 1962), p. 22.

vealed how imperfectly they had thought through the true nature of higher education. The motives that lay behind the establishment of Catholic colleges, and the relation that these schools bore to the seminaries, reflected primarily their founders' apologetic approach, who, it has been said, looked upon the colleges as preparatory schools for youths who might aspire to the priesthood, as centers for missionary activities, and as places where young men who were not to be priests might be afforded the opportunity to cultivate the moral virtues.[78] Bishops and religious superiors demonstrated how secondary in their minds were a love of learning and high academic standards in their employment of the seminarian and the scholastic as teachers of lay students because, as one historian has said, he was "doctrinally orthodox, morally sound, willing to follow directions, and his services cost very little."[79]

It was scarcely surprising, then, that in 1866, the year the hierarchy held its Second Plenary Council in Baltimore, of the sixty Catholic colleges and seven institutions which bore the name of university, not one of the latter had achieved the status of a true university, and that many of those calling themselves colleges failed to measure up to what might be expected of a school bearing that name.[80] Similar conditions obtained among the Catholic theological schools, where off and on for nearly forty years futile attempts had been made to improve matters by centralizing the Church's meager resources in a single or in several institutions. Mention has been made of the discussion of a national seminary at the Baltimore councils of 1829 and 1833, and of the failure of the bishops of the Province of Cincinnati in 1855 to win a degree-granting status for Mount Saint Mary's Seminary of

---

[78] Edward J. Power, *A History of Catholic Higher Education in the United States* (Milwaukee: Bruce Publishing Company. 1958), p. 34.
[79] *Ibid.*, p. 92.
[80] Ellis, *The Formative Years. . . .* p. 22.

the West. A further attempt to do something on a national scale was to meet a like fate in the 1860's.

More than a year before the opening of the plenary council in October, 1866, Martin J. Spalding, Archbishop of Baltimore, who had been born and raised in the Middle West, revealed what he had in mind when he asked the Bishop of Buffalo, John Timon, C.M., "Why should we not have a Catholic University?"[81] Yet in spite of enthusiastic support from men like Isaac T. Hecker, C.S.P., founder of the Paulist Fathers and editor of the *Catholic World*, a combination of circumstances such as the financial difficulties of the American College in Rome, the indifference of many of the bishops, and the failure to find a benefactor who would pledge a substantial sum as an initial fund to begin operations, caused Spalding's hope to fade in 1866. The only consolation that this transplanted mid-westerner had on the score of reform in theological education in the council over which he presided as apostolic delegate, was the hierarchy's expression of a desire for an institute of higher studies in the ecclesiastical sciences when an opportune time should present itself.

Yet during the interval of eighteen years between the second and third plenary councils the idea of some form of advanced instruction in theology for the American Catholic clergy—for the bishops at this time were thinking entirely of the clergy and not the laity—would not die. And of those who figured in the discussion of the 1870's and early 1880's none was more forward looking than the men of the Middle West, and of these none more prominent and more persistent than Archbishop Spalding's own nephew, John Lancaster Spalding, who in 1877 had been consecrated first Bishop of Peoria. As it turned out, two of the most significant happenings in the Catholic Church in this country in the 1880's—

---

[81] Spalding to Timon, Baltimore, August 23, 1865, Copybook of Archbishop Spalding, p. 150, Archives of the Archdiocese of Baltimore.

the convening of the Third Plenary Council (1884) and the establishment of the Catholic University of America (1889) which grew out of it—were owed primarily to the bishops of this region who refused to be put off by the coolness and quiet opposition to another plenary gathering on the part of the leaders of the Church in the East. The man who was destined to preside over the council as apostolic delegate and to be the future university's first chancellor, James Gibbons, admitted the fact when he confided to his diary that John Cardinal McCloskey, Archbishop of New York, was opposed to another council, and then added:

> I gave as my opinion that it would not be expedient to hold a council for some time to come. . . . The Bishops of the West seem to favor a national council, as some of them have intimated to me.[82]

When the western prelates failed to move their eastern colleagues they invoked the assistance of the Congregation de Propaganda Fide at Rome, whereupon the cardinal prefect ordered the American hierarchy to proceed with plans for another plenary council. And once the council opened on November 9, 1884, it was Spalding's famous sermon of the following week on seminary education that placed the problem in its true light, with the mid-westerners, along with eastern prelates like John J. Keane, Bishop of Richmond, becoming the soul and spirit of the movement for the higher education of the clergy.

Were one to seek for the events that brought the university idea into the realm of reality during the council sessions, he would find them in the pledge which Bishop Spalding won from Miss Mary Gweldoline Caldwell to give $300,000 to begin the work, the sermon already mentioned, and the Bishop of Peoria's persistence in seeing that the council did

---

[82] Gibbons Diary, January 4, 1882, p. 158, Archives of the Archdiocese of Baltimore.

not close before the apostolic delegate had appointed a committee to assume charge of the undertaking. In his sermon Spalding first surveyed the leading role played by the Church in medieval university education, the new situation created by the extraordinary scientific advances of the present century, and the nature of a seminary as a vocational school, not a center of broad culture and learning, a theme on which he had spoken and written on several previous occasions. Acknowledging with sincere gratitude the good work that had been accomplished by the seminaries of the American Church, the Bishop of Peoria insisted, nevertheless:

> The ecclesiastical seminary is not a school of intellectual culture, either here in America or elsewhere, and to imagine that it can become the instrument of intellectual culture is to cherish a delusion. . . . Its methods are not such as one would choose who desires to open the mind, to give it breadth, flexibility, strength, refinement, and grace. Its textbooks are written often in a barbarous style, the subjects are discussed in a dry and mechanical way, and the professor, wholly intent upon giving instruction, is frequently indifferent as to the manner in which it is imparted; or else not possessing himself a really cultivated intellect, he holds in slight esteem expansion and refinement of mind, looking upon it as at the best a mere ornament. I am not offering a criticism upon the ecclesiastical seminary, but am simply pointing to the plain fact that it is not a school of intellectual culture, and consequently, if its course were lengthened to five, to six, to eight, to ten years, its students would go forth to their work with a more thorough professional training, but not with more really cultivated minds.[83]

[83] The sermon was published in Spalding's *Means and Ends of Education* (Chicago: A. C. McClurg Company. 1895) under the title, "The Higher Education" (pp. 181-232), the particular passage quoted occurred on pages 212-213. For Spalding's education work in general, see John Tracy Ellis, *John Lancaster Spalding, First Bishop of Peoria, American Educator* (Milwaukee: Bruce Publishing Company. 1961), and the more recent and extensive treatment of David F. Sweeney, O.F.M., *The Life of John Lancaster Spalding, First Bishop of Peoria, 1840-1916* (New York: Herder and Herder. 1965).

As a consequence of the efforts of men like Spalding and John Ireland, Bishop of Saint Paul, before the council closed on December 7, Gibbons, as apostolic delegate, had appointed a committee of the hierarchy to take charge of the project.

This is not the place to detail the difficulties encountered by the committee during the ensuing five years. Suffice it to say, they were altogether real, and at times so formidable as to call in question whether the institution would ever be born. Working in its favor was not only the unflagging zeal of men like Spalding, Ireland, and Keane, but the growing trend in Protestant circles for an improvement of theological education. For example, in the report of President Charles W. Eliot of Harvard to the Board of Overseers in 1882, he had explained the new standards in vogue in the Divinity School as follows:

> The twofold object of these changes is to make the degree of bachelor of divinity inaccessible except to men of thorough training; and to exclude altogether from the School young men who lack the preliminary education necessary to enable them to profit by its teachings, and keep up with its classes.[84]

That was the kind of academic ideal that made an appeal to bishops like Spalding, Ireland, and Keane, who were intent that the Catholic diocesan clergy should be given a similar opportunity to secure training of a high quality.

Within the Catholic community the largest and most influential group in education, the Jesuits, were at this time likewise bestirring themselves in behalf of a reform in theological education for their men. One could see it in such steps as the opening of Woodstock College in Maryland in September, 1869, intended mainly for the eastern states, and

---

[84] "President's Report for 1881-82 to the Board of Overseers," *Annual Reports of the President and Treasurer of Harvard College, 1881-82* (Cambridge: University Press: John Wilson and Son. 1882), p. 27. See also Hugh Hawkins, "Charles W. Eliot, University Reform, and Religious Faith in America, 1869-1909," *Journal of American History*, LI (September, 1964), 191-213.

the establishment at Saint Louis University in 1899 of a
school of theology for western members. For the Society of
Jesus, too, had known its time in the wilderness as was exemplified in a man like James Oliver Van de Velde, a Belgian-born Jesuit who would later be first Bishop of Chicago
and then of Natchez. Van de Velde began his theology at
Georgetown College in 1825 and nine years later at Saint
Louis University he had not yet finished his course. The reason for this long delay was explained by the historian of the
Middle West Jesuits when he stated of Van de Velde:

> He was at once minister, prefect of studies, professor of
> mathematics and Spanish, and for a period treasurer of the
> University. . . . And so the situation persisted unchanged for
> some four or five years longer until finally, without having
> had time to look at the examination-papers, as he declared, he
> presented himself before an examining-board and, it is pleas-
> ing to record, came through the test successfully.[85]

One is reminded here of the words of Scripture, "If in the
case of green wood they do these things, what is to happen
in the case of the dry?"[86]

At length the obstacles that lay in the path of the Catholic
University of America were overcome and on November 13,
1889, the institution was formally dedicated in the national
capital. At first it was exclusively a graduate school of theology with thirty-seven students in residence in Caldwell
Hall, twelve of whom, or just under one-third, were from
the Middle West. The Archdioceses of Chicago and Saint
Paul and the Diocese of Cleveland each sent two men, and
one each came from the Archdioceses of Cincinnati, Milwaukee, and Saint Louis and the Dioceses of Marquette,
Sioux Falls, and Vincennes. For some years, however, progress was very slow at Washington. A year and a half after

---

[85] Gilbert J. Garraghan, S.J., *The Jesuits of the Middle United States* (New
York: America Press. 1938), I, 639.
[86] *Luke*, XXIII, 31.

the opening of the University, an Irish-born priest student
of the Archdiocese of Saint Paul told the president of his
alma mater, All Hallows College, Dublin, that his original
intention had been to study dogmatic and moral theology,
but he had changed to apologetics and church history when
he learned that the professors in the former subjects confined themselves "to one tract a year," and, too, because
these professors were Germans. Revealing his own prejudice,
he remarked, "this premise is wide enough to enable you to
draw a legitimate conclusion." A public disputation had been
held that day over which Cardinal Gibbons had presided as
chancellor, and for which there had been such elaborate
preparations that the student was sure he was going to experience "something extraordinary." As it turned out, it was
he said, "more like a fifteenth century performance than like
a scene enacted in a enlivened and enlightened nineteenth
century."[87]

By this time the new ecclesiastical Province of Saint Paul
had been created by the Holy See and there were, as previously stated, thirty-three dioceses within the area defined
earlier as the Middle West. Within the same area there were
five major seminaries or Catholic theological schools with a
total of 3,554 priests serving an estimated 3,019,921 Catholic
people out of the total of 8,909,000 for the entire United
States.[88] The Middle West still left much to be desired by
way of strong theological schools, but the seminaries of the
region in which most of the candidates were enrolled, as
well as those in the East, in Rome, or in Louvain to which

---

[87]Terence Moore to William Fortune, Washington, March 14, 1891, Archives of All Hallows College, Dublin.

[88] *Sadlier's Catholic Directory, Almanac and Ordo for the Year of Our Lord
1890* (New York: D. & J. Sadlier. 1890), pp. 407-408. In this year the
dioceses of the United States listed a total of 2,132 'ecclesiastical students,' of whom 925 were in the area of the Middle West embraced by
this study; it is impossible, however to distinguish between the students
who were in the major and those who were in the minor seminaries.

a minority were sent, were successful in imparting the basic
spiritual and intellectual training that enabled their products
to guide and direct the mounting numbers of the faithful
who increased their responsibilities each year by natural
increase, by conversion, and most of all by immigration
from abroad. There were—and are—numerous and complex
factors that entered into the making of a priest, but preoccupation with intellectual training should never be permitted to overshadow the importance of the spiritual fashion-
ing of a man for the Christian ministry. What a seminary
was intended to do for a candidate for the priesthood in this
regard was beautifully expressed by Newman when he
preached the sermon at the dedication of Saint Bernard's
Seminary in Birmingham, England, in October, 1873. On
that occasion the great Oratorian stated that a seminary was
"the only true guarantee for the creation of the ecclesiastical
spirit." And in endeavoring to explain what he meant, Newman said:

> In this ecclesiastical spirit, I will but mention a spirit of ser-
> iousness or recollection. We must gain the habit of feeling that
> we are in God's presence, that He sees what we are doing;
> and a liking that He does so, a love of knowing it, a delight in
> the reflection, 'Thou, God, seest me.' A priest who feels this
> deeply will never misbehave himself in mixed society. It will
> keep him from over-familiarity with any of his people; it will
> keep him from too many words, from imprudent or unwise
> speaking; it will teach him to rule his thoughts. It will be a
> principle of detachment between him and even his own
> people; for he who is accustomed to lean on the Unseen God,
> will never be able really to attach himself to any of His crea-
> tures. And thus an elevation of mind will be created, which
> is the true weapon which he must use against the infidelity
> of the world.[89]

---

[89] *Faith and Prejudice and Other Unpublished Sermons of Cardinal Newman.* Edited by the Birmingham Oratory (New York: Sheed & Ward.
1956), pp. 126-127.

MID-WESTERN THEOLOGICAL SCHOOLS FOR THE CATHOLIC DIOCESAN CLERGY 1811-1889*

Diocese	Established	Seminaries	Dates	Clergy in Charge
Bardstown (Louisville after 1841)	1808	Saint Thomas, Howard Farm	1811-1819	Diocesan
		Saint Joseph's, Bardstown	1819-1848	Diocesan
		Saint Mary's, Lebanon	1848-1856	Diocesan
Cincinnati	1821	Saint Francis Xavier, Cincinnati	1829-1840	Diocesan
		Saint Francis Xavier, Brown County	1840-1842	Diocesan
		Saint Francis Xavier, Brown County	1842-1845	Vincentians
		Saint Francis Xavier, Cincinnati	1845-1847	Jesuits
		Mount Saint Mary's of the West, Cincinnati (closed in 1879 and reopend 1887)	1848-	Diocesan
Saint Louis	1826	Saint Mary's of the Barrens, Perryville	1818-1842	Vincentians
		Saint Vincent de Paul, Saint Louis	1842-1848	Vincentians
		Saint Louis, Carondelet	1848-1858	Diocesan
Detroit	1833	House seminary in bishop's residence	1834-1837(?)	Diocesan
		Saint Thomas, Detroit	1846-1854	Diocesan
Vincennes (Indianapolis after 1898)	1834	House seminary adjoining bishop's residence	1836-1840	Diocesan and Eudists
		Saint Charles, Vincennes	1840-1848	Diocesan
		Saint Charles, Vincennes	c. 1853-1860	Diocesan
		Saint Charles, Indianapolis	1874	Diocesan
Dubuque	1837	House seminary in bishop's residence (Saint Raphael's)	1839-1850	Diocesan
		Mount Saint Bernard's, Table Mound	1850-1858	Diocesan

Chicago	1843	Saint Mary of the Lake, Chicago	1844-1868	Diocesan
Milwaukee	1843	House seminary in bishop's residence Saint Francis, Saint Francis	1845-1854 1854	Diocesan Diocesan
Cleveland	1847	House seminary at rear of bishop's residence (Saint Francis de Sales) Saint Mary's, Cleveland	1848-1850 1850-	Diocesan Diocesan
Saint Paul	1850	House seminary in bishop's residence Saint Thomas, Saint Paul	1851-1857 1885-1894	Diocesan Diocesan
Quincy (Alton, 1857-1923; Springfield, 1923—)	1853	House seminary in bishop's residence Saint Francis, Teutopolis	1858-1862 1862-1865	Diocesan Franciscans

* Listed in chronological order according to the year of the establishment of the diocese.

ALTERNATE TYPES OF THEOLOGICAL TRAINING FOR MID-WESTERN DIOCESAN CLERGY 1811-1889

Extra-Diocesan Seminaries		Scholasticates of Religious Orders
Saint Mary's, Baltimore	1791	
Mount Saint Mary's, Emmitsburg	1820	Saint Meinrad Abbey (Diocese of Vincennes, 1861 (?) – Indianapolis after 1898)
American College, Louvain	1857	Saint John's Abbey (Diocese of Saint Paul, 1868 – Saint Cloud after 1889)
American College, Rome	1859	Saint Benedict's Abbey (Diocese of Leavenworth, 1882-1883, Kansas City in Kansas after 1947)

4.

The Seminary in the Shadow of Vatican Council II

PART I

Seminaries have been much in mind of late by reason of the commemoration of the 400th anniversary of the Council of Trent's legislation on that subject and, too, because of the hope and expectation of many that Vatican Council II will approach its consideration of seminary education in the same realistic and imaginative spirit of the aggiornamento that has so splendidly characterized its treatment of the sacred liturgy. More than four centuries have now elapsed since that November of 1555 when there was convoked at the call of Reginald Cardinal Pole, papal legate and soon to be Archbishop of Canterbury, a national council of the English bishops, the eleventh decree of whose legislation stated:

> That in cathedrals there be educated a certain number or beginners, from which, as from a seed bed, priests must be chosen who can worthily be placed in charge of the churches.[1]

Thus did the zeal and forceful leadership of England's cardinal foreshadow the action taken at Trent in July, 1563, when the ecumenical council provided for the universal

---

[1] Quoted in Philip Hughes, *Rome and the Counter-Reformation in England* (London: Burns & Oates, 1942), p. 83.

Church the institution we identify by the word 'seminary,' with Cardinal Pole and Saint Charles Borromeo the chief fonts of its inspiration and the principal architects of its design. In the intervening time the seminary has accomplished so incalculable a service for the Catholic cause that one wonders how during the 1500 years that preceded Pole and Borromeo the Church had done without it.

Yet magnificent as has been its achievement during the last four centuries, like every human enterprise the Tridentine seminary, too, has grown old, and in the judgment of many prudent and respected churchmen and laymen it now stands in need of change. In that regard one is reminded of the singular vision that illumined the mind of Pope Paul VI when he addressed the world from within the sacred precincts of the Church of the Nativity at Bethlehem. Casting his eyes out beyond that hallowed spot, the Holy Father encompassed the entire Catholic family in his thought when he said:

> We are living at the historic hour when the Church of Christ must live its deep and visible unity. . . . We must give the life of the Church new attitudes of mind, new aims, new standards of behaviour, make it rediscover a spiritual beauty in all its aspects: in the sphere of thought and word, in prayer and methods of education, in art and canon law. A unanimous effort is needed in which all groups must offer their cooperation. May everyone hear the call which Christ is making to him through our voice.[2]

Most Americans need no exhortation to heed that call, aware as it is of the spirit that has been moving through most of the Church of the United States during what the pontiff termed this 'historic hour,' as spirit that has prepared his American children for a ready response to the striking summons he gave at Bethlehem. The professional magazines

---

[2] "Faith, Unity, and Peace. Pope Paul's Epiphany Message from Bethlehem," *The Tablet*, CCXVIII (January 11, 1964), 53.

of the ecclesiastical sciences, as well as the Catholic journals of opinion, have been replete of late with programs of renewal, plan of reform, and suggestions for change, all offered in the belief and hope that they will improve and strengthen the seminaries. Some of these may best be described as alterations in emphasis or pace in areas where there is general agreement, for example, the need for reducing the excessive number of class lectures to which students have generally been subjected; others would usher in a sharper break with present practice by locating houses of priestly formation once again near great university centers, and associating them with university life, which was true in the days before Trent; still others of more dubious merit elicit only feeble support, as that which would eschew virtually all compulsory rules in the seminary regime and leave obligations like attendance at daily exercises to students' voluntary response.

Almost inevitably proposals to change patterns that have become deeply fixed in the past give rise to differences among men. Yet if they are put forth with reason and moderation, and with a courteous consideration for others' judgments, they can hardly prove anything but helpful to all concerned. It would be sad, indeed, if in this exchange of opinions about seminary education the truth once expressed by the founder of the American hierarchy to a fellow priest were lost to view. In this instance John Carroll said:

> you will find by experience, that men may think very differently even on subjects interesting to the conduct of religious affairs, without therefore deserving to be utterly distrusted.[3]

A generous mutual recognition of the sincere affection and genuine solicitude for the Church's seminaries that motivate all those who engage in the discussion of this delicate mat-

---

[3] Carroll to Charles Neale, January 19, 1790, John M. Daley, S.J., *Georgetown University: Origin and Early Years* (Washington, Georgetown University Press, 1957), p. 153.

ter, will at the very outset immensely strengthen the common effort. No really priestly heart can today remain altogether untouched by concern, a concern mingled with a mounting anxiety lest the Church should fail to realize her highest potentialities for her encounter with what every alert priest recognizes as a world that has in good measure come to regard her divine mission, as it has all religion, as no more than an irrelevance. A goodly number of earnest men think that a candid reappraisal of the seminary's aims and methods, in the light of contemporary conditions, will assist the priests of the future to achieve their maximum capacity in rendering the Church relevant once again to men of the late twentieth century. In other words, these friendly voices are intent that the danger that overtook the Catholic clergy a half century ago in circumstances not unlike our own, should not find us equally unprepared, a situation which Eudaxe Mignot, Archbishop of Albi, sought to avert when he warned Domenico Cardinal Ferrata, Benedict XV's Secretary of State:

> The perpetuation of this state of things will mean an inferior clergy, more concerned with the externals of worship than with the spiritual realities of interior religion—a clergy which will understand nothing of the intellectual and moral difficulties of the time, or of the movement of ideas, and the Church will be the loser. Such a clergy will stand motionless amidst a world on the march, a world whose light they ought to be.[4]

How, then, should those responsible for seminary education proceed, if they share the belief that an attempt should be made to weigh the validity of the proposed reforms? It would be absurd for one to suppose that he could give an adequate answer to that question at one time. Only after long and patient study, as well as careful analysis of the re-

---

[4] Mignot to Ferrata, October, 1914, Nicolas Fontaine, *Saint Siège, Action française et Catholiques intégraux. Histoire critique avec documents* (Paris: Librairie Universitaire. J. Gamber, 1928), p. 133.

sults of experimentation, on the part of those who have dedicated their lives to seminary administration and teaching, will the varied and complicated factors involved yield a really satisfactory answer. It is proper, however, merely to suggest three points that may merit consideration in the seminary's search for its proper *aggiornamento*. The first two relate to matters of a general nature, the third to a special academic discipline within the seminary curriculum that is intended to prepare the priest for what many believe to be his most critical test in the sensitive functions by which he reveals to men his true spiritual and intellectual depth.

In regard to the first point, the desirability of a stronger emphasis on the intellectual aspects of priestly training, is it not true that there are still too many seminaries where high intellectual achievement is passed over with scant recognition; where relatively little premium is placed on academic distinction, on the use of students' critical faculties, on the merit of that kind of independent inquiry and originality of approach that open and expand the mind; on the exceedingly important need for differentiation of program for superior students, so that they may not be denied the challenge to which their God-given talents entitle them; or where even so commonplace a matter as reading good books is not honored as the vital force that it can become in a student's spiritual and intellectual formation? Has there not been too often a failure to counterbalance the warning against the altogether real danger of intellectual pride with the equally real danger of intellectual sloth?

Several years ago a seminary rector was heard to remark that he did not encourage A students because they were usually troublemakers. A remark of this kind, it is to be hoped, represents no more than an isolated eccentricity, for had the superiors of Thomas Aquinas, Robert Bellarmine, and Jean Mabillon reasoned in this fashion, what a grievous loss would have been sustained by Christian thought and scholarship! Moreover, the founder of the Church's first seminary never betrayed any fidget on this score. On the contrary, in the Sermon on the Mount he told his disciples quite plainly, "let your light shine before men in order that they may see your good works and give glory to your Father in heaven."[5] And in the inscrutable ways of God, he has often seen fit to have the divine glory reflected, so to speak, in the quality of man's effort, and for that reason, as Dom Jean Leclercq has stated, if man

> performs his task poorly, he compromises his reputation and also the cause he serves, the truth he should manifest and the Church whose honor he hopes to enchance.[6]

The American Catholic seminary system has a tremendous accomplishment to its credit since it solidified in the early nineteenth century its first and feeble establishments. Yet on occasion one wonders if the tendency of an Archbishop of Baltimore of that far-off time to foster the spiritual at the expense of the intellectual, is not still more prevalent among some of us than one might wish. In this particular case it was the tendency that prompted the archbishop, in counseling an American priest studying in Paris, to say that if the latter would but imbibe the spirit of Saint Sulpice, then upon his return home, as he expressed it,

> this immense advantage will be for you and for the Church in the United States, infinitely preferable to all the knowledge that you can acquire during your sojourn in Europe.[7]

Needless to say, anyone with the proper understanding of a

---

[5] *Matthew*, V, 16.

[6] *The Love of Learning and the Desire for God* (New York: Fordham University Press, 1961), p. 321.

[7] Archives of the Archdiocese of Baltimore, 21-N-2, Ambrose Maréchal, S.S., to Samuel Eccleston, Baltimore, February 12, 1826, Columba E. Halsey, O.S.B., "The Life of Samuel Eccleston, Fifth Archbishop of Baltimore, 1801-1851," unpublished master's thesis, the Catholic University of America (1963), pp. 19-20.

seminary will never so misconceive its role as to suggest that its principal business is to produce scholars. The seminary is not the graduate school. By the same token, however, it is a house of study, an assembly of men united in pursuit of the noblest ideal known to this world, in the striving for which the cultivation of the intellect is second only to the elevation of the spirit itself.

The second point has to do with the delicate operation whereby the seminarian can be introduced to sufficient fore-knowledge and understanding of the world that he is expected to evangelize, and at the same time be shielded from the type of influence that would gravely injure his sacred calling. Admittedly, it is not easy to achieve the proper balance. Yet if the future priest is to cope with life's grim realities, into which he is plunged immediately following his ordination, it would seem imperative that every effort should be made to condition him psychologically beforehand. Otherwise upon his emergence from the seminary he will be found, as have too many of his predecessors, a grown-up boy and not a man firmly wrapped in the vesture of maturity. In this regard the words that John Henry Newman directed to the first students of the Catholic University of Ireland can, *mutatis mutandis*, be addressed to seminarians. Newman said:

> Gentlemen, if I am called upon to state the difference between a boy and a real man, I should say this—that a boy lives on what is without and around him; the one depends upon others for instruction and amusement, the other is able in great measure to depend upon himself. You come here to learn to pass from the state of boys to the state of men.[8]

It is important, therefore, that the seminary's regime should be so ordered that those who complete its course

---

[8] John Henry Newman, *My Campaign in Ireland.* Edited by William Neville (Aberdeen: Printed for Private Circulation Only, 1896), pp. 317-18. The date of the address was November 5, 1854.

will emerge as more than grown-up boys, but rather as men with all that the term implies by way of maturity of outlook, a keen sense of responsibility, and a consciousness of the realities of life. And if this is to be the case, then avenues of information and lines of communication must be kept open so that the air of the seminary will be redolent with that vitality and freshness that can gain entrance only through the open windows used by the beloved Pope John to revitalize the Church of our time. The unhappy consequences that follow from the contrary policy were graphically described by John Lancaster Spalding, first bishop of Peoria, in a famous sermon preached in Rome at the turn of the century in which he said:

> To forbid men to think along whatever line, is to place oneself in opposition to the deepest and most invincible tendency of the civilized world. Were it possible to compel obedience from Catholics in matters of this kind, the result would be a hardening and sinking of our whole religious life. We should more and more drift away from the vital movements of the age, and find ourselves at last immured in a spiritual ghetto, where no man can breathe pure air, or be joyful or strong or free.[9]

The third and final point found recent and renewed sanction in Vatican Council II when the fathers declared it a principle of the liturgical revival that "the homily . . . is to be esteemed as part of the liturgy itself. . . ."[10] In what course of the seminary curriculum, it may be asked, is there a more favorable opportunity than in homiletics to utilize for the profit of souls the knowledge acquired in the traditional ecclesiastical sciences, to demonstrate the depth with

---

[9] "Education and the Future of Religion," *Religion, Agnosticism and Education* (Chicago: A. C. McClurg and Company, 1902), p. 175.

[10] *Constitution on the Sacred Liturgy* (Huntington, Indiana: Our Sunday Visitor Press, 1964), p. 24.

which the student has mastered the unchanging principles and lessons of Christian asceticism, to reveal the clarity with which he sees men's spiritual needs and the sincerity and determination with which he is intent to satisfy them, to lend guidance and direction to the liturgical and pastoral emphasis so strongly encouraged by Popes John and Paul? Where more effectively can these ends be accomplished than in homiletics, which some have mistakenly regarded as a matter of secondary importance in preparation for the ministry? The thousands of college and university graduates who are now pouring each year like a mighty torrent into the more than 22,000 parishes and missions of the American Church have created an altogther new situation that insistently cries out for professors to give their most serious attention to homiletic instruction, as well as for seminarians to emphasize most urgently its importance for their future lives. If Cardinal Manning could say over eighty years ago of the laity of his time that insofar as sermons are concerned, "They are very quick to perceive, it may be said to feel, whether a priest speaks from his heart or only from his lips,"[11] how much more is that true today!

In any attempt to suggest or evaluate the factors that prompt lay criticism of the clergy one can, of course, speak with certainty only insofar as he has personal knowledge and experience. If I may be pardoned here a personal note, I should say that I am aware of no single aspect of the priestly ministry in the Church of the United States that is the subject of more pointed and sustained criticism than the ill-prepared, commonplace, and at times childish sermons which are still the norm in too many parishes of the land. Much more could be said on the point, but one has no need for belabored argument to be convinced that few features of Catholic life and devotion more readily lend

---

[11] *The Eternal Priesthood* (Baltimore: John Murphy Company, n.d.), p. 186.

themselves to attract the indifferent, distant, and even faint-
ly hostile soul toward the Church than the innate cogency
and beauty of the word of God when it comes adorned in
the habiliments of authoritative knowledge, logical development, and grace of diction. Nowhere does the cultivated
mind, enriched by wide reading and attuned to the best in
contemporary thought, show to greater advantage than in
the pulpit and through the various channels now afforded
by the communications media. It is a golden opportunity,
then, for reaping a harvest of souls which, if neglected by
the seminarian and the priest, may never return.

To say that we live in a time of profound and even revolutionary change in every aspect of human endeavor, is to
state the obvious. And religious circles are no exception, for
the highest reaches of Christian thought outside the Catholic
fold have long been astir, and Vatican Council II has been
responsible, not only for countless new insights breaking
within the Catholic family itself, but, too, for illumining for
other Christians numerous unsuspected features of the
Church of Rome. For certain Protestant and Orthodox
churchmen it has been an unsettling experience, as unsettling
as that felt by some of the more conservative of the sons of
the Roman obedience. Yet those most wedded to the traditional in all communions will not deny the well-nigh miraculous outpouring of charity that has brought in its train a
deeper mutual understanding and enlightened comprehen-
sion such as to destroy many an ancient myth that men have
believed about each other, and to lead to admissions on all
sides that a decade ago would have been unthinkable. For
example, when Karl Barth was asked some years ago to
interpret for his Protestant brethren the changes initiated by
Vatican Council II, among other things he maintained:

> . . . it could very well be possible that we others might find
> more to learn from the Roman Church than Rome for its part

would have to learn from us, as we still assume with undue self-satisfaction.[12]

In our kind of age, therefore, the seminaries assume an importance in the Church's life more compelling and far-reaching, perhaps, than in any age since Trent. For in the hazardous days through which we are now passing, it is to the hands of her clergy that there are, and will be, entrusted decisions which will determine, under God, the fate of the Church for generations to come. To be sure, it is a frightening responsibility, and yet the devoted bishops, priests, and seminarians of the American Church, buoyed up as they and their predecessors have been for well nigh two centuries by the noble and wonderfully generous tradition of her dedicated religious and laity, will not be daunted at the prospect. For amid the sobering circumstances and very real dangers that face them, they also sense the dazzling promise contained in many features of contemporary Catholicism. Their spirits have already been lifted by the wonders wrought within the Church of God in recent years, wonders that move them to feel that theirs, too, is an age such as caused Cardinal Newman at one point in his long and eventful life to declare in an optimistic vien:

The cause of truth, never dominant in this world, has its ebbs and flows. It is pleasant to live in a day, when the tide is coming in. Such is our own day; and, without forgetting that there are many rocks on the shore to throw us back and break our advance for the moment, and to task our patience before we cover them,—that physical force is now on the world's side, and that the world will be provoked to more active enmity against the Church in proportion to her success,—still we may surely encourage ourselves by a thousand tokens all around us now, that this is our hour, whatever be its duration, the hour for great hopes, great schemes, great efforts, great be-

---

[12] Karl Barth, "Thoughts on the Second Vatican Council," *Ecumenical Review*, XV (July, 1963), 365.

ginnings. We may live indeed to see but little built, but we shall see much founded. A new era seems to be at hand, and a bolder policy is showing itself.[13]

PART II

To say that we are living in the most tumultuous age that the Church has experienced since the religious revolution of the sixteenth century, has become almost axiomatic. And what gives this period of profound change a value lacking in that of 400 years ago, is that the force that has engendered the current movement has come largely from the highest ecclesiastical authority rather than from rebellious spirits who have departed from the fold. The factors that have produced this momentous quickening in the realm of the spirit have been numerous, varied, and complicated; but to no single person is more owed for it all than to the beloved John XXIII who eight years ago last January electrified the Catholic world by announcing to the cardinals gathered about him at Saint Paul's Outside the Walls that he had determined to summon an ecumenical council. The knowledge and experience of the previous three months, he said, had encouraged him to initiate the gigantic undertaking, trustful, as he was, in the mediation of the Mother of God, of Saints Peter and Paul, of his special patrons, Saints John the Baptist and John the Evangelist, and of all the heavenly court. "We entreat all of them," said the pontiff "to grant Us a good beginning and continuation and final success in these projects (all of which require hard work) to the enlightenment, edification, and happiness of the whole Christian world, and to the inducement of the faithful of the separated com-

---

[13] John Henry Newman, "Universities and Seminaries. L'Ecole des Hautes Etudes," *Historical Sketches* (Longmans, Green and Company, 1903), III, 251. This essay originally appeared in the *Catholic University Gazette* of Dublin in 1854.

munities to follow Us amicably in this quest for unity and for grace, to which so many souls aspire from all corners of the earth . . ."[14]

I shall not tax your patience by attempting to assess the striking differences that the pope's action has ushered into Catholic life, as contrasted with that of less than a decade ago. They are as sharply limned in your consciousness as they are in mine, for they have intimately touched each one of us in a number of ways—to name only two particulars, in our daily worship and in our relationship to those who are not of our religious faith. That they have inspired a marvelous awakening in men's souls that has already been productive of much good, every Catholic attuned to the religious needs of this second half of the twentieth century recognizes and warmly welcomes. Yet the interpretation at times put on these new ideas and practices, and the innovations with which a small minority have on occasion accompanied them, have sounded certain disquieting notes that could, if widely adopted, do grave damage to the ideals envisioned by the late Holy Father when, in his own colorful phrase, he "opened the windows" to launch the Church's *aggiornamento*. Since this essay marks the jubilee of a major seminary, it would seem fitting to confine what I have in mind to several points that may have special relevance for priests and seminarians, points that can, I believe, be covered under two headings: first, the necessity of retaining respect for authority in the Church as we move forward in this era of change; secondly, the parallel need of holding fast to a sense of history if we are to escape the consequences of mere change for change's sake, or what I would call—if the term be allowed—the curse of "presentism."

No priest or seminarian acquainted with the history of the Church is a stranger to the fact that ecclesiastical au-

---

[14] *The Encyclicals and Other Messages of John XXIII* (Washington: TPS Press, 1964), p. 23.

thority has at times been abused by those to whom it has
been entrusted, nor is he unaware that on occasion bishops
and superiors of religious communities—to say nothing of
popes and cardinals—have made a pretense of governing by
reason and by rule, whereas authority in their hands has more
frequently been a weapon by which they have arbitrarily
threatened and intimidated in order to win their own way.
Moreover, the prevalence of democracy and personal liberty
that today pervade so much of the thinking of the free world
lends a special pertinence to Saint Peter's exhortation to his
fellow presbyters concerning their rule over the people of
God, a rule which they should aim to execute, he said, by
"governing not by constraint, . . . nor yet as lording it over
your charges, but becoming from the heart a pattern to the
flock."[15] But the misuse of a moral power that is good in
itself lends no warrant to deny the validity of that power,
or to act as though one denied it, to flaunt it, or to forget
that the ultimate integrity of both ecclesiastical and civil
society depends on a hierarchy of persons as well as a hierarchy of values and ideas, if order in both Church and State
is not to degenerate into anarchy.

Perhaps I can best illustrate what I mean in the words of
two internationally famous French Jesuits, both of whom
have had more acute personal experience with ecclesiastical
authority than most priests of our day, just as both have
given more serious consideration than most of us to delineating the role of authority in the mystical body of Christ. In
his wonderful book, *The Splendor of the Church*, Father
Henri de Lubac is fond of describing the apostolic Catholic,
be he priest or layman, as the "man of the Church." Speaking
of the mission of this "man of the Church," he says that
while obedience can never oblige him to do anything evil,
it can cause him to interrupt or to omit the good that he is

---

[15] 1 *Peter* 5:2-4.

doing or wishes to do. This the "man of the Church" knows in advance, says de Lubac, and he knows it with what is termed "a conviction of faith which nothing can shake." The learned author then continues:

> Even if this truth is in certain cases a hard one, it is, as far as he is concerned, first and foremost a 'wonderful truth.' Certainly, as long as the order is not final he will not abandon the responsibilities with which he has been invested by his office or circumstances. He will, if it should be necessary, do all that he can to enlighten authority; that is something which is not merely a right but also a duty; the discharge of which will sometimes oblige him to heroism. But the last word does not rest with him. The Church, which is his home, is a 'house of obedience.'[16]

Here, surely, is no benighted discouragement to the priest and the seminarian from speaking his mind candidly to his superiors, nor does Father de Lubac suggest that they should refrain from criticism and from the thought of changing the established order of things in the Church. But by the same token, here, too, is the saving principle that provides ecclesiastical society with its ultimate safeguard, namely, that while the "man of the Church" may, indeed, voice his critical judgments, and that to the point where at times it may constitute a painful and heroic duty, "the last word does not rest with him," since the Church that is his home is, as de Lubac expressed it, a "house of obedience."

Still more widely known than Father de Lubac was his late confrère, Pierre Teilhard de Chardin, whose name has become synonymous with the most advanced thought in both scientific and religious circles. In fact, it is hardly an exaggeration to say that this man's scholarly achievements probably accomplished more to repair the injury done to the image of the Church in the minds of the world's sci-

---

16 Henri de Lubac, S.J., *The Splendor of the Church*. (New York: Sheed and Ward, 1956), pp. 194-195.

entists by the Galileo case and similar disasters, than any single Catholic of the present century. Upon the eve of Father Teilhard de Chardin's departure from South Africa in October, 1951, after several months of scientific investigation, he wrote a letter to the late General of the Society of Jesus, Johannes Janssens, in order to let him know, as he put it, "what I am thinking and where I stand." He went into considerable detail about his theories of the universe and his personal religious views, and he then closed with a paragraph that read as follows:

> It is on this important point of formal loyalty and obedience that I am particularly anxious—it is in fact my real reason for writing this letter—to assure you that, in spite of any apparent evidence to the contrary, I am resolved to remain a "child of obedience."[17]

And as such, we may add, did he remain until death took him in New York three and a half years later.

If so eminent a scientist and so distinguished a priest as Teilhard de Chardin felt it not personally demeaning to bear such striking witness to the worth of humility and to a steadfast dedication to an ideal to which he had pledged himself in his youth, is there not here something of value for you and me, true disciples of the *aggiornamento* as we hope that we are? And might not the lesson be stated something along these lines: that at a time when a few of the Church's more restive sons would seem to have become a trifle intoxicated with the heady wine of the new-found freedom within her fold, to the point of almost suggesting that they are calling in question authority itself, that at such a time you and I might well post a guard over what we think, and say, and do? The posting of this guard, so to speak, may thus prevent us from lending support to a heedless attitude

---

[17] Teilhard de Chardin to Janssens, Cape Town, October 12, 1951, Bernard Wall (Ed.), *Pierre Teilhard de Chardin, Letters from a Traveller.* (New York: Harper and Row, 1962), p. 43.

toward the indispensable and sacred character of authority in human affairs, and likewise prevent us, perhaps, from unwittingly helping to hasten the return of a time about which Saint Paul warned Saint Timothy nineteen centuries ago when he said, "they will not endure the sound doctrine . . . "and will turn away their hearing from the truth and turn aside rather to fables."[18]

Were one to seek a recent example of the extremes to which a cold irreverence or defiance of legitimate authority can lead, he need not look beyond the Berkeley campus of the University of California. As the Dean of the Pacific School of Religion stated in writing of the student riots, "At the heart of all this confusion lies the value vacuum . . ., the total lack of any moral authority anywhere." And he went on to say: "Surely this means that students enjoy the rights to which they are entitled, as they accept the legal penalties which they have earned. It must also mean . . . a fresh establishment of the moral authority which alone can undergird any other authority . . ."[19]

It need hardly be said that I am far from suggesting that any individual priest or seminarian, or any group of such, has been guilty of the excesses perpetrated by the brash student minority on the Berkeley campus, even if one seminary chapel was the scene of a novelty called a "pray-in" to hasten the faculty's commitment to the *aggiornamento* of Pope John! What I am trying to convey is rather that the concept of authority is a delicate one, that ideas in general are subtle things, and that the human spirit is capable of startling reactions to influences that play upon it. I am reminded here of a famous passage in Taine where he drew a picture of how the French upper classes of the late eighteenth century played with the ideas of the Enlightenment as

---

[18] 2 *Timothy* 4:3-4.
[19] Robert E. Fitch, "Extremism in the Defense of . . . ," *The Christian Century LXXXII* (January 6, 1965), 15.

they would with a toy, little realizing the effect these same
ideas were to have when they reached the level of those
beneath them in social station. "On the upper story of the
house," said Taine,

> ideas, in rooms beautifully gilded, have served merely as an
> evening illumination, as parlor fire-crackers and pretty Bengal
> lights; the company have had their fun with them and then,
> with a laugh, have thrown them from the windows. Gathered
> up on the ground floor, borne off into shops, storehouses and
> counting-rooms, they have found in these plenty of com-
> bustible material, heaps of dry wood that have gradually
> accumulated, and here the flame kindles and spreads.[20]

In our participation in the dialogue of our time—and
participate we certainly should, whether that be with those
outside or within the Church—it may prove helpful to re-
mind ourselves now and then that to each of us God has
given what Newman once called "a certain power of influencing others . . . a certain circle of persons, larger or
smaller, who depend on us, whom our words and our actions
affect for good or for evil. . . ."[21] And the simple remem-
brance of that sobering fact should be sufficient to restrain
us from ever betraying our trust by, as it were, lightheartedly
tossing ideas out of the windows of our minds before their
merit has been weighed in the balance of good sense and
sound judgment.

A further assistance in our fulfillment of that obligation
will I believe, be gained from what I should like to call
one's fidelity to a sense of history. Some years ago Barbara
Ward stated, "Nothing is more dangerous to the survival of
a free Western society than the increasing neglect of history

---

[20] Hippolyte Adolphe Taine, *The Ancient Regime*. Tr. John Durand, new
rev. ed. (New York: Henry Holt and Company, 1896), p. 327.
[21] *Faith and Prejudice and Other Unpublished Sermons of Cardinal Newman*. Edited by the Birmingham Oratory. (New York: Sheed and Ward,
1956), p. 101.

in our teaching and our interests." She went on to explain that loss of interest in history is as fatal to society as loss of memory is to the individual man. And what she remarked in relation to civil society can, I think you will agree, be applied *mutatis mutandis* with equal force to the ecclesiastical society in which you and I dwell, for is it not as true in the Church as it is in the State that, as this gifted lady declared:

> The record of the struggles and hopes and faiths and fears that have created our free society is as much a part of us as the experiences and beliefs and trials by which adult man reaches maturity of character and judgment.[22]

That being the case, is it not evidence of the loss of a sense of the Church's historic doctrines—to use no harsher word—when a recently ordained priest is heard to voice his disapproval of an especially artistic tabernacle on the altar of a city church, because objects of this kind lend encouragement to what he styles the "blessed Sacrament cult"? Is there not a pathetic blackout—again to employ no more severe term—concerning the record of heavenly favors gained through well-nigh seven centuries, when a priest ordained less than four years greets the suggestion of a fellow priest that they recite the rosary with the retort, "No thanks. I consider that a repetitious and childish devotion"? Has not a priest or seminarian who would refer to the holy Sacrifice in the traditional Latin tongue of the western Church as the "mumbo-jumbo of the Mass" at least given cause for bewilderment and confusion to the faithful, to say nothing of his apparent ignorance of the hostile overtones of an expression used so frequently by enemies of Catholicism? Is it too much to say that these men have been victimized by the vogue of "change for change's sake," and that the curse of "present-

---

22 "The Battleground is Here," *New York Times Magazine* (January 27, 1952), p. 7.

ism," of which I previously spoke, has laid its hold upon them?"

I should regret it, however, if what I have said in criticism of disrespect for authority and misguided zeal were to be misinterpreted as a suggestion that we should turn our backs on the gains made since October, 1962, in what the then Abbot of Downside called "this almost miraculous Council."[23] Nor do I mean to imply that the examples cited and similar abberations are typical. Thanks be to God, they are exceptions to the rule. Moreover, it should be noted that they can be matched by comparable abuses on the part of some who—with less excuse because they are generally older and generally occupy positions of greater authority in the Church —show a lack of respect for authority by denigrating, for example, the council's decisions in matters liturgical or in the field of ecumenism, or who belittle or obstruct the admirably zealous efforts of younger priests to implement not only the letter but the spirit of these decisions. In other words, disrespect for authority is not synonymous with a youthful spirit of rebellion or a misguided hankering for change in pastoral practices.

On the contrary, not only should we cherish the *aggiornamento's* achievements to date, but each one of us, of whatever rank or station, be he bishop, priest, or seminarian, should regard it as a sacred duty insofar as we are able, to hold high the hands of the conciliar fathers by our prayers and petitions that their labors may be crowned by ultimate success in the vital questions on which they legislated.

---

[23] Basil Christopher Butler, O.S.B., "Divine Revelation," *The Tablet* *CCXVIII* (October 10, 1964), 1135.

5.

The Seminary Today

"There is an appointed time for everything . . ." said the author of *Ecclesiastes*, "a time to be silent, and a time to speak."[1] When one considers the handicaps that confront a writer who attempts at this juncture to say something constructive and helpful about the present seminary and its prospects for the future, he might well feel that it was 'a time to be silent.' Scarcely a seminary in the Catholic world has not already experienced, or is not now experiencing, a prevading spirit of uneasiness as it sets about the inauguration of a series of changes, as yet not fully tested, with a view to adapting the training of the Church's future priests to the age that dawned with Vatican Council II. In some instances so grave a situation has been created by this uneasiness and unrest as to call in question the ability of the institution to function in a normal way. Thus on the eve of the new academic year in the autumn of 1966 the threat of student rebellion against the old order was serious enough to cause the Archbishop of Barcelona in Spain and the Archbishop of Mariana in Brazil to announce that their seminaries would remain closed until such time as the problems posed by the threatened student revolts could be resolved.

And if the state of flux in which most seminaries now find themselves was not sufficient to deter a writer, the fact that

---

[1] *Ecclesiastes*, 3: 1,8.

everything worthwhile on the subject would seem to have
been said, should give him pause. For no institution in the
Church in recent years has been the subject of a more search-
ing scrutiny and more widespread criticism than the seminaries, with the result that a writer finds himself at his wits'
end when he tries to say anything even moderately fresh
and original. And if the same writer should resort to drawing a blueprint of what the character and shape of the
seminary of the future may be, he will quite rightly lose the
best of his reading audience, for they will be fully aware that
he has taken leave of the real world and entered a make-
believe universe where, if he is honest with himself and with
his readers, he will admit that his views have no claim to the
validity that might invite the respect of serious readers.

What, then, is a writer to do who has been asked to prepare an essay that will view the seminary in the light of
Vatican Council II, both as it appears today and as he thinks
it may appear some years hence? His choice is a narrow one
that would seem to be restricted along the following lines.
First, since he has only a limited space he must presume a
reasonable acquaintance with the numerous and complicated
problems that have made the 1960's a time of ferment for
most seminaries; he will take it for granted, therefore, that
the reader will neither need nor expect a detailed explanation of the causes of this unrest. Secondly, he may well seek
out the most recent authoritative directive for bringing the
seminary into the main stream of the Church's *aggiornamento*, and in that regard he will be well served in the *Decree
on Priestly Formation* promulgated by the Vatican Council
on October 28, 1965.[2] Thirdly, with this conciliar decree as
his principal guideline he can emphasize what, in his judgment, are its main points, and make such comment thereon
as he may consider of value. In brief, that is what the present

---

[2] Walter M. Abbott, S.J., and Joseph Gallagher (Eds.), *The Documents
of Vatican II* (New York: Guild Press. 1966), pp. 437-461.

essay attempts to do, the writer being fully conscious of the pitfalls that it entails; all things considered, however, he does not know a better method of procedure for the task in hand.

Vatican II and The Seminary

The Catholic Church is now passing through the most profound revolution she has known since the Protestant Revolt. Over the years there had accumulated a set of circumstances throughout the Church in general, and in seminaries in particular, that gave rise to a deep discontent, and it was Vatican Council II that afforded an outlet for the open expression of this widespread desire for alteration of the old order of things. Obviously, the radical changes that have come about since the Council's opening in October, 1962, could not have taken place had not a large majority of bishops, priests, religious, and laity lent them strong support. Confining the present discussion solely to the seminary, the general failure of these institutions to keep an open mind about the desirability of adaptation to the demands of a new age, contributed largely to the seminary becoming fossilized, so to speak, while the march of life passed it by. This static quality in the seminary system had taken its rise from a variety of causes. With no thought of their order of importance, the following may be said to have played a major part in the seminary's confinement and aloofness from a world in which its graduates were expected to exercise their ministry.

First, the siege mentality that overtook the entire Church in the wake of the Protestant Revolt was nowhere more evident than in the training centers for the clergy. From having had no seminaries in the strict sense before the late sixteenth century, the decrees enacted at the Council of Trent in July, 1563, ultimately became the warrant for a system that was centrally administered from Rome and that left slight margin for creative thought or adaptation. Adding to the unreality of the situation was the fact that the original legislation itself had dealt largely with methods of seminary administration—approximately three out of four printed pages—and had said relatively little about the spiritual and intellectual standards that should govern these houses of priestly formation.[3] That being true, it is more understandable why the chief architects of the system as it evolved from the early seventeenth century should have broken with the prescriptions of Trent, just as it is understandable how the concept of the Tridentine seminary, based in good measure on a myth, should have made its own contribution to the checkered history of these institutions. Moreover, the fixity of what were regarded as the postulates of Trent were periodically reaffirmed in one particular or another by the Congregation of Seminaries and Universities which stood guard to protect the system against alteration. It was a different type of mentality from that of Archbishop Gabriel Garrone, Pro-Prefect of the Congregation of Seminaries and Universities, who in an address at Assisi on August 26, 1966, called for a priestly formation that would be "pastoral and dynamic" and which could be best brought about through an "habitual dialog" between the bishops and seminary authorities.[4]

Aligned against the forces opposed to seminary reform, however, were other factors actively at work for the change dictated by the vastly different society into which men enter today upon ordination, in contrast to that of their predecessors of the first half of this century. In the sequel of this conflict of opinions the proponents of change gradually overtook the defenders of the 'static' seminary, and even be-

---

[3] H[enry] J. Schroeder, O.P. (Trans. and Ed.), *Canons and Decrees of the Council of Trent, Original Text with English Translation* (Saint Louis: B. Herder Book Company. 1941), pp. 175-179.

[4] *Delmarva Dialog* (Wilmington), September 2, 1966, p. 2.

fore the recent ecumenical council certain seminaries had begun the laborious and painful ascent toward the new age that was dawning for the Church. To name only one—and there have been others—Saint Meinrad Seminary in Indiana underwent in 1960 a thorough self-scrutiny as a preliminary step to inspection by the North Central Association of Colleges and Secondary Schools. The goal of accreditation was achieved in March, 1961, and in the process some distinct improvements were introduced, for example, elimination of an absurd situation that had previously compelled first-year theologians to attend twenty-one hours of class a week—not counting chant and education—spread over seven courses requiring seven separate examinations. By a skillful telescoping of related disciplines, such as church history and patrology, class hours were reduced to fifteen for the week and distributed through three basic courses.[5]

Necessity for Intellectual Competence

Moreover, it has not been just the number of class hours and the quantity of material for which seminarians have been held responsible that have been undergoing close analysis. The quality and content of theological instruction have likewise been rethought in some of the leading institutions. Aware that Catholic theology had become isolated from the real world, as was evident from the fact that it was largely ignored, and that theologians were asking themselves

---

[5] Adrian Fuerst, O.S.B., and Polycarp Sherwood, O.S.B., "Academic Renewal in a School of Theology," *American Ecclesiastical Review*, CLI (November, 1964), 293-294. The Benedictine scholastics and candidates for the diocesan priesthood at Saint Meinrad have recently been joined by the scholastics of the Middle West province of the Passionists and the candidates for the Glenmary Home Missioners, as well as by students for the first time from the Archdiocese of Atlanta and the Dioceses of Joilet and Pittsburgh which brought the enrollment in September, 1966, up forty percent from 121 to 166 students. Adrian Fuerst, O.S.B., to the writer, Saint Meinrad, September 19, 1966.

questions that had long since lost any relevance for our time, a growing number have of late been casting about for a seminary theology that would have, in the words of one theologian, "a much more strongly pronounced kerygmatic flavour," in that it would be more directly tied in with preaching and catechetical instruction. No one who has given serious thought to these matters would gainsay this writer when he declared that seminary theology has hitherto been "cluttered up with many questions that the seminarists will never have occasion to think of again, while other matters of great pastoral importance are comparatively neglected."[6] In that connection those who are trying to breathe new life into the theological curriculum were furnished with a *gratia adjuvans* in the Vatican Council's emphasis on the scriptural and historical approach to theology. In the judgment of one of the council's non-Catholic observers, Warren A. Quanbeck, professor of systematic theology in the Lutheran Theological Seminary of Saint Paul, this is a point of special importance since, as he says:

> The Council's will to relate to the contemporary world will be set forward more by taking this seriously than by anything else which could be mentioned.[7]

The conciliar *Decree on Priestly Formation*, as has been said, will afford those interested in the seminary of today a helpful guideline. That is indeed, true, but it is important to note the remark of Alexander Carter, Bishop of Sault Sainte Marie, in his introduction to this decree to the effect that while the document furnishes counsel, directives, and suggestions, those directly involved like bishops, seminary administrators, and faculty, but "most of all the seminarians

---

[6] Charles Davis, "Theology in Seminary Confinement," *Downside Review*, LXXXI (October, 1963), 316.
[7] Abbott-Gallager, *op. cit.*, p. 460.

themselves," must, nonetheless, as he said, "use their ingenuity and will and must respond to the grace of Christ to work out the solution."[8] In other words, the Council's decree can only point the way; it cannot conduct the seminary's administrators, professors, and students over the road to renewal. And here, it seems to me, is one of the initial tests of the seminarian today, one of the prime challenges to his maturing process, namely, to know and to make his own this conciliar document. But more important still, the seminiarian must manfully accept Bishop Carter's counsel when he says that he, the seminarian, is the captain of his own ship, and that it is he, and he alone, with the grace of God, who can pilot that ship safely into the port of an effective ministry. From the very nature of the document, and by reason of the many hands from which it sprang and the myriad minds to which it is addressed, it has necessarily dealt in the main with broad propositions and abstract principles.

Yet the decree of Vatican Council II is by no means confined to glittering generalities as can be seen, for example, in what is said about the selection of members of the seminary faculty. In that regard it stated:

> Since the training of seminarians hinges, to a very large extent, on wise regulations and on suitable teachers, seminary directors and professors should be chosen from among the best, and be painstakingly prepared by solid doctrine, appropriate pastoral experience, and special spiritual and pedagogical training,[9]

and the Council reinforced this point by reference to Pius XI's encyclical, *Ad Catholici sacerdotii*, of December 30, 1935, in which the pontiff exhorted the bishops to be particularly vigilant in the choice of professors for their semin-

---

[8] *Ibid.*, p. 436.
[9] *Ibid.*, pp. 442-443.

aries. They should, of course, be priests "endowed with the greatest virtue," to which the pope then added:

> and do not hesitate to remove them from duties which, though in appearance of much greater import, can in no way be compared with this foremost duty, whose elements are supplied by nothing else.[10]

Anyone who is acquainted with the casual and at times haphazard manner in which professors are chosen for seminary faculties, or the length of time through which those who have proven that they have neither the qualities of mind nor of heart for the task, are permitted to inflict the consequences of their ineptitude and mediocrity on generations of seminarians, can easily envision what Pius XI and the fathers of Vatican Council II may have had in mind. Had the bishops of the world and their seminary rectors scrupulously followed the papal directive of 1935, instead of being in all too many cases parties to its quiet burial, it would have assisted tremendously in absorbing many of the seminaries' problems. For the decisions of an alert bishop and of a highly perceptive seminary rector in weighing with the utmost care the choice of those who were appointed to teach, would have headed off many a storm and anticipated many a trouble spot before it was allowed to cause serious damage to students' intellectual life and morale. Superior instruction in the classroom will normally induce a quick and warm response from seminarians, and lead them on to a genuine love of learning that will preoccupy them and profitably fill otherwise empty and aimless hours. And when perceptive administration and stimulating instruction are crowned, so to speak, by prudent and enlightened spiritual counsel and direction, many of the seminarian's difficulties

---

[10] *The Catholic Priesthood, Encyclical Letter (Ad Catholici Sacerdotii) of His Holiness, Pope Pius XI* (Washington: National Catholic Welfare Conference. 1936), p. 43.

will have been met and satisfactorily resolved before they can become deep-seated personal crises which all too frequently bring on the doubt and discouragement that, in turn, beget the dropout and thus cause the Church to sustain another casualty to her ministry.

Lest the foregoing strictures should give rise to misunderstanding, it should be said that they are in no sense meant as a generalization, for that would be grossly unfair to the numerous enlightened and dedicated seminary professors whom almost every priest and seminarian recalls with a genuine sense of gratitude. But it does mean that altogether too many priests have been entrusted with this sacred duty who clearly had no qualifications either by intelligence, temperament, or training for the work; and that they left an indelible mark on the lives of countless priests who were compelled to pass agonizing hours in their classrooms, is a melancholy fact to which again almost every priest will bear witness. In the relatively small community of most seminaries, it is by no means difficult to arrive at a consensus about a man's teaching ability, and when that consensus points unmistakably to defective, dull, and indifferent instruction, he should be removed and assigned to another type of work. By the same token the principle enunciated by Pius XI and Vatican Council II is violated when a priest of superior talent and professional training who enjoys his work and whose students are virtually unanimous in their enthusiasm about his classes, is taken from the seminary on the whim of a bishop who may think it a 'promotion' to name him pastor of a neighboring church. The history of American Catholic seminaries reveals the presence of a considerable number of genuinely superior administrators and professors, even if few can ever hope to achieve the enviable record of a John B. Hogan, S.S., first Rector of Saint John's Seminary, Brighton, of whom Austin Dowling, one of his former students who was destined to become Archbishop of Saint

Paul, stated shortly after Hogan's death in September, 1901:

> He was forever whetting the appetite for knowledge, chal-
> lenging the impatient, prodding the slow. His method was the
> same, whether we met him in class or on the walk or in his
> room. It was his business to set us thinking—an occupation
> which he would never admit was highly superfluous in the
> life of a priest. Often he would seem to go to the very limit
> of daring in the vigor with which he plied us with objections,
> annihilated all our arguments and then walked off without
> vouchsafing an answer to our difficulties.
>
> But, sure of his own faith, he had no fear of ours, while
> he did fear the vicious effect of the smug satisfaction which
> a boy may feel—and never afterwards lose—in dealing filp-
> pantly with the grave problem of thought. . . .
>
> No doubt, at times, this fine temper of his mind left him
> open to misunderstanding and exposed him to the suspicion of
> being a 'liberal,' and liberal he was if by liberty we mean
> freedom from narrowness and pettiness and the fussiness of
> those who are always in terror lest the Bark of St. Peter shall
> founder. He had no such terror, nor did he think that truth
> had anything to fear from investigation. It was, perhaps, his
> childlike faith so serene, so secure, so full of charity that made
> him so absolutely fearless of error that he always met it, not
> with strategy, but in faith and open fight.
>
> Not his least attractive feature was his characteristically
> youthful mind. It never aged. His experience widened; his
> knowledge increased; his powers were developed, but he still
> confronted the field of science with the frank curiosity of a
> child. His mind, like his heart, was always wide open. . . .[11]

The Abbé Hogan, as he was familiarly called, was the
kind of man who would have given enthusiastic support to
the Vatican Council's proposition that

> the very manner of teaching should inspire in students a love
> of seeking, honoring, and defending the truth vigorously, along

---

[11] *A Garland of Affectionate Tributes to the Memory of the Very Rev.
John Baptist Hogan, D.D., S. S.* (Boston: Alumni Saint John's Seminary. 1906), pp. 32-35.

with an honest recognition of the limitations of human understanding.[12]

In the same manner he would have been cheered by the conciliar directive that "excessive multiplying of subjects and classes is to be avoided,"[13] as he would have delighted in seeing the Catholic seminaries of his country improve their academic status by seeking the approval of the secular accrediting agencies. Moreover, Hogan possessed the magnanimity and the sense of the Universal Church that are required if Catholic theological education is to be strengthened by collaboration like that inaugurated recently at Saint Meinrad where Passionist professors and students, as well as candidates for the Glenmary Home Missioners, mingle daily with the Benedictine monks and clerics of the archabbey. This type of collaboration was also urged over thirty years ago by Pius XI wherever resources were not sufficient to enable a single diocese or religious community to impart a superior theological training. As the pontiff said:

> We have never let pass an opportunity to favour and encourage and foster such efforts. Often, in fact, We have suggested and recommended them. . . .[14]

COORDINATION IN SEMINARY EDUCATION

As was true in the choice of professors for the seminary, so also in the proliferation of small and weak seminaries, had Pius XI's suggestions of 1933 received in the United States the consideration they merited, American Catholics in 1966 would have been spared the burden of supporting 607 seminaries—diocesan and religious, major and minor—thirty-six more than were recorded for 1964, although in the intervening two years the overall enrollment had dropped by more

---

12 Abbott-Gallagher, *op. cit.*, pp. 450-451.
13 *Ibid.*, p. 453.
14 *The Catholic Priesthood*, pp. 44-45.

than 700 students.[15] Nor is it easy to see how it can be
reckoned as anything but a loss to Catholic scholarship when
extraordinary opportunities for widening the intellectual
horizons of both theology professors and students are either
neglected by the group in question or forbidden by higher
ecclesiastical authority. There come to mind in that connection two recent examples when Saint Michael's College
became affiliated with the four non-Catholic institutions
that make up the Toronto Graduate School of Theological
Studies on the campus of the University of Toronto, and the
partnership entered into by Saint Patrick's Seminary, Menlo
Park, the Jesuits of Alma College, and the Dominican friars
with the six Protestant institutions represented in the Graduate Theological Union near the campus of the University of
California at Berkeley. If Catholic theological education is
ever to achieve here the standard warranted by the Church's
numerical and financial strength, there will have to be many
more combined efforts along the lines now being pursued in
The Netherlands. There present plans envision, besides the
experimental seminary at Rothem, only three major seminaries for the nation's seven dioceses, as well as for the students of nine religious orders and nine missionary congregations.[16] Fortunately, a more realistic attitude about all these
matters would seem to be gaining ground of late in seminary
circles, for the time has not passed when clerical smugness—
not infrequently sparked by a touch of arrogance—can carry
the day. Thus the views of a majority of today's priests and

---

[15] *Official Catholic Directory Anno Domini 1966* (New York: P. J. Kenedy
& Sons. 1966), General Summary, p. 1. The proliferation of seminaries
has been a widespread abuse in the Church. For example, in England
between 1873 and 1891 there were seven diocesan seminaries established
of which only two survived, namely, Saint John's, Wonersh, and Saint
Joseph's Upholland. David Milburn, *A History of Ushaw College* (Durham: Ushaw Bookshop. 1964), pp. 263-264.
[16] *The Tablet* (London), CCXX (July 16, 1966), 823; (August 13, 1966),
928.

seminarians would find nothing in common with those of a
writer in a Catholic journal a century ago who stated:

> Heavier and more extensive studies are required for the Priest-
> hood than for any other profession in this country, and as a
> body, the Catholic Clergy are undoubtedly the most learned
> class in their sphere to be found in the country.[17]

THE LIBRARY: A RESOURCE CENTER

Needless to say, one of the best indications of the seminary's changing concept toward the entire learning process
is the increased emphasis—and budgetary allowance—now
directed toward the library. It is still, of course, the exception when one finds a separate library building on a seminary
campus with trained librarians in charge, as has been the
case—to name only two—at Saint John's Seminary in Brighton
and Saint Thomas Seminary in Denver. It takes no special
brand of wisdom to perceive that the library is the heart of
any educational institution, and it is heartening to observe,
therefore, that the shameful neglect of the library that was
characteristic of so many seminaries until a very recent date,
is now gradually being remedied. The seminary library's
very openness and accessibility is a relatively recent phenomenon, for there were all too many of these institutions
where the students' use of books was not encouraged, even
if they did not go as far as a sign read by Sir Francis Head
in 1852 on a visit to Saint Patrick's College, Maynooth, which
said: "Whoever takes a book out of this Library incurs ex-
communication *ipso facto!*"[18] In that connection Professor
Quanbeck's remarks in his response to the conciliar *Decree*

---

[17] "Clerical Seminaries," *The Monthly*, I (June, 1965), 411. The author
of the article in this single issue of the journal of the University of Saint
Mary of the Lake, Chicago, was unnamed.
[18] Denis Meehan, *Window on Maynooth* (Dublin: Clonmore and Reynolds. 1949), p. 123.

on Priestly Formation could be pondered with profit by both bishops and seminary officials. He said:

> Virtually nothing is said about a most important tool of theological education, the library. If the Council's impulse for the renewal of the Church is to be realized, students must certainly have access not only to their own heritage but also to the theological interpretations of other traditions and even to the questions raised by earnest men who belong to no Church. It is rumored that not all bishops are poignantly aware of the importance of libraries, so some specifics on this topic could be helpful.[19]

MOVING TO THE UNIVERSITY CAMPUS

Catholic churchmen in this age know better than to advance an opinion such as that held by the Chicago writer of 1865, as they likewise recognize the incongruity of the sign in the Maynooth library back in 1852. The improved attitude is seen in the welcome that the more thoughtful among them have accorded to changes in the seminary system, such as enabling students during their preparatory training for theology to major in subjects other than philosophy. The same is true for what shows signs of becoming a seminary trend toward university centers as, for example, the Bellarmine School of Theology which moved from its rural site in Indiana to North Aurora, Illinois, within relatively easy reach of Loyola University in Chicago. For the same reason relocation is contemplated for Saint Mary's College, Kansas, to be near Saint Louis University and for Alma College, Los Gatos, California, the urban site of which has yet to be fully determined. Action of this kind will help to overcome the

---

[19] Abbott-Gallagher, *op. cit.*, p. 460. Allan M. Cartter's widely discussed study, *An Assessment of Quality in Graduate Education* (Washington: American Council on Education. 1966), likewise speaks of the library as "the heart of the university," and in that connection it is said, "no other single nonhuman factor is as closely related to the quality of graduate education." (p. 114).

handicaps induced by isolating the seminary in remote areas, the unhappy effects of which were well summarized by the late E. Allison Peers. Speaking of the thorough secularization that had taken place in the Spanish universities in which at the time (1939) there was not a single faculty of theology, he remarked:

As an alumnus of a University which teaches theology who has spent nearly all his adult life in another which does not, I can testify how greatly the Spanish Universities suffer by this secularization. But the worst sufferer is the Church; for her future ministers, instead of joining freely, at the most impressionable age, in the life of a University, are relegated to seminaries, completely cut off from lay thought and lay ideals, neither themselves leavening the academic world nor receiving from it that influence without which the priest is apt to become narrow in his interests, in his outlook upon life and in his judgments of his fellows.[20]

Walter J. Burghardt, S.J., put the same idea in a positive framework in his call for a pilot program that would embrace several regions of the country with seminaries to be established on university campuses, "here a Catholic campus, there a secular campus," which led him to say:

Put the seminarian in contact with lay students in at least some of his classes. Let him see at first hand how lay people sacrifice for an education. Let him compete with them for marks, academic standing, scholarships. Let him come into personal contact with atheism and agnosticism and existentialism and positivism, with technology and science—even with women! Let him see that the life of the intellect is not simply

---

[20] *Spain, the Church and the Orders* (London: Eyre and Spottiswoode, 1939), p. 39. The story of how the Jesuits happened to locate their combined American scholasticate on a farm near Woodstock, Maryland —perhaps for the first time in a rural area in the 300 years of the Society —is told in brief by F. Gerard Drummond, S.J., "The Origins of Woodstock College: 1859-1869," *The Philosopher*, XI [Student publication of the College of Philosophy and Letters, Fordham University] (May, 1964), 101-106. The farm was purchased in January, 1866, and the college opened on September 23, 1869.

theory, that the world of ideas is terribly real, that ideas can and do move the world, but that, to move the world, his ideas must first move *him*.[21]

Arrangements of the kind suggested by Father Burghardt have for some years been in operation at a number of Catholic institutions like Borromeo Hall at Carroll College in Helena and a similar residential hall for ecclesiastical students at Saint Ambrose College in Davenport. But the idea should be implemented within the American Church on a far wider scale than it is at present, which raises the question if this is not a plan far better attuned to the needs and the mood of our time than the traditional minor seminary or the philosophy department of the major seminary.

The Spirit of Sacrifice

It is doubtful if there is now a seminary anywhere in the Catholic world that has not undergone in some fashion one or other of the changes mentioned regarding its program of studies, and, too, changes in its disciplinary code to carry out the new academic approach. Yet every conceivable improvement in the seminary's intellectual fare, as well as an accompanying liberalization of its discipline, will not in themselves resolve the crisis through which these institutions are passing. For that the first requisite must be a reasoned and intelligent assent and acceptance on the part of a seminarian of the sacrifice, yes, even the suffering, entailed in the life of a priest. Without this acceptance there is little hope of an enduring transformation of the old into the new and better order that every conscientious man is seeking. Put in another way, the seminarian must in a truly magnanimous spirit make his own the words quoted from Saint Augustine by the *Decree on Priestly Formation* to the effect that, "A man

---

[21] "The Intellectual Formation of the Future Priest," *National Catholic Educational Association Bulletin*, LXI (August, 1964), 67.

possesses the Holy Spirit to the measure of his love for Christ's Church."[22] And Christ's Church is made up of persons, of the seminary rector, the spiritual director, and the professors to whom a fundamental respect is owed and to whom obedience is offered when their commands are not clearly in conflict with the Church's welfare. Moreover, as the conciliar decree stated, Christ's Church is the poor, the ill, the sinful, and the unbelieving, either by enrollment or by desire and, therefore, the Church is not only the young, the attractive, the well-to-do, and the passing heroes and heroines of a current ideology. To serve any or all of these entails sacrifice of time, comfort, and personal pleasure; indeed, to serve them as Christian wisdom would on occasion dictate, entails suffering.

In the purely human and natural order, no one welcomes sacrifice or suffering. And in the present discipline of the Latin Church one source of that sacrifice and suffering can be the deprivation of the joy of conjugal love and the consequent loneliness that is often the lot of the seminarian and the priest. Or the suffering may take the form of the personal betrayal and hostility of his associates, a cross borne by the great French Dominican, Henri Jean-Baptiste Lacordaire, who in a note of July 22, 1846, stated:

> In proportion to my vocation in the Church, God has heaped upon me during almost twenty years an unbroken succession of painful trials. From my entrance to the seminary in 1824 up to my assignment to Paris in 1844, I have been the butt of a stubborn hostility on the part of a certain number of men capable of inflicting great damage, and who have neglected nothing in order to ruin my reputation and to drive me to extremes. Twenty years of patience, of kindness, and of perseverance have been needed to arrive at a little peace which will endure as long as it may please God.[23]

---

22 Abbott-Gallagher, *op. cit.*, p. 446.
23 Le Comte de Montalembert, *Le Père Lacordaire* (Paris: Charles Douniol. 1862), p. 170.

Hundreds of similar instances could be cited from the lives of able men who dedicated their efforts to furthering what they felt in conscience to be the Church's best interests. True, not all seminarians and priests are called upon to suffer as Lacordaire did, yet if a seminarian is to be honest and clear about his future, must he not ask himself the question: Is the maturity upon which my peers place so much stress possible without a measure of sacrifice and suffering? Are they not part of the maturing process of every human being? Do they not partake of what Adrian van Kaam had in mind in his oft-quoted phrase that "Life is a mystery to be lived, not a problem to be solved"?[24]

THE PAST: AN EXPERIENTIAL VALUE

The fathers of Vatican Council II spoke pointedly of the seminarian's need to develop during his student days the maximum of maturity which, they maintained, was attested by "a certain emotional stability, by an ability to make considered decisions, and by a right manner of passing judgment on events and people." Moreover, they advanced the formula for the seminarian's ultimate goal, that is, a successful execution of the priestly ministry *vis-à-vis* his fellowmen when they said he should grasp the importance of prizing those qualities on which men set high store in a minister of Christ, that is, "sincerity of heart, a constant concern for justice, fidelity to one's word, courtesy of manner, restraint, and kindliness of speech."[25] Attributes of that kind, to be sure, are only the external manifestations of something that lies hidden within the recesses of the seminarian's soul, and that is faith in Christ and in the mystery of His Person and His Church. Thus in addressing seminarians about the prime requisites in a priest, Bernard Cooke, S.J., stated:

---

[24] *Religion and Personality* (Englewood Cliffs, New Jersey: Prentice Hall Inc. 1964), p. 13.
[25] Abbott-Gallagher, *op. cit.*, p. 448.

If he is to function as a guide for his fellow Christians, he will have to possess a mature faith and powers of adult decision. Unless his own faith assent is a living acceptance of the mystery of Christ, unless it is a realistic and fearless personal commitment to Christian living, he will not have the psychological security necessary to deal honestly and openly with the problems posed for faith in the contemporary world.[26]

There is no certain road by which his elders may assure the seminarian that he can achieve success in his priesthood, but surely he will find one very helpful set of guidelines in the collective experience of those who have traversed the same road upon whch he has set out. As one might expect of so extraordinary a mind, Pierre Teilhard de Chardin had a deep respect for the past experience of mankind, and he never made the mistake, of which not a few seminarians have been guilty in recent years, of decrying the past as antiquated and unprofitable, or of acting as though it had never been. On the contrary, Teilhard de Chardin set a high premium on the past for the revealing light it shed on the present and the future. Yet he was no mere antiquarian cherishing the past simply for itself, for as he once told his brother Joseph, he had learned from historical research:

> that there is only one real road . . . it is to build the future. It's perfectly simple, but there are still so many people who behave as though the past were interesting in itself, and treat it as only the future deserves to be treated.[27]

Knowledge of and respect for the past help to balance a man's judgments and prevent him from falling victim to 'presentism,' or from becoming an alarmist about the grim happenings of his own time. Perhaps, too much seminary in-

---

[26] "Theological Education of Seminarians," *Chicago Studies,* V (Summer, 1966), 44-45.
[27] Letter written on board the *Cathay,* September 14, 1935, bound for Bombay, Bernard Wall (Ed.), *Letters from a Traveller* (New York: Harper & Brothers. 1962), p. 209.

struction has heretofore treated the past as though it were 'interesting in itself,' and this may have been a contributing cause to making so many of today's seminarians—reacting to this influence—seem to suffer from any excessive preoccupation with the new and a proneness to cast into the discard all that is old. In any case, this is a fatal error which every discerning mind will recognize, for as Yves Congar, O.P., has said:

> The faith did not begin with the present generation any more than the Church did. As we study the tide of ideas we have ridden on in the last twenty-five years, we notice, first and foremost, the break with the past and the novelty of the themes; we are struck by the discoveries or the rediscoveries. But the more we know and think, the better we see how closely successive eras are bound together and to what extent each young generation is borne by its elders, who, in turn, owe everything to those who preceded them. . . . We are always building on the foundations others have laid and reaping the fruits of what others have sown.[28]

Paul J. Hallinan, Archbishop of Atlanta, expressed the same idea with his customary acuteness when he remarked, "The higher man rides on the shoulders of the past, the more likelihood that his perspective of the present will be clear."[29]

No seminarian, therefore, who is at all *au courant* with the conflicting currents that are now swirling about the Bark of Peter, and who at the same time has some knowledge of what ungoverned conflict of opinion has in times past cost the Church, will question the wisdom of Pope Paul VI when he cautioned the students of the North American College on his visit to their summer villa on September 5, 1965. *Inter alia* he said:

---

[28] Preface to Louis Evely, *That Man Is You* (Westminster: Newman Press, 1964), pp. viii-ix.
[29] "The American Bishops and the Vatican Councils," *Catholic Historical Review*, LI (October, 1965), 380.

These are challenging and changing times. Old methods will have to be transformed but always in the light of past lessons. Sometimes new solutions are proposed but these are not always in keeping with Catholic teachings and principles.[30]

Like the majority of their fellow citizens, most American seminarians display a strong tendency to conform to what is believed to be the vogue of the moment, and this urge to conform has led some of them during the present decade into serious errors concerning the advisability of change in fundamental matters and in their general attitude toward ecclesiastical authority. Some have even gone to the point of questioning in a heedless manner both doctrine (Real Presence) and discipline (ecclesiastical celibacy), which though they do, indeed, admit of discussion, should be treated in a sober and responsible way. In fact, by their very conformity these seminarians have disappointed those who looked to them for the hallmark of true leadership and courage. Abraham Kaplan put his finger on this characteristic weakness of Americans and the high price it exacts when he said:

> The final cost of the code of conformity is the sacrifice of leadership. The role of the leader it assigns to the most successful follower, the man whose features can best reflect at every moment the changing face of the crowd. . . . Leadership requires the maintenance of a certain distance from the followers, enough to give scope for independent judgment and decisive action. But this in turn calls for courage and self-confidence, not the sheepish virtues of conformity to a pre-formed opinion. Such a man may not always be liked; he may even expect to make some enemies. But to be able to lead others a man must be willing to go forward alone.[31]

One is reminded here of the remark of John Ireland, Arch-

---

[30] *L'Osservatore Romano*, September 6, 1965, p. 1.
[31] *American Ethics and Public Policy* (New York: Oxford University Press. 1963), p. 70.

bishop of Saint Paul, "The timid move in crowds, the brave in single file."[32]

CHURCH MAGISTERIUM

One of the popular ideas now current in American seminaries is that it is 'camp' to fight shy of the past, and that one is warranted in becoming a trifle impatient when he is told that there are old ideas and practices that have an enduring validity. Yet reminders of this kind should on occasion be expressed, for as Cardinal Suhard stated in his memorable pastoral letter, *Priests Among Men,* "One of the priest's first services to the world is to tell it the truth."[33] Thus among the first services of the first of all Catholic priests, the Vicar of Christ, is to tell the rest of us the truth as he sees it from the vantage point of his unique observation post, that as Saint Paul remarked to the Ephesians centuries ago, "we may be now no longer children, tossed to and fro and carried about by every wind of doctrine. . . ."[34] Paul VI has been performing that service with mounting emphasis of late, for example, on October 1, 1966, in the warning he gave to nearly 1,400 theologians gathered in audience after their international congress at Rome. "To wander away from the magisterium in your investigations along personal arbitrary paths would," said the pontiff:

> easily expose you to the danger of being alone—teachers without faithful—and laboring in vain without producing vital fruits for the community. It might even expose you to the danger of deviating from the correct way, choosing your own judgment as preferable to the thinking of the Church as a criterion of truth. This would be arbitrary choice—the road toward heresy.[35]

---

[32] "The Mission of Catholics in America," *The Church and Modern Society. Lectures and Addresses* (Saint Paul: Pioneer Press. 1905), I, 90.

[33] (Notre Dame: Fides Publishers, Inc. 1960), p. 40.

[34] *Ephesians,* 4: 12-14.

[35] *The Monitor* (San Francisco), October 6, 1966, p. 9.

INDIVIDUAL RESPONSIBILITY

To pursue one's personal arbitrary paths can be as damaging for the seminarian as it can for the theologian, that is, to act otherwise than with the respect that is owed the past, or in a manner that would suggest that everything that is outdated, according to one's own judgment, should be cast aside. To proceed in this fashion in the face of the problems that now beset the seminary is *mutatis mutandis,* to invite the kind of disaster that has overtaken so many innocent people in China since the late summer of 1966 when the militant youths known as Red Guards were urged by Marshal Lin Piao to destroy, as it was said, four 'olds': old ideas, old culture, old customs, and old habits. In consequence of this campaign hundreds of persons were driven from their homes, religious houses were ransacked, and dozens of nuns were herded into exile from their schools and charitable enterprises—all by insensate youths fired by open contempt for China's past.[36] A similar though less costly exhibition of this absurd determination to uproot the old and to supplant it with the new, was staged by the 250 youths in attendance at the annual conference of the British Liberal Party at Brighton in late September, 1966, where in the words of a UPI dispatch, they "startled the other 950 delegates at the conference by presenting a political program the Kremlin would have warmly approved."[37]

Yet words of caution from a pope, a cardinal or a bishop should in no sense be interpreted by Catholics in general, and by seminarians in particular, as the herald of a return to the antiquated ideas and methods of a bygone era. Even if high churchmen wished to turn back the hands of the clock to the relatively quiet days of a quarter century ago—which the majority quite frankly do not—they would re-

---

[36] Los Angeles *Times,* September 1, 1966, Part I, pp. 21 and 23.
[37] *San Francisco Sunday Examiner and Chronicle,* October 2, 1966, Section II, p. 6.

semble nothing so much as Canute at the seashore striving
to prevent the waves from rolling in. The gains made by the
Church's *aggiornamento* are here to stay, painful as that
truth may be to certain members of the Roman Curia who
in the pre-conciliar period could trample with impunity on
the individual freedom of an author or the freedom of a
group, and deny fundamental rights to distant men without
so much as an explanation.

FREEDOM AND OBEDIENCE

The new dispensation was never more conspicuous than
in Vatican Council II's *Declaration on Religious Freedom*
which in time will probably be seen as having inaugurated
a new era in the history of the Catholic Church. Even now
with its principal premises resting firmly on the foundation
of official teaching, the ramifications have begun to extend
beyond the key questions of the freedom necessary for the
individual act of faith and the union or separation of Church
and State. American Catholics felt a justifiable pride in the
major role played by their countrymen in bringing about that
conciliar document, and they were equally proud when the
new freedom was splendidly championed once again by two
of their own in the International Congress on the Theology
of Vatican Council II summoned by Paul VI and held at
Rome between September 26 and October 1, 1966. On this
occasion the theology of freedom found eloquent voices in
John J. Wright, Bishop of Pittsburgh, and John Courtney
Murray, S.J., of Woodstock College. From what might be
called the font of the council's declaration the seminary like
every phase of the Church's life is destined to be nourished
and informed. True, it will require a delicate balance and a
prudent courage to implement what Bishop Wright in his
Roman address called "a freedom which is salutary because
it is obedient," while maintaining "an obedience which is

salutary because it is free."[38] But the Catholic seminaries of the United States might well be thought unworthy of their high calling were they compelled to confess their lack of sufficient intelligence and resourcefulness within their respective communities to warrant the hope that they too can profit directly, as the Bishop of Pittsburgh said, from the atmosphere foreshadowed in the council's declaration when, in treating the necessity of freedom for the act of faith, it added:

> In consequence, the principle of religious freedom makes no small contribution to the creation of an environment in which men can without hindrance be invited to Christian faith, and embrace it of their own free will, and profess it effectively in their whole manner of life.[39]

THE CREATION OF AN ENVIRONMENT

That the 'creation of an environment' of which the council fathers spoke as a consequence of the *Declaration on Religious Freedom,* may be extended during these post-conciliar days to all the Church's varied undertakings, would seem entirely reasonable. For as Father Murray, principal author of the declaration, said:

> The conciliar affirmation of the principle of freedom was narrowly limited—in the text. But the text itself was flung into a pool whose shores are wide as the universal Church. The ripples will run far.[40]

And that these 'ripples' have already run far can be illustrated by the clean break that some have been making with the traditional seminary system. The Seminary of Pope John XXIII, opened at Louvain in 1964 at the request of Cardinal Léon-Joseph Suenens, Archbishop of Malines-Brussels, and

---

[38] *The Monitor* (San Francisco), October 6, 1966, p. 9.
[39] Abbott-Gallagher, *op. cit.,* p. 690.
[40] *Ibid.,* p. 674.

presided over by a Belgian canon who holds a doctorate in
English from Yale University, is a case in point. Here philosophy students, formerly trained at the major seminary in
Malines, take their courses in the university city with its
obvious advantages. In neighboring Holland another experimental seminary called the Institut voor Europese Priester-
hulp, located in the little town of Rothem, receives students
from any country with a surplus of vocations and then later
sends them to less favored lands. Judged by the customary
seminary discipline, the Europa Seminar, as it is sometimes
called, is permeated by an atmosphere of freedom, one
American visitor observing that almost everyone "seemed to
be reading Camus and Sartre, Heidegger and Jaspers, and
wondering what American students thought about these
men."[41] Still other novel approaches to priestly training are
seen in the *freies jahr* or free year during which students
may leave certain German seminaries to attend a university
of their choice; the seminary at Pontigny in France where
professors and students spend time working in shops and
factories; the Archdiocese of Munich where Cardinal Julius
Doepfner, President of the National Conference of German
Bishops, has closed the theology department of his seminary
and sent the students to the Catholic Faculty of Theology
of the University of Munich; and the seminary of Mainz
whose rector, Josef Maria Reuss, auxiliary bishop of the
diocese, presides over an institution which has witnessed
numerous reforms, the spirit of which the rector conveyed
when he said:

> It would be a very poor system of education which would try
> to make candidates for the priesthood conform to a standard
> formula without taking into account their personality. One
> single norm is essential: disposition and behavior must con-
> form to Jesus Christ. The candidate himself can only approach

---

[41] Willard F. Jabusch, "New Seminaries in Europe," *The Commonweal*,
LXXXV (October 7, 1966), 18.

this norm by a slow growth on the lines of his own individuality, with his faults and shortcomings and with the help of God's grace.[42]

EXPERIMENTATION: A NECESSARY RISK

Needless to say, it does not follow that each and every one of these experiments will prove to have been successful; but at least they are a sign that there are seminaries in the Catholic world that are not afraid to risk change—and to risk making a mistake—and the bishops and seminary authorities who have inspired, approved, and executed these changes should be credited with the imagination and creativeness to sense that experimentation is demanded today, even if some of their innovations may later have to be modified or abandoned in the light of experience. The current mentality governing the more advanced seminaries was also exemplified by the five Catholic institutions that sought and gained associate membership in the formerly all-Protestant American Association of Theological Schools, something that would have been unthinkable a generation ago, as well as by Catholics' formal participation in the graduate theological unions in Toronto and Berkeley previously mentioned. In fact, so free and open is this new environment in relation to problems bearing on the seminary that a recognized sociologist, Joseph H. Fichter, S.J., suggested in September, 1966, to the National Conference of Diocesan Vocation Directors at Milwaukee that the Church should

---

[42] *Ibid.*, p. 21. One of the most recent experiments is that inaugurated by Bernhard Stein, Bishop of Trier, which has been summarized as follows: In their first year of major seminary life, students will live in the seminary and follow regular classes. In their second year, however, they will live in a local town and do part-time work in a parish. Third year studies will be made at an area university, while students in their fourth year will have the option of living either at the seminary or in town. [*Delmarva Dialog* (Wilmington), August 4, 1967, p. 10].

begin to give serious thought to ordaining married men and women as well.[43]

THE LESSON OF HISTORY

A conscientious effort is, then, being made in many seminaries to bring about an up-to-date curriculum that will take cognizance of the realities of a priest's life in the second half of the twentieth century, just as they have introduced changes in their disciplinary regulations. In all of this there has been much high purpose and good will, as there has been much doubt and uncertainty. For who can predict the final effect that these changes will have on the priesthood of the future, any more than one can foretell how the winds of doctrine and discipline may blow within the Church, to say nothing of the far more radical winds that are almost certain to rise out of the secular society in which she makes her home? Losses there have been, to be sure; they are occurring at the present moment, and they will continue to occur. For Vatican II is no exception to the ecumenical councils that preceded it where in virtually every instance heavy losses were sustained in the wake of new doctrines and new disciplinary rules introduced by these conciliar gatherings. Thus after the Council of Nicaea in 325, eighty bishops separated from the Church and, as Cardinal Manning said, "carried multitudes with them."[44] Following the Council of Ephesus in 431, thirty bishops and their flocks departed as disciples of Nestorius, and twenty years later the Council of Chalcedon witnessed the Monophysites break from obedience to Rome. All this is to say nothing of the countless lapses from the Roman Church that took place before, during, and after the Council of Trent in the sixteenth century. Compared to the casualties suffered after

---

[43] *Georgia Bulletin* (Atlanta), September 29, 1966, p. 7.
[44] *The True Story of the Vatican Council* 2nd ed. (London: Burns & Oates, Ltd., 1877), p. 204.

these councils, those incurred in the wake of Vatican Councils I and II have been trivial. The loss of even a single member of the visible Church, to be sure, is cause for sincere lament, but to date, inasfar as one can at this moment gauge the situation, relatively few have gone out as a consequence of the council held in 1962-1965.

Among the many lessons that history teaches is that the painful purging which accompanies periods of the kind through which the Church is now passing, are not infrequently the prelude to a 'second spring' when she emerges with fresh vigor and flourishes anew. Every informed seminarian and priest is aware of the rottenness of the ecclesiastical fabric of the late fifteenth and early sixteenth centuries, as he is aware of the vibrant Church that gradually grew out of the Catholic Reformation. The point may best be illustrated, perhaps, in France where the frightful thirty years of civil war over religion that ended in 1598 with the Edict of Nantes were the forerunner of the glorious revival of French Catholicism that marked the early seventeenth century. In the same way the decadent and sterile Catholicism into which France and the German states had again lapsed by the late eighteenth century needed the cleansing fires of the French Revolution and the secularization of the German ecclesiastical princedoms to give birth, in turn, to a movement that produced a Lacordaire and a Montalembert in France and a Möhler and a Görres in Germany.

The Church In The Secular City

As the Church goes, so goes the seminary. Thus the dropouts from the latter, the defections from the priesthood, and the losses among the laity are part of the price that the Church must pay for her presence in the age of the 'secular city' with all that this term has come to imply. And, indeed, it is an age that will in all likelihood exact an even heavier toll in Catholic ranks before there dawns a true renaissance of the spirit among the people of God who constitute His Church. Furthermore, in the Church of the secular city the relationship between the clergy and those whom they are trained and expected to serve has likewise undergone a sharp alteration. It were well, therefore, if every bishop, priest, and seminarian would from time to time meditate on that somber fact, for as a leading English Catholic layman has reminded us:

> The priesthood of tomorrow, like the episcopate of tomorrow, is likely to find itself sharing many of the experiences long painfully familiar to Protestant parsons and bishops, that they are listened to selectively, approved and commended by those who like what they say, and politely disregarded by those in the pews who withhold their assent on that point.[45]

THE REALITY OF OPTIMISM

It does not follow, however, that there is cause or need for despair or discouragement on the part of those now enrolled in the seminaries, for as Pope John said on that October morning of 1962 when he opened the twenty-first ecumenical council, "we must disagree with those prophets of gloom, who are always forecasting disaster, as though the end of the world were at hand."[46] Could those who were seminarians in past ages now return and speak to their successors of the 1960's as they surveyed the Church in her present setting, I wonder if they would not be likely to say, 'We have been here before.' In terms of the old French axiom, *'plus ca change', plus c'est la même chose!'* Few men of our time understood this profound truth better than the beloved John XXIII who often drew on his knowledge of the Church's history to point a lesson and to instill a serenity of mind in those made uneasy by the ferment about them as

---

45 Douglas Woodruff, "The Fathers Disperse and Reflect on Whence They Came," *The Tablet* (London), CCXIX (December 10, 1965), 1377.
46 Abbott-Gallagher, *op. cit.*, p. 712.

well as to moderate those who might be borne up by a false hope of what the future had in store for them. The old pontiff reflected this blend of wisdom and realism which the world found so attractive on April 6, 1961, when he received in audience a group of Italian seminarians. Certain words addressed to the young levites on that occasion may appropriately bring to a close this essay written in the main for seminarians and for priests. He said:

> I want to recommend to you a clear, cool view of present reality; a reality which is full of anxieties, just as it has always been. The Pope should lead, and you are called to follow, in the way of the Cross, which is the way of the Eternal Priest. Today in the seminary you are not preparing yourself for service in an ideal chimerical world; if you have been thinking this you are in for bitter disillusionment. Make no mistake about it. The true priest of the Lord does not live by nourishing dreams of unattainable earthly happiness, much less of comfort and well-being. Nor does he waste time lamenting past happy ages, which never were in reality. It is the same today as it was yesterday and always will be: we shall have to fight, and to remain solid in faith and charity.[47]

---

[47] *The Tablet* (London), CCXVI (April 15, 1961), 369.

6.

The Priest as Intellectual

"If all other factors remain constant, in the course of the next century the Catholic priesthood might almost disappear."[1] A decade ago anyone who would make that assertion would be thought to have taken leave of his senses. In the intervening ten years, however, the alarming decrease in vocations to the priesthood, the rising tide of dropouts from the seminaries, and the well grounded suspicion of an increasing number of defections from the priesthood itself, have given Father McNally's somber prediction a note of reality in the minds of thoughtful Catholics. Here, then, is a prime justification for devoting a chapter of this book to the priest's intellectual life, in the hope of assessing the principal causes for its unsatisfactory character and of suggesting a few ideas for its improvement. For the lower the proportion of priests to the people, the more will inevitably be demanded of those in the ministry. And that this proportion is steadily declining is evident from many sources, among them a study issued by the Congregation of Seminaries and Universities for the years 1959-1960 which revealed that in the thirty-nine countries surveyed the lay Catholic population increased over two percent while the growth in the number of priests was well under one percent.[2]

---

[1] Robert E. McNally, "The Disappearing Priesthood," *America*, CXIV (June 25, 1966), 877.
[2] *L'Attività della Santa Sede nel 1961* (Città del Vaticano: Tipografia

A second justification is closely related to the first. The informed Catholic, whose number is rapidly on the increase, does not need to be told about the altered status of the Church's laity, and what their greatly improved education, financial standing, and social sophistication implies by way of a more educated and cultivated clergy. Should there be any lingering doubt on that score, a recent address by Daniel Patrick Moynihan, former Assistant Secretary of Labor, who is now Director of the Joint Center for Urban Studies at Harvard University and M.I.T., should resolve the doubt. Deploring the failure of the American Catholic clergy to reveal a true intellectual and aesthetic standard, Mr. Moynihan warned of the loss of the "best and most vibrant souls," and he then asked:

> Is there any way to bring our bishops and pastors to see this? Surely there must be. The great task of the educated laity at this moment is to begin to ask, even to insist on a share in judgments of this kind, on an opportunity to bring into the life of the Church the standards of taste, and rigor and excellence as they are perceived by the best minds and spirits of the age. . . .
> Protest is in order. The time has come to walk out on sermons that are so puerile as to threaten the very bases of faith, or at least to arrange gestures of mass inattention. . . . The time has come to suffer mediocrity less than gladly: and to make known to those who try harder that we appreciate it more than they may have sensed.[3]

This is very plain speaking, indeed, and there is every reason to believe that more of the same will be heard in the

Poliglotta Vaticana. 1962), pp. 262-263; for the more recent figures of 1965, see *ibid.*, (1966), pp. 696-697. For the problem of dropouts in American seminaries, see Cornelius M. Cuyler, S.S., "Perseverance Trends in the Seminary," *National Catholic Educational Association Bulletin*, LXIII (August, 1966), 151-156; and William J. Lee, S.S., "Perseverance Trends in Major Seminaries," *ibid.*, pp. 156-166.

3 "Art-less Catholics. 'What Kind of Faith Built the National Shrine?'" *The Commonweal*, LXXXIV (July 1, 1966), 408-409.

days ahead. In the words of the old adage, 'a word to the wise is sufficient!'

At the outset it should be clearly stated that this essay is directed to the great majority of American diocesan priests, and not to those whose ministry has been cast in the world of scholarship and research. In other words, it is neither necessary nor desirable that the parochial clergy, or even those who serve in most special diocesan assignments, should be intellectuals in the strict sense. For the latter, by reason of the nature of their work, are often insulated from effective communication with the people, and direct and constant rapport is imperative if there is to be a successful fulfillment of the duties of the parochial office. Informed Catholics in the United States have no need of an American counterpart to Michael de Saint Pierre's controversial novel, *The New Priests*, to prove that point for them. Rather what is intended here is a survey of the factors that have impeded the general body of priests in this country from maintaining a lively interest in intellectual matters and in public questions, with several suggestions as to how the situation may be remedied. If it does not imply the desirability of priests trying to become scholars, it does, however, imply an earnest cultivation of study on the part of priests so that they may be truly informed as they move among the growing number of enlightened and sophisticated laity who constitute the people of God in this second half of the twentieth century. Thus the priest will be recognized and respected as the authentic voice of the apostolate which it is his vocation to advance.

Obviously, it is impossible to treat this broad topic in a fully adequate way in a brief essay, and for that reason what follows will be limited to certain aspects of the problem. First, one should listen to the voice of history, for as Pierre Teilhard de Chardin once remarked—a statement that I have repeatedly employed—whether one studies man or man's world, he is forced to the same conclusion that "everything is the sum of the past and that nothing is comprehensible except through its history."[4] Training for the Catholic priesthood has been no exception to that rule, and whenever one thinks of priestly training it at once suggests a seminary. Yet for roughly 1500 years of the Church's history, properly speaking, there were no seminaries.[5] Only with the action of the Council of Trent in July, 1563, did the idea gradually emerge of a special institution for each diocese in which candidates for the priesthood should be educated, and even then vicissitudes of one kind or another prevented the seminary system from becoming widely accepted until well into the seventeenth century.

It was that century's extraordinary religious revival in France that produced the principal architects of the seminary as it has been known in the modern Church, that is, men like Cardinal Pierre de Bérulle, Jean-Jacques Olier, Vincent de Paul, and Jean Eudes. And it was the disciples of these religious founders who made the diocesan seminary not only an established part of the French Church, but who introduced the system to the United States when the Sulpicians opened Saint Mary's Seminary in Baltimore in 1791 and Saint Joseph's near Bardstown, Kentucky, twenty years later, while the Vincentians inaugurated the American chapter of their seminary history at Saint Mary of the Barrens in Missouri in 1818. True, many candidates for the diocesan priesthood were trained under other auspices, for example, in this country by the Benedictines and other religious orders, as well as by secular priests—often Irish-born or German-born—who had themselves been educated in their native countries. Likewise a good number of Americans studied in Europe after 1788, the year that the first two students from the United

---

[4] *The Future of Man.* (New York and Evanston: Harper & Row, Publishers. 1964), p. 12.

[5] For a brief history of education for candidates to the priesthood, see the first two chapters of this book.

States enrolled at the Urban College of the Propaganda in Rome. And the foreign trained priests increased with the establishment of the American College at Louvain where David Russell of Louisville was the first American to arrive in 1858, the year after the college opened.

Meanwhile a much larger number—including a significant percentage of the American hierarchy—were to study in the Eternal City, especially in the years following 1859 when the North American College was founded. From that year until 1932 these students attended classes at the Urban College of the Propaganda, and from the latter date until the present at the Gregorian University. According to the historian of the college, there was little difficulty in adjustment when the change came in 1932, "for the methods followed by the Jesuit Fathers were practically the same as those followed by the Urban College professors."[6] One would like to believe, although until a very recent date the supporting evidence for such a view has not been impressive, that the methods improved over those which Newman found at Propaganda in the 1840's. The famous convert was on the whole quite happy during the time he studied in Rome, but it did not take his perceptive mind long to discover how thoroughly the siege mentality had permeated the Roman clerican atmosphere. Late in 1846 he confided to a friend:

> One thing however has struck me here and every where; (though I am ashamed to introduce it with an 'however'— ashamed to introduce it at all) the monstrous absurdity of supposing that the Catholic Priests are not most absolute and utter believers in the divinity of their own system. They are believers so as to be bigots—their fault is that they generally cannot conceive how educated Englishmen can be Anglicans with a good conscience—but they have a profound confidence in the truth of Catholicism—indeed it would be shocking to

---

[6] Robert F. McNamara, *The American College in Rome, 1855-1955.* (Rochester: Christopher Press, Inc. 1956), p. 521.

entertain the question, except that it is so commonly asked in England.[7]

And a few months later Newman summarized his impressions of Roman ecclesiastical education to another friend when he told him:

> Again (let me say it to *yourself*, for I don't like to say it aloud) you will not, cannot, get education here—not simply from the many objects there are to take you off your studies, but be-¬ cause you are not a boy. The lecturers are men quite up with their subject, but the course takes *four* years—if you don't stay that time, you only go through a part of it—and any how you go, lecture after lecture, to drawl through a few tedious pages —All this is quite necessary for boys, not for grown men. I should think (still in confidence) you will do as much sitting at home at Maryvale.[8]

To return to the seminary origins in the United States, among Catholic seminary educators, generally speaking, the two groups that occupied the most prominent place were the Sulpicians and the Vincentians. Thus one may with good reason concentrate on the attitude toward the intellectual life of their respective founders and the consequent tradi-tions to which it gave rise among their followers.

The point of view of Vincent de Paul and Olier toward the things of the mind was largely conditioned by two pain-ful facts in the religious conditions of France in their life-time: first, the deplorable state of both morals and knowl-edge among the clergy; secondly, the widespread ignorance and neglect of religion among the laity, especially among the poor and the destitute. Both men would have heartily agreed with Pope Adrian VI who sent an instruction to his nuncio, Francesco Chieregati, late in 1522 for use at the

---

[7] Newman to Henry Wilberforce, Rome, December 13, 1846, Charles Stephen Dessain (Ed.), *The Letters and Diaries of John Henry New-man.* (New York: Thomas Nelson and Sons. 1961), XI, 295.

[8] Newman to Richard Stanton, Rome, February 21, 1847, *ibid.*, XII, 48.

Diet of Nuremberg, in which he stated that Chieregati was to acknowledge frankly that the revolt of the Protestants against the Church had arisen on account of the sins of men, "and especially of prelates and clergy. . . . Holy Scripture declares aloud," said the pontiff, "that the sins of the people are the outcome of the sins of the priesthood. . . ."[9] So preoccupied were Saint Vincent and Father Olier with the urgent need for a clergy who might set an example of good morals for the laity and afford the latter simple instruction in the basic teachings of the Church, that study was assigned a quite secondary role to piety, when they did not seem to view it as actually harmful to advancement in the spiritual life.

True, the situation with which these religious founders had to deal was pathetically real, and the desperate need of the French Church for good priests to administer the sacraments and to teach the bare essentials of the faith to a religiously illiterate people, was constantly before their eyes. Given these circumstances, it was understandable how men of Vincent and Olier's deeply spiritual nature should have come to possess a 'holy obsession' for piety in the clergy. Yet it was unfortunate that the impression should have been created of a downgrading of study and learning in the hierarchy of clerical values taught to their immediate subjects, and through the latter and their successors, to the candidates for the priesthood who enrolled in their seminaries. Both founders had themselves been well educated, Vincent having taken his bachelor's degree in theology at the University of Toulouse and Olier having passed his examination for the same degree in 1629 at the Sorbonne. Yet their deter-

---

[9] Ludwig Pastor, *The History of the Popes.* 3rd ed. (Saint Louis: B. Herder Book Company. 1923); IX, 134. Pastor described the document as "unique in the history of the Papacy" (IX, 132); and of those who accused the pope of exaggeration, he said: "The charge of exaggeration cannot be sustained: the corruption in Rome was undoubtedly as great as Adrian described it to be." (IX. 136-137).

mination for the moral renewal of the clergy made them suspicious of learning, and Vincent told one of his men in 1659, "A general knowledge [*la médiocrité*] suffices, and what one wishes to have beyond that is rather to be feared than to be desired by workers of the gospel because it is dangerous. . . ."[10]

Father Olier had been deeply influenced by Saint Vincent de Paul and had made the retreat for ordinands which the latter had instituted in France. The Sulpician founder's attitude toward the intellectual life could not, perhaps, be summarized as succinctly as the quotation above is said by one of Vincent's spiritual sons and latest historians to have summed up his views on this subject.[11] Olier was at pains to provide not only a general theological course for his seminarians, but to enroll a certain number of them in the courses offered at the Sorbonne. Yet to him, as to Vincent de Paul, study was viewed only as a mode of advancing in holiness, and that he was in substantial agreement with the latter was evident when he stated:

> If you study from any other motive than that of piety, all your knowledge will serve only to make you more vain, more full of yourselves, more self-opinionated and attached to your own private judgment; in a word, the more learned you become, the drier will be your devotion. . . . This pride, this vanity of the intellect, is the most dangerous, the most deadly of all; it is a vanity from which a man scarcely ever recovers, for human learning goes on increasing with age and experience.[12]

---

10 Vincent de Paul to Gaspard Stelle, Paris, July 18, 1659, Pierre Coste (Ed.), *Saint Vincent de Paul, Correspondence, Entretiens, Documents.* I. *Correspondence.* (Paris: Librairie Lecoffre. J. Gabalda. 1923), VIII, 33.

11 Maurice A. Roche, C.M., states that Vincent's "over-all view is summed up" in the statement in the letter to Stelle, *Saint Vincent de Paul and the Formation of Clerics* (Fribourg: University Press. 1964), p. 84.

12 Quoted in Edward Healy Thompson, *The Life of Jean-Jacques Olier, Founder of the Seminary of St. Sulpice.* New and enlarged edition (London: Burns and Oates. 1886), pp. 462-463. In this and other mat-

Saint Vincent de Paul and Jean-Jacques Olier were, however, neither the originators nor the most prominent representatives of this point of view. For at least three-quarters
of a century before Olier's ordination (1633), a siege mentality had taken possession of the central government of
the Church as a consequence of fears induced by the Protestants' revolt from Rome. It was the same mentality that
has accounted in good measure for the lack of enthusiasm
for intellectual pursuits—when it has not actually fostered
anti-intellectualism—among large segments of the Catholic
clergy down to the present decade. The story of the Catholic
or Counter Reformation is filled with the triumphs of this
type of mind among high ecclesiastics. In a certain sense
the outcome was foreshadowed when the advantage enjoyed
by the humanists in the earlier sessions of the Council of
Trent, men who thought in terms of faculties of theology in
the urban universities as the best training schools for priests,
was lost. It would be historically inaccurate, however, to
attribute the departure from the cities to the proponents of
a revitalized scholasticism who gained the ascendancy in the
later sessions at Trent. The conciliar decree establishing the
diocesan seminary stated that it was to be located "near the
said churches [cathedral] or in some other suitable place to
be chosen by the bishop."[13] As it turned out, in time more
and more bishops were of the mind that the proper place to

---

ters Olier had been strongly influenced by Charles de Condren, second
Superior General of the French Oratory. For example, in a letter to his
subjects at Dieppe, de Condren stated that he was not writing with the
idea of depriving them of study, but rather of teaching them to study
in a Christian way, so that they would not be led astray "by the vanity
of the human spirit and the love of profane letters. . . ." de Condren to
the Dieppe Oratorians, Paris, April 12, 1631, Paul Auvray and André
Jouffrey (Eds.), *Lettres du Père Charles de Condren, 1588-1641* (Paris:
Editions du Cerf. 1943), p. 81; the same thought was expressed in his
letter entitled "De l'etude," (No. 146), *ibid.*, pp. 445-446.

[13] H. J. Schroeder, O.P. (Trans. and Ed.), *Canons and Decrees of the
Council of Trent. Original Text with English Translation* (Saint Louis:
B. Herder Book Company. 1941), p. 175.

educate future priests was not in the theological faculties of the universities but rather in private seminaries often located remote from the centers of learning.

A similar spirit was manifest in many of the post-conciliar measures taken to implement the reform legislation. For example, in March, 1564, Pope Pius IV issued a bull that brought into being the Index of Prohibited Books, a document that contained a set of rules for reading the Bible in the vernacular that must have discouraged many a seminarian and priest whose deficient knowledge of Hebrew, Greek, and Latin prevented them from making much sense of the Word of God in these ancient languages. Vernacular versions of the Scriptures could be read only with the written permission of the bishop and the advice of the pastor or confessor, and the directive closed by saying:

> But he who dares to read or possess Scripture without this permission cannot receive absolution from his sins until he has returned the Bible to the ordinary. . . .[14]

Nor did the breviary revised by Cardinal Francisco de Quiñones with a view to eliminating dubious material regarding the saints as well as basing the contents more firmly in the Scriptures, fare much better. Although it had been published in 1535 with Pope Paul III's approval and had won widespread popularity, it was ordered set aside in August, 1558, by Pope Paul IV in favor of a return to the traditional breviary of the Roman Curia as it had been issued since 1474.[15]

---

14 Quoted by Robert E. McNally, S.J., "The Council of Trent and Vernacular Bibles," *Theological Studies*, XXVII (June, 1966), 226-227.

15 Robert E. McNally, S.J., *The Unreformed Church* (New York: Sheed and Ward. 1965), pp. 138-140. Father McNally gives another instance of the same kind a century later in Pope Alexander VII's brief of January 12, 1661, condemning a French translation of the Roman Missal in which *inter alia* he said:

> We have learned with great sorrow that in the kingdom of France certain sons of perdition, itching with novelties detrimental to souls,

That the ecclesiastics of the late sixteenth and early seventeenth centuries should have shown a tendency to dig in and to hold the line against further losses among the Catholic faithful, was understandable. As it turned out, however, their efforts to save what was left of Catholic Christendom created an atmosphere that stifled individual initiative and originality of thought. As a result the clergy found little incentive to aspire to intellectual distinction in the ecclesiastical sciences or in any other branch of knowledge. The lack of incentive was reflected in the *Catechism of the Council of Trent for Parish Priests* which appeared in 1566 and which contained a chapter devoted to holy orders with a section entitled 'Qualifications for the Priesthood.' Holiness of life was rightly placed first; but under the heading of 'competent knowledge,' aside from the special training recognized for the study of Scripture, one finds no real premium placed on study. The priest should know how to administer the sacraments and, too, be versed in the Scriptures so as to enable him to instruct the people, but the general tenor was conveyed in the conclusion to the item which read:

> Now to fulfill the first of these duties it is enough for him to be endowed with a moderate share of knowledge. As for the second, it is no more ordinary, but very special knowledge that is required. At the same time, however, it should be remembered that a profound knowledge of abstruse questions is not demanded of all priests in an equal degree. It is enough that each one know all that is necessary for the discharge of his office and ministry.[16]

---

and despising the laws and practice of the Church, have lately come to such madness as to dare to translate the Roman Missal . . . into French . . . and to hand it over to persons of every rank and sex. Thus they have attempted by their rash action to degrade the most sacred rites, to lower the majesty which the Latin language gives to them, and to expose the divine mysteries to the common gaze. . . . (p. 116).

[16] John A. McHugh, O.P. and Charles J. Callan, O.P. (Trans. and Eds.), *Catechism of the Council of Trent for Parish Priests* (New York: Joseph F. Wagner, Inc. 1934), p. 336.

The spirit represented by these examples from the 1560's became more pronounced throughout the Church as time passed, and it was this cast of mind, together with the local religious conditions in France already mentioned, that helped to shape the attitudes of the Vincentian and Sulpician founders. While the problems of Cistercians and Benedictines did not relate directly to the diocesan clergy, the latter were not uninfluenced by what transpired in monastic circles. since it was the monks' works that often furnished the spiritual reading of the diocesan clergy. They would not have been altogther unaffected, therefore, by one of the more notorious instances of clerical anti-intellectualism which occurred in 1683. In that year Jean-Armand de Rancé, Abbot of La Trappe, was persuaded by Bossuet to publish *La Sainteté et les Devoirs de la Vie Monastique*, a treatise that espoused the thesis that study was the greatest obstacle to the life of self-denial to which monks had vowed themselves. So sharp a challenge to all that the learned Benedictines of the Congregation of Saint Maur had stood for could hardly go unanswered, and after considerable hesitation Jean Mabillion, O.S.B., the famous historian, was prevailed on to publish a reply in 1691. In the foreword to his *Traité des Études Monastiques*, Mabillon stated that studies "far from being absolutely opposed to monastic life, are in some instances even necessary for the preservation of religious communities."[17]

One would have thought that the highly useful and productive careers of so many priest-scholars would have supplied sufficient evidence to offset a tendency toward anti-intellectualism among the Catholic clergy. To name a single example, the only Englishman to be proclaimed a doctor of the Church, Saint Bede, in describing his daily routine near the end of his life stated that he had meditated on the

---

[17] Alcuin Siebenand, O.S.B., Isidore Botz, O.S.B., and Maurice Weber, O.S.B. (Trans. and Eds.), "Traité des Etudes Monastiques of Dom Jean Mabillon, O.S.B.," *Scriptorium*, XVII (January, 1958), 10.

Scriptures, observed the monastic discipline, and sang the divine office, and he then added, "the rest of my time, I was delighted always, to learn of others, to teach myself, or else to write."[18] While it would be possible to cite numerous priests, both diocesan and religious, who were holy men and at the same time learned men, it would be foolish to try to maintain that it was the learned priest who set the pattern. Throughout the whole of the modern history of the Church and down to the present time, all too frequently the pattern has been fixed by those who, as a contemporary priest-scholar has said, viewed any effort at investigation as "pride of intellect," a type that would be inclined, as he remarked, to view "laziness of the intelligence as a form of faith."[19]

Was it not this type of clerical mind, lazy and at the same time excessively concerned over the 'safety' of doctrine, that explained why an investigator some years ago found that among about twenty-five theological manuals written in the period 1880-1900, all but three or four condemned the theory of evolution as heresy? As John L. McKenzie, S.J., has pointedly asked, "Did these men serve the Church better than those who denied that the theory is heresy?" Granted, as he said, that they were trying to defend the truth, the latter cannot be defended by falsehood, and while their misjudgment of the theory of evolution can be pardoned, "their assurance in their misjudgment cannot."[20]

Even the most elementary awareness of human nature is sufficient to enable one to recognize the dangers of intellectual pride, especially for men of outstanding talent. Yet as Dom Leclercq maintains, if this talent is placed at the

18 Thomas Stapleton (Trans.) and Philip Hereford (Ed.), *The Ecclesiastical History of the English People by the Venerable Bede* (London: Burns, Oates & Washbourne Ltd. 1935), p. 334.

19 Jean Leclercq, O.S.B., *The Love of Learning and the Desire for God* (New York: Fordham University Press. 1961), p. 256.

20 John L. McKenzie, S.J., *Myths and Realities: Studies in Biblical Theology* (Milwaukee: Bruce Publishing Company. 1963), p. 6.

disposal of God's service and not employed for the purpose of enhancing a man's own reputation, it can lead to the
increase of God's glory, which in His providence is often
made to depend on the personal reputation of an author.
On the other hand, if the latter performs his task in a shabby
manner, as Leclercq says

> he compromises his reputation and also the cause he serves,
> the truth he should manifest and the Church whose honor he
> hopes to enhance. It is therefore quite usual and permissible
> for an author to be concerned about his reputation insofar as
> it depends on him. To the extent that it depends upon others,
> he must place it in God's hands and submit to criticism. And
> this will never be lacking.[21]

This is not the place to relate the varying fortunes of the
intellectual life among the clergy of the Universal Church
during the more than three centuries since the time of Vincent de Paul and Olier. Yet since these essays are concerned in the main with the priests of the United States, it
will be appropriate to speak of the American scene. Every
informed and honest Catholic in this country will admit that
the intellectual and cultural achievements and interests of all
too many of the American clergy leave much to be desired.
What, then, have been the chief causes behind this situation,
and the growing emphasis of late on the widening gap and
contrast between the educational and cultural interests of
the laity and those of the clergy? First, it should be mentioned that Catholics, whether clerical or lay, have like other
Americans been influenced by a national ethos which, as
Richard Hofstadter has made evident,[22] has not provided a
hospitable atmosphere for the things of the mind. Speaking
here solely of the clergy, it is difficult to escape the conclusion that the seminary must bear a major share of the

---

[21] Leclercq, *op. cit.*, p. 321.
[22] *Anti-Intellectualism in American Life* (New York: Alfred A. Knopf.
1963).

blame. Granted that it is not a graduate school or a research
institute intended for the training and support of scholars,
as the late Cardinal Meyer stated in Vatican Council II,
"The end . . . of all seminary formation is the apostolate,
however this apostolate is going to be exercised."[23] The
apostolate demands the best that a priest has to give at any
time, but especially in this age of an articulate and exacting
laity, and quite simply no man can produce his 'best' unless
a portion of his time is allotted to study in one form or
another.

In ruminating on the hindrances to the success of the
Catholic apostolate in England in the twilight of his life,
Cardinal Manning noted the superiority of the Anglican to
the Catholic clergy in a knowledge of history and constitu-
tional law, an interest in public affairs, and in a promotion
of the civic life of the people. "It is here," he said, "that
we are wanting, and mischievously wanting."[24] The present
is a much more demanding age than that of Manning, and
yet many American priests are 'mischievously wanting' in
the matters he mentioned. It would be difficult, however, to
see how the clergy of either Manning's time or of our own
could hope to meet a high standard in these particulars when
one reflects on how little intellectual stimulation they received in the seminary, and, indeed, how often their pursuit
of knowledge beyond the textbook level may have even
been discouraged. The mentality that has dominated these

---

[23] "Cardinal Meyer's Interventions at the Vatican Council," translated by
Vincent A. Yzermans, *Chicago Studies*, V (Spring, 1966), 110.

[24] Notes made in a private journal, July 17, 1890, Edmund Sheridan Purcell *Life of Cardinal Manning, Archbishop of Westminster* (New York:
Macmillan and Company. 1896), II, 774. Two years later an English
priest, Canon William Barry, wrote along similar lines in speaking of the
founder of the Paulist Fathers. He said: "Laymen and men of the world
will never be influenced for long by those who seem to them below their
own level in acquirements and general culture . . . and if they detect,
as it appears to them, ignorance or narrow-mindedness in respect of matters outside the sanctuary, we may rest assured that they will turn a
deaf ear to the preacher when he mounts the pulpit." "Isaac Hecker,"
Dublin Review, Fourth Series, II (July, 1892), 84.

institutions from the seventeenth century to the present
decade was more reminiscent of the cloister than it was of
a school for clerics intended for an active parochial ministry.
The ideals of the spiritual life likewise far more befitted the
monk and the friar than they did the parish priest, and the
man who was thought to have isolated himself from the evil
encroachments of the secular world was not infrequently
presented as the model.

Nor were matters in this regard improved by a notion,
both then and now quite widespread in Catholic circles, that
the diocesan clergy were not expected to meet the spiritual
and intellectual standards maintained by members of the
religious orders. For example, when the subject of a national university was under debate at Baltimore in the Third
Plenary Council in November, 1884, Robert Fulton, S.J.,
Provincial of the New York-Maryland Province, openly
scoffed at the idea of the diocesan clergy conducting a university. Many years later Thomas S. Byrne, by that time
Bishop of Nashville, recounted the episode for a friend.
Byrne had been present in 1884 and he challenged the
Jesuit provincial who, he stated, had contended that the
diocesan clergy

> were not intended to be an educated Clergy or at least a
> learned and erudite body . . . and that the proper custodians,
> cultivators, and representatives of learning in the Church
> were Religious Orders to whom alone Universities should be
> entrusted.[25]

---

[25] Byrne to Sister Mary Agnes McCann, n.p., December 3, 1917, John
Tracy Ellis, *The Formative Years of the Catholic University of America*
(Washington: American Catholic Historical Association. 1946), p. 104.
That Fulton did not speak for all the American Jesuits seemed to be
evident from a statement made by the Provincial of the Missouri Province,
Leopold Bushart, S.J., to James Gibbons, Archbishop of Baltimore, at
the time of the Fulton-Byrne encounter. Bushart had been present and
he said, "I wish to state to your Grace, that Father Fulton has expressed
his own private opinion and by no means the opinion of the Fathers of
our Society as far as I have been able to ascertain." Bushart to Gibbons,
Baltimore, November 26, 1884, Ellis, *op. cit.*, p. 108.

A generation ago a leading moral theologian manifested a similar spirit when writing on the vocation of the diocesan clergy. Arthur M. Vermeersch, S.J., admitted that the state of the diocesan priests far surpassed that of the laity because, as he put it, of "the vow of chastity they have taken and in virtue of their holy ministry." This "excellent state" was, indeed, to be "positively approved," he said, for those who had the talent and character, but who at the same time were scarcely fitted for religious obedience or community life. There would always be many who would shrink from the additional self-denial demanded of the religious life since, said Vermeersch, men are little inclined "to such complete voluntary surrender of self." The Gregorian University professor then declared:

> The confessor, speaking in the name of Christ, must express the sentiments of Christ. Therefore, he must beware of persuading individuals to join the secular clergy, or of concealing the better things in such a manner that individuals are turned away from the religious state.[26]

It is not difficult to see how this sort of judgment would lower the diocesan priesthood in the minds of many readers, any more than it is to envision the unfortunate reactions to which it would give rise among seminarians and diocesan priests themselves.

Apart, however, from the real and alleged differences between the diocesan and religious clergy, the environment that permeated most seminaries and scholasticates tended

---

[26] *Religious and Ecclesiastical Vocation* (Saint Louis: B. Herder Book Company. 1930), pp. 71-72. Another moral theologian of the same period was distinctly annoyed at Vermeersch's position and made his mind known. Edward J. Mahoney of Saint Edmund's College, Ware, commented that moral theologians were accustomed to "having their little joke," and he added, "The kindest way of regarding this extraordinary doctrine is to treat it as a joke, out of place, indeed, in such a context, but clearly not to be taken seriously." *The Secular Priesthood* (Saint Louis: B. Herder Book Company. 1930), p. 239.

to isolate both faculty and students from the currents of thought and discussion prevalent in their time. The situation was illustrated by the ban on reading newspapers and periodicals which obtained until quite recently, a rule that served to stifle intellectual curiosity, to say nothing of keeping seminarians in the dark about public questions of vital concern to the Church.

A further factor that helps to explain the low state of the intellectual life among the priests of the United States is that in too many cases the natural tendency to intellectual laziness and sloth was not combatted in the seminary by the professors' insistence on extensive and deep collateral reading, on the writing of research papers, and by active encouragement to students to use their critical faculties and to give rein to their intellectual curiosity. In other words, generally speaking, there has been no such serious approach to the learning process as one finds at Reed College, where a statement in the catalogue reprinted annually since 1911, the year the institution opened, reads as follows:

> Intercollegiate athletics, fraternities, sororities, and most of the diversions that men are pleased to call 'college life' as distinguished from college work, have no place at Reed College. . . . Only those who want to work, and to work hard, and to gain the greatest possible benefits from their studies are welcomed.[27]

To be sure, there is not a perfect parallel here, and yet Reed College and Catholic seminaries share enough common characteristics as institutions for the cultivation of the mind to allow the example, for anyone who knows the seminaries of the American Church will attest that they, too, have their own type of 'diversions,' even if they are not fraternities and sororities! The lesson in this instance comes home when one recalls that Reed has led the nation in the ratio of

---

[27] *Reed College Bulletin* (Portland: Reed College. 1965), p. 4.

Rhodes Scholarships won, in the percentage of students who have gained Woodrow Wilson Fellowships, and in the percentage of graduates who have gone on to become college and university teachers.[28] As the 'houses of intellect' they should be, therefore, Catholic seminaries would profit immensely from Reed's brand of emphasis rather than the casual attitude toward study that has all too frequently been their hallmark.

Indeed, the pedagogical procedures of which Wilfrid Ward was a witness during his brief time (1877-1878) as a student of the Urban College of the Propaganda has—again until within the very recent past—been typical of the seminary system of the American Church. Speaking of the philosophy courses in which he was enrolled, Ward said:

> But philosophy was taught to us in Rome in a way which seemed to me equally a *reductio ad absurdum* of the human reason. In the one case reason is pressed to a point which discredits itself, in the other authority held the field so exclusively that it was evoked to prove the reasons alleged for its validity — an equal disparagement of the functions and powers of reason. We were taught the various philosophical positions as the 'right view' and if any of us did not find those positions convincing we were accounted heterodox. Thus philosophy which professed to prove the rational duty of accepting Theism and revelation was not really enforced by reason but by authority. It was really learnt by rote and by sheer memory. Those students were best thought of who learnt best by heart. Genuine philosophic thought annoyed our Professors. The man with whom I had the opportunity of arguing at close quarters was Don Corti, our clever little *Ripetitore*, and I was equally impressed by his readiness in replying and by his failure ever really to understand or even to consider one's objections.[29]

---

[28] "A Thinking Reed," *Time*, LXXX (December 28, 1962), 38.
[29] From a memoir for the years 1877-1882 reprinted by Ward's daughter in Maisie Ward, *The Wilfrid Wards and the Transition* (New York: Sheed & Ward. 1934), p. 66.

Given the spirit and method of the instruction imparted in most seminaries, therefore, it should occasion no surprise that relatively few priests have come out with a keen and sustained interest in the things of the mind. And lest there should be created a misconception of their proper role, it should be repeated that it is not the purpose or function of a seminary to turn out productive scholars. But it is hardly asking too much to expect that priests, whose ministry automatically thrusts them into a position of leadership, should have a lively interest in intellectual and cultural affairs, lively enough at least to prompt them to assemble a good personal library and to make active use of it. In the Church of the United States there have been prelates like Archbishop Francis Patrick Kenrick and Bishop John Lancaster Spalding who have set an admirable example in this regard, as there have been diocesan priests who were seminary professors like James A. Corcoran of the last century and John A. Ryan of the present century—to name only two—who left behind them a lasting memorial in their written works as well as the example of lives supremely dedicated to the intellectual apostolate. But the paucity of publications among the Catholic seminary faculties in this country is one of the most tell-tale aspects of their history, allowing always for the few notable exceptions. Nothing refines one's knowledge and produces a more effective and contagious enthusiasm for the truth than research and writing, but here in general the seminary faculties have been sadly remiss.

In all of this, needless to say, it must be kept in mind that there have been notable exceptions, outstanding seminary men who not only taught and wrote extensively, but who were responsible for arousing the intellectual interests of their students. Such a man was the first Rector of Saint John's Seminary in Brighton, John B. Hogan, S.S. Of relatively few could it be said, as it was said of Hogan, that he had "the rare gift of filling the student's mind with the unrest of

inquiry." At a memorial service some months after the Sulpician's death one of his former students, Austin Dowling,
later Archbishop of Saint Paul, paid him an extraordinary
tribute that is worth quoting at some length. He said:

> He was forever whetting the appetite for knowledge, chal-
> lenging the impatient, prodding the slow. His method was the
> same, whether we met him in class or on the walk or in his
> room. It was his business to set us thinking—an occupation
> which he would never admit was highly superfluous in the
> life of a priest. Often he would seem to go to the very limit of
> daring in the vigor with which he plied us with objections,
> annihilated all our arguments and then walked off without
> vouchsafing an answer to our difficulties.
>
> But, sure of his own faith, he had no fear of ours, while he
> did fear the vicious effect of the smug satisfaction which a boy
> may feel—and never afterwards lose—in dealing flippantly with
> the grave problem of thought. . . .
>
> No doubt, at times, this fine temper of his mind left him open
> to misunderstanding and exposed him to the suspicion of be-
> ing a 'liberal,' and liberal he was if by liberty we mean free-
> dom from narrowness and pettiness and the fussiness of those
> who are always in terror lest the Bark of St. Peter shall
> founder. He had no such terror, nor did he think that truth
> had anything to fear from investigation. It was, perhaps, his
> child-like faith so serene, so secure, so full of charity that
> made him so absolutely fearless of error that he always met
> it, not with strategy, but in fair and open fight.
>
> Not his least attractive feature was his characteristically youth-
> ful mind. It never aged. His experience widened; his knowl-
> edge increased; his powers were developed, but he still con-
> fronted the field of science with the frank curiosity of a child.
> His mind, like his heart, was always wide open. . . .[30]

---

[30] A Garland of Affectionate Tributes to the Memory of the Very Rev.
John Baptist Hogan, D.D., S.S. (Boston: Alumni Saint John's Seminary.
1906), pp. 32-35. For the comments on seminary training of Patrick
Sheehan, author of the widely read novels of clerical life and a contemporary of Hogan's, see Herman J. Heuser, Canon Sheehan of Don-
eraile (New York: Longmans, Green and Company. 1917), pp. 38-44.

A further deterrent to a vibrant intellectual life among the Catholic clergy generally has been the lack of freedom of thought and expression in ecclesiastical circles. The Church's priest-scholars have experienced it more directly than priests in the active ministry, but when the scholars are seriously impeded the inhibiting factor is not long in being felt among those who often constitute the scholars' immediate audience, for both are subject to the same ecclesiastical authority. The point was well summarized by Newman when he declared:

> I say, then, that it is a matter of primary importance in the cultivation of those sciences, in which truth is discoverable by the human intellect, that the investigator should be free, independent, unshackled in his movements; that he should be allowed and enabled, without impediment, to fix his mind intently, nay, exclusively, on his special object, without the risk of being distracted every other minute in the process and progress of his inquiry, by charges of temerariousness, or by warnings against extravagance or scandal.[31]

One of the reasons for this unsatisfactory situation may, indeed, arise from the failure to distinguish in a sufficiently clear manner between the pastoral and the intellectual, or academic, life within the Church. There has been too much of a tendency on the part of some to impose pastoral norms and operations, that is, caring for the sacramental and emotional needs of the people, on the intellectual aspects of the priestly ministry. As a consequence of this confusion of purpose, and the absence of sharper lines of limitation between the two, in turn there has occurred an imposition of unnecessary restrictions on the investigation, inquiry, creativity, and initiative that constitute the life blood, so to speak, of those whose apostolate lies in the academic world. The pastoral approach, of paramount importance in the administration of

---

[31] John Henry Newman, *The Idea of a University* (New York: Longmans, Green and Company. 1923), p. 471.

the sacraments to individual souls, cannot be applied uni-
vocally in an academic context, since it tends to stifle true
intellectual investigation. In brief, the proper distinction
must be made between these two quite legitimate areas of
priestly endeavor, they must be made to function according-
ly, with the simultaneous realization that the one effects the
other and that if each is kept within its proper orbit there
will be no conflict.

There is no need to review here the disastrous results to
the Church's relationship to the intellectual life that followed from the Inquisition, the Galileo case, the Index, and the
witchhunt that came after the condemnation of modernism
in 1907. One has only to scan the directives issued by Pope
Pius X and his Secretary of State, Cardinal Raphael Merry
del Val, between 1903 and 1913 regarding ecclesiastical
studies, to get a vivid impression of the negative approach
as well as the restrictions imposed during these years by the
highest authorities in the Church. Granted that there was
merit in the official encouragement given to thomism, the
wisdom of making it the sole system of thought to be followed in Catholic institutions was surely open to question. Likewise the zeal displayed in stamping out the modernist heresy
was, indeed, commendable, but, unfortunately, the situation
got badly out of hand when the implementation of this laud-
able goal was put at the mercy of a group of unscrupulous
agents called integralists headed by Monsignor Humberto
Benigni. When month after month witnessed communications from the Holy See breathing the spirit of the samples
given below, and striking at honored names in the ecclesiastical learned world, it is understandable why Catholic scholarship should have been brought to a virtual standstill in the
period prior to World War I. The following summaries are
typical of the tone and content of most of these documents:

1. A letter of the Secretary of State to Canon J. Lahitton (September 6, 1909) praising his work, *La vocation sacerdotale*. The principal sign of a vocation is aptitude. In order to develop this aptitude and suitableness, superiors and directors of Seminaries should make their students apply themselves with care to a vigorous intellectual formation by the constant use of the Latin language and by a profound study of scholastic philosophy, as well as a moral discipline impregnated by the habit of obedience. . . ., and a filial eagerness for the opinions and pronouncements of the bishop, the guardian of faith and moderator of conduct.

2. The letter *Redditae sunt Nobis* (December 12, 1909) to M. Henry Garriguet, Superior General of the Society of Saint Sulpice, to congratulate him on faithfully following the directives of the Holy See in the formation of clerics. The ecclesiastical youths will thus be drawn to the school of Saint Thomas from which they will immunize themselves against all the new errors.

3. Letter of the Consistorial Congregation (September 1, 1911) to the bishops of Italy forbidding the reading in their Seminaries of the *Storia della Chiesa antica,* the Italian version of *l'Histoire ancienne de l'Eglise* of Monsignor Louis Duchesne.

4. Letter of the Secretary of State (April 22, 1912) to [Frédéric E.] Fuzet, Archbishop of Rouen, to thank him for sending his letter on the apostolicity of the Churches of Provence. After having pointed out the contagious effects of the more or less subtle poison of modernism and the more or less disguised venom of the higher criticism, the letter invites courageous writers, animated by the spirit of God, to unite their efforts against the assertions of a temerarious science and to raise the cry of alarm against the false wisdom of the century.

5. A circular letter of the Consistorial Congregation to the bishops of Italy on the textbooks [*les manuels de classe ou d'étude*] of Seminarians (October 17, 1913). The circular of July 16, 1912, of the Consistorial Congregation relative

to the choice of textbooks in the Seminaries has produced
the desired results, but there still remain some books
which merit censure and which are dangerous. Consequently the following are forbidden: *Il primo passo alla
philosophia* of Luigi Ambrosini, the manuals of ecclesiastical history of F. X. Funk and F. X. Kraus, the patrology
manual of Rauscher, and the *Légends hagiographiques* of
Père Delehaye.[32]

In fact, our own generation has been a witness to a wave of
censorship of this kind that became rampant in the 1950's
and that extended into the present decade. It was highlighted
in this country in the spring of 1963 by the banning of the
four theologians at the Catholic University of America, and
the attempt about the same time of the Congregation of
Seminaries and Universities to control the granting of hon-
orary degrees at Catholic institutions of higher learning.[33]
In the judgment of one writer the former episode, "marked
not only a new high point in the intransigence of the con-
servatives but also a turning point in the history of freedom
in the Catholic Church in America."[34] Two years after these
events a remarkable intervention in Vatican Council II (October 1, 1965) was in part directed against this evil spirit so
frequently manifested within the modern Church. After
sketching certain characteristics of the phenomenon, Michele
Pellegrino, Archbishop of Turin, stated in the aula of Saint
Peter's:

Such things do not belong only to the past; a few years ago
I found a religious living in involuntary exile for having ex-

---

[32] "Principaux actes des derniers Papes concernant les études et la défense
de la doctrine sacrée," *La Documentation Catholique*, XII (November
22, 1924), cols, 990-1006.
[33] "Roman Catholics. Clear it With the Vatican," *Time*, LXXXII (September
20, 1963), 72. For a brief general discussion of this problem, see the
writer's *A Commitment To Truth* (Latrobe: Archabbey Press. 1966).
[34] Leonard Swidler, "The Catholic Historian and Freedom," *American
Benedictine Review*, XVII (June, 1966), 152.

pressed opinions which today we read in papal and conciliar documents; this was not a unique case.

Progress of research in the theological sciences, he went on to say, as in other fields necessitates periodic revision, and the sphere and range of knowledge subject to change of this kind is much broader, said the archbishop, "than those who have not experienced the hard and often dangerous work of research may think." On the other hand, if the Church's scholars are aware that they may express themselves freely, they will act, said Archbishop Pellegrino:

> with the straightforwardness and sincerity that should shine in the Church; otherwise the abominable plague of dishonesty and hyprocrisy can hardly be avoided.[35]

What adds to the difficulty of the intellectual virtues finding the defense and support they sometimes require from high authority is that few bishops and major religious superiors seem fully to comprehend their importance. That being true, they attach relatively little weight to these aspects of clerical life, and with the absence of a strong sanction from above all too many seminarians and priests conclude that intellectual pursuits really do not matter. Even so generally enlightened a prelate as Patrick W. Riordan, second Archbishop of San Francisco, revealed the practical turn of mind so characteristic of the majority of American bishops—to say nothing of a lack of understanding of the purpose of a university—in questions relating to the graduate training of their priests. In the autumn of 1909 he complained to Thomas J. Shahan, Rector of the Catholic University of America, about the way the institution was being conducted and *inter alia* he said:

> The young students are not trained for the ministry such as they must exercise when they come back to their respective

---

[35] *The Tablet* (London), CCXIX (October 9, 1965), 1113.

dioceses. Very few of them will ever be professors. Nearly all of them will be employed in the active ministry of parish work, and for that reason they should be taught how to preach and how to conduct the services of our holy religion.[36]

No one will gainsay the point that priests should learn how to preach and to administer the sacraments, but that is scarcely the aim that bishops should have in mind in assigning priests to graduate studies.

To be sure, ever since the consecration in 1790 of John Carroll, the first of their number, most American bishops have had little respite from the incessant round of official duties and, therefore, they have had relatively brief time themselves to read and to cultivate the intellectual virtues. But might not many of these practical administrative tasks that absorbed so much of their energies have been performed just as competently by subordinates, either clerical or lay? One gets the impression that pragmatic as most Americans are, with many bishops this national characteristic is so strong that the arts of administration have far more appeal than do the things of the mind. In any case, in the American Church there has been extremely little of what Charles Davis called "espiscopal theology," thinking of the great fathers and doctors of the Church, a point that he illustrated when he said, "The pastoral letters of Cardinal Suhard are an example of what can be achieved when pastoral concern and theological insight are wedded."[37] But in contrast to the hierarchies of other countries, especially of Belgium, Holland, Germany, and France, the bishops of the United States, with a few notable exceptions, failed to make

[36] Riordan to Shahan, San Francisco, September 18, 1909, copy. Archives of the Archdiocese of San Francisco. The writer owes this reference to the kindness of his friend, the Reverend James P. Gaffey, Superintendent of Schools of the Diocese of Santa Rosa.

[37] "Theology in Seminary Confinement," *Downside Review*, LXXXI (October, 1963), 310.

the kind of impression at Vatican Council II that one associates with the happy combination mentioned by Davis or with deep study and reflection.

Like every other group or community of men, the Catholic clergy look to the top for guidance or direction, and it is the bishops and the major religious superiors whose decisions usually fix the pattern or set the pace in the intellectual as well as in other avenues of clerical activity. What the late H. Outram Evennett of Trinity College, Cambridge, once remarked of the failure of the Church in England, can *mutatis mutandis* be applied to the Church in the United States. The intellectual life, he said, would not flourish among the clergy until

> we have become accustomed to the notion of scholarship as a priestly work and are prepared to recognize that gifted amateurs with insecurity of tenure in their facilities for regular study cannot build up a first-class tradition or make an adequate mark in the world of learning. . . .[38]

Moreover, those priests who do try in a general way to keep abreast of intellectual movements, as well as those who may elect a career in scholarship, must be reconciled ahead of time to paying a high price, for to borrow David Knowles' term, they may often find themselves "ploughing a lonely furrow." Many a priest who has become involved in these pursuits will find a familiar echo in Knowles' words when he says:

> Men of action and administration are apt to regard him as one shunning the real things of life, or as pursuing a hobby. He will be fortunate, if sooner or later, and sooner rather than later, he is not called forth to be useful, to stop a gap in a school or a parish, and to stay there. He himself will have a

[38] "Catholics and the Universities, 1850-1950," George Andrew Beck, A.A. (Ed.), *The English Catholics, 1850-1950* (London: Burns Oates. 1950), p. 314.

demon within disguised as an angel of light, a voice to ask,
in those days of loneliness and frustration that come to all
scholars, whether he is justified in standing aside from the
labour and heats of the day, from the direct service of souls,
whether his work will ever have issue, whether in fine it is
really worthy of his priestly vocation.[39]

Vatican Council II suggested a corrective that, if translated into a living policy throughout every diocese, would
prevent situations of this kind arising. Under the heading of
the unity that should obtain among priests, it was stated:

> All priests are sent forth as co-workers in the same undertak-
> ing, whether they are engaged in a parochial or supraparochial
> ministry, whether they devote their efforts to scientific re-
> search or teaching. . . . or whether they fulfill any other
> apostolic tasks or labors related to the apostolate.[40]

And so on the day that the council closed, among the particular greetings directed to various groups by one or other
of the fathers, there was a special message from Cardinal
Paul-Emile Léger 'To Men of Thought and Science.' The
Archbishop of Montreal illustrated superbly what, one may
hope, will become the accepted approach of all high prelates
of the Church when he asked why there should be a special
greeting to scholars, and then proceeded to say:

> Because all of us here, bishops and Fathers of the Council,
> are on the lookout for truth. . . . Hence our paths could not
> fail to cross. Your road is ours. Your paths are never foreign
> to ours. We are the friends of your vocation as searchers,
> companions in your fatigues, admirers of your successes, and,
> if necessary, consolers in your discouragement and your fail-
> ures.[41]

---

[39] "The Need for Catholic Historical Scholarship," *Dublin Review*,
CCXXXII (Summer, 1958), 128.
[40] "Decree on the Ministry and Life of Priests," Walter M. Abbott, S.J.
and Joseph Gallagher (Eds.), *The Documents of Vatican II* (New York:
Guild Press. 1966), pp. 549-550.
[41] *Ibid.*, pp. 730-731.

There is scarcely a priest in the United States who has not known of cases such as those mentioned by Dom Knowles, and the most notorious recent instance in the Universal Church was the prolonged and acute ordeal to which a priest was submitted who possessed what the learned world may ultimately recognize as the greatest mind of our time, Pierre Teilhard de Chardin. After the latter's death an intimate friend revealed that the "most agonizing trial" for the famous Jesuit scientist had been "not being understood, seeing himself disclaimed, even practically abandoned." Yet through all his suffering Teilhard de Chardin never lost sight of the priestly ideal, for as this same friend, Frédéric-Marie Bernounioux, O.F.M., professor of geology in the Catholic Institute of Toulouse, remarked in describing their last meeting in New York, the Jesuit's final words to him were, "Pray for me, that I may not die embittered."[42]

One of the gravest losses sustained by the Church in consequence of ecclesiastical superiors' lack of awareness in these matters arises from the unused talents and special aptitudes and skills of their priests. Not only are the latter's initiative and originality often stifled by an excessive authoritarianism, but the tendency to view priests simply as functionaries takes no cognizance of the creativity that many of these men could bring to the solution of the phenomenally varied and complex problems of contemporary society. One need only think of the multiple evidences of the social malaise which afflicts men today in the inner-city, in suburbia, and in rural areas as well to know what is meant. And beneath the surface of these baffling moral and social ills lies the supreme problem for all priests in the present hour, namely, to relate Christ to a people whose lives are so involved in the myraid and complicated circumstances of the

---

[42] *L'âme sacerdotale du Père Teilhard de Chardin* quoted in Claude Cuénot, *Teilhard de Chardin. A Biographical Study* (London: Burns & Oates. 1965), p. 368.

material world that our Lord and His Church have been rendered largely irrelevant. In these conditions, then, the Church stands in desperate need of the most highly trained and skilled spokesmen, priests whose expert knowledge in a variety of fields will help others to illumine the intricate problems of their lives and to heal the deep wounds, whether of a personal or a social nature, with which so many souls are now afflicted. For the Church to afford the maximum service, however, bishops must know the particular gifts of their priests, and in such a way that they can make real in their dioceses what Thomas Corbishley, S.J., had in mind when he told a group of religious, "We have the responsibility of seeing that the unique qualities which each of them possesses are developed to the full."[43]

A century ago life in the American Church was infinitely more simple than it is today, a fact that is illustrated by the mandatory decrees of Baltimore's Second Plenary Council of October, 1866, that each diocese must have a chancery and a regular set of diocesan officials.[44] But the problems of the 1960's do not admit of solution by a handful of churchmen operating from the sheltered recesses of a diocesan chancery. Now the situations with which virtually every American diocese is faced can only hope to be improved by the active and constant efforts of a larger number of trained priests who, upon the completion of special studies, are not only permitted to execute policy, but who are also made parties to its formation. Embodied within the 36,419 diocesan priests of the United States (as of January 1, 1966, when the priests of religious orders numbered 22,774) are tremendous latent talents of which the Church is in many instances making almost no use. In fact, so much is this the case, that it is

---

[43] "The Intellectual Formation of the Religious," *Wiseman Review*, No. 493 (Autumn, 1962), 267.

[44] *Concilii Plenarii Baltimorensis II. . . . Acta et Decreta* (Baltimore: John Murphy Company. 1868), pp. 53-58.

difficult to take seriously some of the flattering impressions of the Church's general efficiency left by the audits of the American Institute of Management.[45]

American Catholics have heard so much about the well educated laity of this second half of the twentieth century and their 'emergence' that many must have grown a bit weary of the theme. But relatively little has been said about the numerous gifted priests whose potential has scarcely been tapped, because it is not known and has never been sought out in a systematic way within their own diocese. How many of these priests there are who, fully aware as any intelligent being must be of his God-given talents which their Church and their superiors largely ignore, must at times have felt a certain kinship to Thoreau's men who led "lives of quiet desperation." Likewise of how many of them might it not be said that if their talents and gifts were recognized in a way that made them feel like active participants in diocesan policy and performance, the therapeutic effect would enable them psychologically to sublimate their loneliness with some creative and productive good for their fellowmen? For it is hardly open to question that had every bishop been alert to this factor and taken the pains to know his priests and, whenever possible, to place them in assignments where their natural talents could flourish and their temperaments find a favorable response, not a few priests who today are living as laymen in this country might have been retained in the priestly ministry.

Common sense, to be sure, dictates that the majority of diocesan priests should not and cannot aim at duplicating the careers of men like Erasmus, John Fisher, Alban Butler, John Lingard, Johannes Janssen, and Louis Duchesne, to name only a few of the host of secular clergy whose literary

---

45 *Nineteen Centuries of the Roman Catholic Church . . . A Portfolio of Three Management Audits, 1956, 1960, 1962* (New York: American Institute of Management. 1956-1962).

work brought them lasting fame. Nor can they hope to re-
peat the accomplishments of more recent figures like Georges
Lemaitre, a priest of the Archdiocese of Malines-Brussels,
professor emeritus of the Catholic University of Louvain and
President of the Papal Academy of Sciences, who died in
June, 1966. It was in the difficult terrain of mathematics and
the natural sciences that Lemaitre earned his reputation,
fields remote from the normal surroundings of the ecclesiastical world. Yet who would question that Lemaitre was every
bit as much a witness to Christ as his distinguished Louvain
colleagues, Roger Aubert, the church historian, and Charles
Moeller, canonist now at Rome as an official of the Congregation of the Doctrine of the Faith.

For many priests both here and abroad it is obviously too
late to begin a cultivation of the intellectual virtues. But
those students at present enrolled in the seminaries who persist in their calling will have no excuse, for the Church's
training schools have granted to them an unprecedented
freedom. And the supreme test of this new-found freedom
may well be how profitably they employ it in deepening
their intellectual lives, along with attending to their spiritual,
social, and physical well being. Probably no single group of
Catholics has been reminded more frequently and more
forcefully than these same seminarians of the new type of
laity that is now found among the people of God. These
future priests cannot say, therefore, that they were not
warned about what awaited them. As Pope Paul VI told the
students of the North American College on the occasion of
his visit of September 5, 1965, to their summer villa:

> Your future ministry offers you a challenge now, a challenge
> to prepare yourselves as well as you can for the demanding
> tasks before you. We urge you to prepare yourselves intellect-
> ually very well because the community looks to the priests
> for guidance and leadership more than ever before.[46]

---

[46] *L'Osservatore Romano*, September 6, 1965, p. 1.

That preparation entails, needless to say, hard work, long hours of reading, and generous time allotted to intellectual pursuits during which a seminarian or a priest can gradually carve out, so to speak, manageable areas of knowledge in which he can become proficient, while at the same time excusing himself as he should, from trying to become an expert in the sense that one associates with research scholars and university professors.

Whether it be seminarians, young priests, or priests in middle age, however, the surrender of easy-going ways and deeply ingrained habits in order to initiate a program of study in their lives, will exact a sacrifice, even at times a measure of suffering. But the priest who is honest with himself will admit that almost everything in the life of Christ suggested suffering and sacrifice and nothing ran counter to it; in fact, the priest who is without some touch of it in his daily living may well feel a certain uneasiness. And if the will to self-discipline is there, this exercise in adult education can find its fulfillment, nor is it possible to see how in the years ahead a genuine execution of a priest's ministry can be realized without it. Failure of priests to bring about their own intellectual *aggiornamento*, then, will grow more costly as the stream of a superior educated laity swells, and the latter become more and more restive with clerical bungling and ignorance, impatient with clerical immaturity, and intolerant of clerical indifference to the intellectual and cultural values that are the hallmark of every cultivated mind.

The personal witness to Christ, or the individual ministry of many priests, in the coming time may find its most critical test in this very area. For like any man who has a deep sense of personal integrity, a priest cannot continue indefinitely in a post where he has a daily feeling of inadequacy in performing its duties in a manner that meets with the approval of his fellowmen. An honest man instinctively withdraws from a situation where he believes that he is playing a disguised role, where pretense is stronger than reality, and where in the final analysis falsehood may be served more frequently than truth. To be at peace with himself the priest like all other men must feel reasonably equal to his assignment and able to cope with its demands; anything short of this will multiply frustrations to the point where one's life commitment is imperiled. Reduced to simple terms, for some it could mean the difference between success and failure in this life and, perhaps, even the difference between ultimate salvation and its eternal loss. The essence of it all was expressed by the present pontiff on the occasion of the fourth centennial of Trent's establishment of seminaries when he said:

> in his dealings with others the man who wants to bear witness before the world—with Christ and for Christ—to that truth which brings freedom must be trained in the virtue of truth in word and action, and so must cultivate sincerity, loyalty, integrity, fidelity.[47]

---

[47] *Summi Dei Verbum. Apostolic Letter of His Holiness Pope Paul VI on the Occasion of the Fourth Centenary of the Establishment of Seminaries by the Council of Trent. November 4, 1963* (Washington: National Catholic Welfare Conference. 1963), p. 13.

Index